The Bedside Book

The
Bedside Book

Edited by Julian Shuckburgh

WINDWARD

First published in Great Britain 1979
by WHS Distributors (a division of W. H. Smith & Son Ltd),
Burne House, 88/89 High Holborn,
London WC1V 6LS

ISBN 0 7112 0014 9

Typesetting by SX Composing Ltd, Rayleigh, Essex
Printed and bound in Great Britain by Morrison & Gibb Ltd,
Edinburgh and London

Conceived and designed by Shuckburgh Reynolds Ltd,
8 Northumberland Place,
London W2 5BS

Designer: Roger Pring

Illustrations by Rene Eyre, Lucina Della Rocca Hay,
Kathryn Hunt, Carole Johnson, Sheilagh Noble,
Sarah and Roger Pring

CONTENTS

CONTENTS

INTRODUCTION

A bedside book is defined in Chambers' dictionary as one "suitable for sleepless nights", and the pieces offered here have primarily been chosen to lift the spirits of the insomniac in the small hours, when worldly troubles seem most heavy, and the sleeve of care is liable to unravel uncontrollably. The anthology includes few searching studies of economic or political affairs, accounts of blood-curdling crime, analyses of international relations, or other daytime concerns of the conscientious citizen. There is, in fact, a detectable bias towards nostalgia and other forms of sentimentality, on the grounds that the vulnerable non-sleeper cannot bear very much reality.

The greater part of *The Bedside Book* contains extracts from recently published books. If the net is cast widely enough a remarkable variety of good and unusual fish can be caught; and the reader may find foretastes and appetisers from a number of books which he will not yet have come across, as well as reminders of the good things read in the last year or two.

This rule has not been followed with regard to fiction. Instead the aim has been to resurrect some older stories of high quality, often ones which have been unjustly neglected or forgotten. The short story occupies an uneasy place among the literary genres. There are few regular outlets for the single story, and publishers will rarely touch a volume of them (unless the author is distinguished enough to insist). The examples reprinted here may help to confirm what a high form of art, and how entertaining, the short story can be. Also among the fiction will be found the occasional extract from recently published novels.

There is also a problem with poetry. Anthologies of this kind used to contain a good deal of verse; but very few poets are widely read today, and very few readers read poetry regularly. It is hard to disagree with Lord David Cecil's remark that the later twentieth century does not provide a natural and congenial element for poets to live in, or even with his description of some of their work: "brief, breathless, effortful and cacophonous!" Yet in the last few years some slim volumes of excellent verse have appeared, often by older poets who have retained their sense of humour, and it is from these that a selection has been made.

The arrangement of pieces throughout *The Bedside Book* is not wholly haphazard. From time to time the reader may be amused or enlightened by the juxtaposition of pieces with a common theme. An obvious example is Edward VIII's abdication. The fine account by Frances Donaldson reprinted here (her book was the source for a highly successful recent television drama series on the subject) is accompanied by a little group of quotations which give added perspective to the story. Another example is Christopher Matthew's very funny new book *Diary of a Somebody*, which is here made to stand direct comparison with the Grossmiths' masterpiece. And the temptation was irresistible, having reproduced Katherine Mansfield's short story "Psychology", to include Virginia Woolf's psychologically revealing diary entry written on her death (and published recently in the second volume of the Virginia Woolf diaries). There are many more juxtapositions of this kind in the book, and it would spoil the fun to point out too many of them; but for this reason it is suggested that *The Bedside Book* should be read consecutively, and not only dipped into at random like a Christmas bran-tub.

A small group of pieces has been specially commissioned for this volume: Colin Wilson's fascinating survey of latest developments in the study of the paranormal, which discusses material too new to have been included in his recent book *Mysteries*; Marina Vaizey's lively account of the state of contemporary art; and Dilys Powell's reflections on the trends among recent films.

Should *The Bedside Book* be successful enough to fulfil its publisher's hopes, a second volume is planned for publication in 1980. An anthology of this kind inevitably reflects the personal taste and preferences of its editor, who in collecting pieces for a second instalment would greatly welcome the suggestions of readers in order to reduce the personal bias and make the choice as catholic as possible.

Finally, the editor would like to record his gratitude to the staffs of Paddington Library and of the London Library for their efficient, kindly and patient assistance during the preparation of this book.

J.S.
June 1979

PARADISE
LAURIE LEE

I T seems to me that the game of choosing one's Paradise is rarely
a rewarding pastime; it either produces images of vast banality,
or boredom on a cosmic scale: sometimes a kind of Killarney
between showers, ringing with Irish tenors, or a perpetual Butlin's
rigged for everlasting Bingo; for others an exclusive developed
area in Stock Exchange marble surrounded by cottonwool and
celestial grass. This last—perhaps the most popular and longest
sold in the series—has always had its own unimaginable horror,
where, in the glaring blue-white of the adman's heaven, the
starched inmates have nothing whatever to do except sit down,

stand up, walk around the draughty halls, or hide behind the classical pillars.

Indeed, through the ages, man's various conceptions of Paradise have seemed more often than not to teeter on the brink of hell. And with the common element of eternity thrown in, there wouldn't be all that much to choose between them— except that hell would seem to promise more entertainment.

Paradise, in the past, as a piece of Christian propaganda, never really got off the ground. Too chaste, too disinfected, too much on its best behaviour, it received little more than a dutiful nod from the faithful. Hell, on the other hand, was always a good crowd-raiser, having ninety per cent of the action—high colours, high temperatures, intricate devilries and always the most interesting company available. In the eyes of priest, prophet, poet and painter, Hades has always been a better bet than heaven. Milton's best-seller was *Paradise Lost* (while *Paradise Regained* was just a plate of cold potatoes). The sulphurous visions of Savonarola, Dante and Hieronymus Bosch are something by which we have always been willingly and vigorously haunted. Of all the arts, only certain rare passages of music seem ever to have touched the fringes of a credible Paradise.

The difficulty of trying to suggest in any detail what one's personal Paradise should be is like suddenly coming into enormous wealth. There are no limits or disciplines to contain one's grandiose plans, and the results are generally unfortunate.

Having said that, and declared some of the flaws in the game, the time has come for me to outline my own banality. Paradise, for me, is a holding on to the familiar contained within some ideal scale of the past—an eighteenth-century·thing, perhaps, in its grace and order (without its squalor and tribulations). I would have a landscape shelving gently between mountains to the sea, with pastures and woods between them. There would be a small city on the coast, a couple of villages in the hills, and a hermitage hanging from one of the distant crags—a place of sonorous mystery, never to be visited, but from which oracles would be issued once a week. The city would be walled, terraced and luminescent, intimate and without wheeled traffic. From its centre, the countryside would always be visible and could comfortably be reached on foot. Temperatures would be constant: 68 to 74 with no wind except a breeze from the sea. No rain either, except for unseen showers in the night, just enough to keep things green; or festive "summer-rain days", known and predictable, when a light warm mist would drift through the streets and gardens, and lovers would fasten their shutters and spend long whispering afternoons accompanied by the sound of moistures dripping from rose to rose.

Weather, in Paradise, would be varied, yet tactful, never attempting to achieve any monotonous perfections. There would also be long Nordic twilights for walks in the country, beside river or reeded lake, whose rustling waters, standing with tall grave birds, would reflect the sky's slow shade towards night. The pastoral landscape itself would be lightened by tall flowering grasses, bee-orchids, button mushrooms and snails. Apart from songbirds, who would sing only at dawn and evening and the whisper of river and ocean—no noise: no explosion, public announcement, radio, hammering of buildings, motor-car, jetplane—only the deep, forgotten primeval silence which, like true darkness itself, is a natural balm of which man is now almost totally deprived.

Breaking this silence, or course, there would have to be music, for any place without music is a hearth without fire; not music of brass, I think, but music of reed and strings whose sounds are the most potent ravishers of the senses. This music would be based in the skull, to be switched on at will, and inaudible to others unless they wished to share it.

But what about people? Well mine would be a First Day Paradise, for a very solid reason. In it one would have no past, nor future, only the new-peeled light of the present, and so put the unthinkableness of eternity out of one's mind. The people of the city, fields and mountains—wits, sages, children, lovers— would shine for you with the original magic of first sight, as you yourself would shine for them. Recognition, but no remembrance, would ensure that they were members of a familiar society whom you could never accuse of repeating themselves; while their pleasure in the newness of you would spare you the purgatory of knowing that you might be boring them. It might be agreeable to imagine that everyone grew imperceptibly younger, like Cary Grant in his old TV films, but having no recollection, this wouldn't matter—each day would bring its fresh confrontation, each love would be first and only.

Paradise would also restore some of the powers we lost in that long descent from childhood to death.

Senses that failed would be returned to the keen, high level of their beginnings. The child's animal sharpness of taste and smell

—which the adult knows only too well he's lost when he hears the adman trying to prove he still has them—the ability to take in the whiff of heat from summer grass in the morning, the oils in a leaf, the white dust on a daisy, the different spirits in wood, in clay, in iron, all of which allows the child to bind himself intimately to these objects, but from which the adult is inexorably exiled. Paradise would bring back these senses and the contacts they offer—the special aura of a house as you open its door, a tang which tells you its history and the character of all the people in it; the awareness of an invisible animal close at hand in a wood; the girlish texture of a young calf's mouth: and taste; the brutality of nursery medicines, the delight in a common caramel, the sharp bitter milk of the dandelion root, the acrid horse-breath of straw in a barn.

Surely, with the handing back of these powers, one might reasonably ask also for the restoration of appetite. Sacred appetite, so readily blunted on earth—at least, three parts of one's time to denying it, whether it be for food or love, not for puritanical reasons but in order to sharpen it to the edge when it could best celebrate the thing it longed for.

But one needn't bother to ask what one would do in Paradise. Timeless, without memory or sense of future, one would live out each day new. An ideal landscape; mountains, fields and woods, and the sea throwing up its light. A deep green silence outside the walls of the city, or occasional sweet airs that delight and harm not; within the city, companionship, the sibilant pleasure of bare feet on marble; wine, oil, the smell of herbs, brown skin; oceans mirrored in eyes that would be the only eternity.

Above all, I think I'd wish for one exclusive indulgence—the power to take off as one does in dreams, to rise and float soundlessly over the bright tiles of the city, over the oak groves and nibbling sheep, to jostle with falcons on mountain crags and then sweep out over the purple sea.

On the rooftops, as I returned, silver storks, wings folded, would stand catching the evening light. There would be children in the patios playing with sleepy leopards, girls in the windows preparing their lamps. Alighting on this terrace of heaven I would join my unjealous friends and choose one for the long cool twilight. Asking no more of the day than that I should be reminded of my body by some brief and passing pain; and perhaps

be allowed one twinge of regret at the thought of the other world
I'd lived in, a sense of loss without which no Paradise is perfect.

From
I Can't Stay Long

THE MYSTERIES OF THE KINGDOM
EDWARD NORMAN

WHAT Christians most need in our day is to see that the
complicated mixture of the Infinite in the structures of time
is explicable according to the spiritual interpretations of religious
tradition—and does not require them to turn, instead, to the
inappropriate explanations of secular culture. Both in daily life
and in the worship of the church, the prevailing emphasis upon
the transformation of the material world has robbed men of their
bridge to eternity. Around them, as in every age, they hear the
clatter of disintegrating structures and the shouts of distressed
humanity. But the priest in the sanctuary no longer speaks to
them of the evidences of the unseen world, discovered amid the
rubble of this present one. He refers them, instead, to intellectual-
ised interpretations of the wrong social practices and political
principles which have, in the view of conventional wisdom,
brought suffering to the society of men. Around us, however, the
materials of eternity lie thick upon the ground, ambiguous in
relation to time, lucid as pointers to the celestial forces. For the
mysteries of the Kingdom are not the commonplaces of the mere
inquirer, but the pearl of great price, which only they possess who
dispose of all their other goods.

From the Reith Lectures, 1978

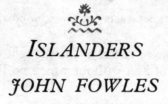

ISLANDERS
JOHN FOWLES

I first began to feel the releasing power of *The Tempest* when I lived on my island in Greece—the lack of a Prospero, the need of a Prospero, the desire to play Daedalus. It is the first guidebook anyone should take who is to be an islander; or since we are all islanders of a kind, perhaps the first guidebook, at least to the self-inquiring. More and more we lose the ability to think as poets think, across frontiers and consecrated limits. More and more we think—or are brainwashed into thinking—in terms of verifiable facts, like money, time, personal pleasure, established knowledge. One reason I love islands so much is that of their nature they question such lack of imagination; that properly experienced, they make us stop and think a little: why am I here, what am I about, what is it all about, what has gone wrong?

Modern wreck-divers use the word "crud", a dialect form of curd, to describe the coagulated minerals that form round any long-sunken metal object, and that have to be laboriously chipped and leached away before it can be exposed to sight again. Islands strip and dissolve the crud of our pretensions and cultural accretions, the Odyssean mask of victim we all wear: I am this because life has made me like this, not because I really want to be like this. There is in all puritanism a violent hostility to all that does not promise personal profit. Of course the definition of profit changes. "It may be thought," wrote Cromwell to the House of Commons after he had helped reduce the city of Bristol in 1645, "that some praises are due to those gallant men, of whose valour so much mention is made: their humble suit to you and all that have an interest in this blessing is that in the remembrance of God's praises they be forgotten." The profit then lay in eternity and the ticket to that was to be bought by an arrogant extreme of self-denial.

We have in our own century lost all faith in the remembrance of God's praises. The profit now is tallied in personal pleasure; but we remain puritan in our adamant pursuit of it. Purveying recipes for pleasure has become a mainstay of popular publishing and journalism: where to go, what to enjoy, how to enjoy, when to enjoy, to such a clogging, blurring extent that our modern duty to enjoy is nowadays almost as peremptory—and destructive—as the old puritan's need to *renounce* pleasure . . . to ban the play, dance, the graven image and everything else that makes present life agreeable. It is all very well creating a permissive society. But we have not created the essential corollary of a pagan mind.

The true pagan mind, from Homer on, always knew that the laws of pleasure have very little to do with endless consumption, endless exhortation to experience, endless attempts to tell the individual in what his pleasure consists and to guide him through the labyrinth whose deepest values can only be self-discovered. We cannot all be labyrinth-makers; but we can all learn to explore and trace them for ourselves. There used to be a guide to the famous maze at Hampton Court that showed the quickest route to take. Nobody who used it ever reached the centre; which lies not in the unravelled, but the unravelling.

From
Islands

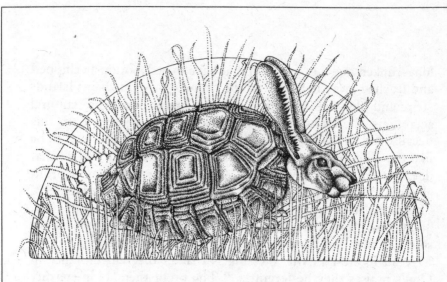

GEORGE MOORE

TOM STOPPARD

The hero of Tom Stoppard's play Jumpers *is a
Professor of Moral Philosophy (apparently at
London university) called George Moore. He is
attempting, amid an extraordinary variety of
interruptions, to write a paper for a symposium
debating the existence of a moral absolute. In the
scene which follows he is dictating his lecture to a
secretary, while from the next room violent cries are
to be heard from his wife Dotty, a beautiful young
musical-comedy star.*

GEORGE: To begin at the beginning: is God? *(Pause.)* I prefer to
put the question in this form because to ask, "Does God
exist?" appears to presuppose the existence of a God who
may not, and I do not propose this late evening to follow
my friend Russell, this evening to follow my late friend
Russell, to follow my good friend the late Lord Russell,
necrophiliac rubbish!, to begin at the beginning: is God?
(He ponders a moment.) To ask, "Is God?" appears to
presuppose a Being who perhaps isn't . . . and thus is open
to the same objection as the question, "Does God exist?" . . .
but until the difficulty is pointed out it does not have the
same propensity to confuse language with meaning and to
conjure up a God who may have any number of predicates

including omniscience, perfection and four-wheel-drive but
not, as it happens, existence. This confusion, which indicates
only that language is an approximation of meaning and not a
logical symbolism for it, began with Plato and was not ended
by Bertrand Russell's theory that existence could only be
asserted of descriptions and not of individuals, but I do not
propose this evening to follow into the Theory of
Descriptions my very old friend—now dead, of course—
ach!—to follow into the Theory of Descriptions, the late
Lord Russell——!
(He continues smoothly, improvising off-script.)
—if I may so refer to an old friend for whom punctuality
was no less a predicate than existence, and a good deal more
so, he would have had us believe, though why we should
believe that existence could be asserted of the author of
"Principia Mathematica" but not of Bertrand Russell, he
never had time, despite his punctuality, not to mention his
existence, to explain, very good, keep to the point, to begin
at the beginning: *is God? (To* SECRETARY.*)* Leave a space.
Secondly! A small number of men, by the exercise of their
intellects and by the study of the works both of nature and
of other intellects before them, have been able to argue
coherently against the existence of God. A much larger
number of men, by the exercise of their emotional and
psychological states, have affirmed that this is the correct
view. This view derives partly from what is known as
common sense, whose virtue, uniquely among virtues, is
that everybody has it, and partly from the mounting
implausibility of a technological age as having divine origins
—for while a man might believe that the providence of
sheep's wool was made in heaven, he finds it harder to
believe the same of Terylene mixture. *(He leans into
the mirror intently.)* Well, the tide is running his way, and it
is a tide which has turned only once in human history. . . .
There is presumably a calendar date—a *moment*—when the
onus of proof passed from the atheist to the believer, when,
quite suddenly, secretly, the noes had it. *(And squeezes a
blackhead in the imaginary mirror. Then he straightens up and
is the lecturer again.)* It is now nearly fifty years since
Professor Ramsay described theology and ethics as two
subjects without an object, and yet, as though to defy
reason, as though to flaunt a divine indestructibility, the

question will not go away: is God?

DOTTY *(off)*: Rape!

GEORGE: And then again, I sometimes wonder whether the question ought not to be, "Are God?" Because it is to account for two quite unconnected mysteries that the human mind looks beyond humanity and it is two of him that philosophy obligingly provides. There is, first, the God of Creation to account for existence, and, second, the God of Goodness to account for moral values. I say they are unconnected because there is no logical reason why the fountainhead of goodness in the universe should have necessarily created the universe in the first place; nor is it necessary, on the other hand, that a Creator should care tuppence about the behaviour of his creations. Still, at least in the Judaeo–Christian tradition, nothing is heard either of a God who created the universe and then washed his hands of it, or, alternatively, a God who merely took a comparatively recent interest in the chance product of universal gases. In practice, people admit a Creator to give authority to moral values, and admit moral values to give point to the Creation. But when we place the existence of God within the discipline of a philosophical inquiry, we find these two independent mysteries: the how and the why of the overwhelming question:——

DOTTY *(off)*: *Is anybody there?*

GEORGE *(pause)*: Perhaps all mystical experience is a form of coincidence. Or vice versa, of course.

(DOTTY screams. It sounds in earnest. Of course, nothing can be seen.)

(Murmurs.) Wolf. . . .

DOTTY *(off)*: Wolves!—Look out!

(GEORGE throws his manuscript down furiously.)

(Off.) Murder—Rape—Wolves!

(GEORGE opens his door and shouts at the enclosed Bedroom door.)

GEORGE: Dorothy, I will not have my work interrupted by these gratuitous acts of lupine delinquency!

(The Procession Music, which had been allowed to fade out, is brought up by the opening of the Study Door.)

And turn that thing down!—you are deliberately feigning an interest in brass band music to distract me from my lecture!

(He closes his door, and from behind it produces a quiver of arrows and a bow. These he brings downstage and places them on his desk.)
(Pleasantly.) Does, for the sake of argument, God, so to speak, exist?
(He returns upstage and finds an archery target, which he leans up against the upstage bookcase, resting on the day-bed.)
(To mirror.) My method of inquiry this evening into certain aspects of this hardy perennial may strike some of you as overly engaging, but experience has taught me that to attempt to sustain the attention of rival schools of academics by argument alone is tantamount to constructing a Gothic arch out of junket.
(He extracts an arrow from the quiver.)
Putting aside the God of Goodness, to whom we will return, and taking first the God of Creation—or to give him his chief philosophical *raison d'être*, the First Cause—we see that a supernatural or divine origin is the logical consequence of the assumption that one thing leads to another, and that this series must have had a first term; that, if you like, though chickens and eggs may alternate back through the millennia, ultimately, we arrive at something which, while perhaps no longer resembling either a chicken or an egg, is nevertheless the first term of that series and can itself only be attributed to a First Cause—or to give it its theological soubriquet, God. How well founded is such an assumption? Could it be, for instance, that chickens and eggs have been succeeding each other in one form or another literally for ever? My old friend—Mathematicians are quick to point out that they are familiar with many series which have no first term—such as the series of proper fractions between nought and one. What, they ask is the first, that is the smallest, of these fractions? A billionth? A trillionth? Obviously not: Cantor's proof that there is no greatest number ensures that there is no smallest fraction. There is no beginning.
(With a certain relish he notches his arrow into the bowstring.)
But it was precisely this notion of infinite series which in the sixth century BC led the Greek philosopher Zeno to conclude that since an arrow shot towards a target first had to cover half the distance, and then half the remainder, and then half the remainder after that, and so on *ad infinitum*, the result was, as I will now demonstrate, that though an

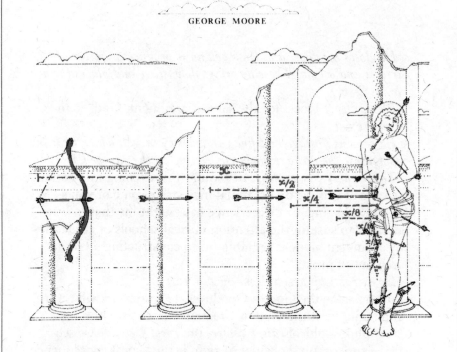

arrow is always approaching its target, it never quite gets there, and Saint Sebastian died of fright.

(He is about to fire the arrow, but changes his mind, and turns back to the mirror.)

Furthermore, by a similar argument he showed that *before* reaching the half-way point, the arrow had to reach the quarter-mark, and before that the eighth, and before that the sixteenth, and so on, with the result, remembering Cantor's proof, that the arrow *could not move at all!*

DOTTY *(off)*: *Fire!*

(GEORGE fires, startled before he was ready, and the arrow disappears over the top of the wardrobe.)

Help—rescue—fire!

GEORGE *(shouts furiously)*: Will you stop this childish nonsense! Thanks to you I have lost the element of surprise!

(He tosses the bow away, tries to peer on tiptoe over the wardrobe, which is too high, and desists. He picks up his script, and then puts it down again, and sits on the corner of his desk, one leg swinging, arms folded. He notices that his socks do not match. The SECRETARY, unruffled, waits patiently, her pencil is poised. (It may as well be stated now that she never speaks.))

(Subdued at first.) Look. . . . Consider my left sock. My left sock exists but it need not have done so. It is, we say, not necessary, but contingent. Why does my sock exist? Because

a sock-maker made it, in one sense; because, in another, at some point previously, the conception of a sock arrived in the human brain; to keep my foot warm in a third, to make a profit in a fourth. There is reason and there is cause and there is the question, who made the sock-maker's maker? etcetera, very well, next! see, see, I move my foot which moves my sock. *(Walks.)* I and my foot and my sock all move round the room, which moves round the sun, which also moves, as Aristotle said, though not round the earth, he was wrong about that. There is reason and there is cause and there is motion, each in infinite regress towards a moment of origin and a point of ultimate reference—and one day!—as we stare into the fire at the mouth of our cave, suddenly! in an instant of grateful terror, we get it!—the one and only, sufficient unto himself, outside the action, uniquely immobile!—the Necessary Being, the First Cause, the Unmoved Mover!!

(He takes a climactic drink from his tumbler, which however contains only pencils. He puts the tumbler down, leaving a pencil in his mouth.)

(Indistinctly.) St. Thomas Aquinas. . . .

(He drops the pencil back into the tumbler.)

(Quietly.) Of the five proofs of God's existence put forward by St. Thomas Aquinas, three depended on the simple idea that if an apparently endless line of dominoes is knocking itself over one by one then somewhere there is a domino which was *nudged*. And as regards dominoes, I haven't got any further than St. Thomas.

(The music from the TV Procession has been quietly re-establishing itself in the background.)

Everything has to begin somewhere and there is no answer to *that*. Except, of course, why does it? Why, since we accept the notion of infinity without end, should we not accept the logically identical notion of infinity without beginning? My old—— Consider the series of proper fractions. Etcetera. (*To* SECRETARY.) Then Cantor, then no beginning, etcetera, then Zeno. Insert: But the fact is, the first term of the series is not an infinite fraction but *zero*. It exists. God, so to speak, is nought. Interesting. Continue. By missing the point of a converging series Zeno overlooked the fallacy which is exemplified at its most picturesque in his famous paradoxes, which showed in every

way but experience that an arrow could never reach its
target, and that a tortoise given a head start in a race with,
say, a hare, could never be overtaken—and by way of
regaining your attention I will now demonstrate the nature
of the fallacy; to which end I have brought with me a
specially trained tortoise—*(which he takes from the smaller
wooden box)*—and a similarly trained, damn and blast!——
*(He has opened the larger box and found it empty. He looks
round.)*
Thumper! Thumper, where are you, boy?
*(Failing to find Thumper under the desks or the bed, he leaves
the room and, carrying the tortoise, enters the Bedroom, opening
the door wide and leaving it open as the Bedroom lights up.
Procession on Screen. Procession music loud now, as though we
travelled with him. The body of the JUMPER is nowhere in sight.
However, DOTTY's nude body is sprawled face down, and
apparently lifeless on the bed. GEORGE takes in the room at a
glance, ignores DOTTY, and still calling for Thumper goes to
look in the bathroom.*
*GEORGE reappears from the Bathroom after a second or two.
Mixed in with the TV music now is a snatch of commentary.)*
TV VOICE: . . . beautiful blue sky for the fly-past, and here they
come!
*(Very loud: the jet planes scream and thunder on the sound
track and scream and thunder across the SCREEN. In mid-flight
they are cut off—— GEORGE has turned off the TV: silence and
white Screen. GEORGE still moving towards the door, from the
bed where the TV switch is lying.)*
GEORGE: Are you a proverb?
DOTTY: No, I'm a book.
GEORGE: *The Naked and the Dead.*

From
Jumpers

PHILOSOPHY

ISAIAH BERLIN AND BRIAN MAGEE

MAGEE Can you . . . give a straightforward example of a philosophical question which is moral as distinct from political?

BERLIN Well, let me tell you a story which somebody told me about his experiences in the Second World War. He was a British Intelligence officer in France who, towards the end of the war, had to interrogate a French traitor whom the French Resistance had caught. The traitor had worked for the Gestapo, and the Resistance group was about to execute him. The British Intelligence officer asked for permission to interrogate him first, because he had reason to believe that the man might be able to give him information which might help to save innocent people from death or torture. Well, he went to see this Gestapo agent, a very young man, who said to him: "Why should I answer your questions? If you can promise me my life, I'll answer. But I know that these people intend to kill me tomorrow, and if you cannot promise me my life, why on earth should I talk at all?" In those circumstances, what should the British officer have done? His duty as an Intelligence Officer was to extract as much information as he could—the lives of innocent people might depend on it—yet he could do this only by lying. It would have been no use saying: "I'll do my best to persuade them to let you live", or anything like that. He knew that he could do nothing to save the man from execution, and the man would have seen through any effort to evade making a straight promise. If the officer had said definitely: "If you talk to me, I'll save your life", the young man when he discovered he had been deceived would have cursed him with his dying breath.

This seems to me an example of a moral problem, the kind of thing morality is about. A Utilitarian might say: "Of course you must tell a lie, if it is likely to increase human happiness or diminish human misery." The same conclusion would be reached by those who accord supreme value to military or patriotic duty, particularly in wartime. But there may be other considerations: absolute religious commandments; the voice of conscience; relations between one human being and another: how can one tell an appalling lie to a man condemned to death? Has his behaviour deprived him of all rights to be treated as a human being? Are there not ultimate human claims? One of Dostoevsky's heroes says that if he were asked whether he was prepared to purchase the happiness of millions of people at the price of the torture of one innocent child, he would refuse. Was his answer obviously wrong? A Utilitarian would be forced to say: "Yes, it was obviously wrong—sentimental and wrong." But, of course, we do not all think that; some of us think a man is perfectly entitled to say: "I will not torture an innocent child. I don't know what will happen next, but there are certain things which no man may do, no matter what the cost."

Well, here are two philosophies in conflict. One is perhaps, in the noblest sense, utilitarian (or patriotic), the other founded on recognition of absolute universal rules. It is not the job of the moral philosopher to order a man which of these to make his own: but it is very much his job to explain to him what are the issues and values that are involved, to examine, and adjudicate between, the arguments for and against various conclusions, to make clear the forms of life which have come into collision, the ends of life, and perhaps the costs, which he has to decide between. In the end, of course, a man has to accept personal responsibility, and do what he thinks is right: his choice will be rational if he realises the principles on which it is made, and free if he could have chosen otherwise. Such choices can be very agonising. Obeying orders without reflection is easier.

MAGEE One good thing about the examples of moral and political problems which you've just given is that there's absolutely nothing linguistic about them. I wish that were more often the case with the problems discussed by moral philosophers in print—at least till recently. One thing which astonishes many laymen who try reading philosophy, and puts many of them off, is the discovery that so much philosophical discussion is about words, about language. Can you explain, in terms which would justify it to the layman, why this is so?

BERLIN I'll do my best. Modern philosophers, some of them, have done themselves a disservice, so far as the public is concerned, by insisting that they are mainly concerned with language. People then think that there must be something trivial about what they do—that they are concerned about language in the sense in which lexicographers or grammarians or linguists understand it, in which case the lexicographers and grammarians are better at it.

Yet they *are* concerned with language, because they believe that we think in words, that words are sometimes themselves acts, and therefore that the examination of language is the examination of thought, indeed of entire outlooks, ways of life. When one is faced by these difficult philosophical questions, to which there is no obvious answer, one can begin by asking oneself: "What *kind* of question is this? What sort of answer are we looking for?

Is it like this sort of question, or is it like that sort of question? Is it a question of fact? Is it a question of logic, of the relation between concepts? Or a mixture of these? Or like none of them?" This sorting out of concepts and categories is quite a difficult thing to do; but all good philosophers have done and are doing it, whatever they may call it: there is nothing wrong—save that it has misled the unwary or the ill-intentioned—with calling it the clearing up of linguistic confusions. Confusions of this kind can lead to muddles in people's heads—and this, in its turn, can lead to barbarism in practice.

MAGEE The Nazis' beliefs about race rested on muddles of many kinds, including muddles of this kind, didn't they?

BERLIN Yes—these muddles were partly empirical, partly not. The very notion of a sub-man—the very notion that there exist certain sub-human creatures—Jews, or Gypsies, or Slavs, or Negroes, or whoever it might be, and that they are a terrible danger to society, and ought therefore to be exterminated—this horrible conviction was no doubt in part founded on false empirical beliefs about the nature of the behaviour of these men and women. But the notion of sub-humanity, of what it means to be sub-human, and, in relation to this, what we mean by the word "human", what human nature is, what constitutes a human being, what it is to be inferior and superior; and, of course, what follows from it, what justifies torturing or killing the "inferior"—these are philosophical, not empirical, questions. Those who complain that they are trivial, a mere examination of language and linguistic usage, should reflect that people's lives depended—and still depend—on them.

MAGEE Some language philosophers have claimed that by analysing our use of language they are freeing us from the spell of language. In other words, it's not they who are under its spell, but we.

BERLIN Indeed. I should say that this was one of their major services to mankind. That is why they are regarded as dangerous people by those who want the original use of language to be kept, and fear that to analyse it is to weaken its influence. It was the German poet Heine who told us not to ignore the quiet philosopher in his study, since he can be a powerful and formidable figure; that to regard him as a mere harmless pedant, engaged on a lot of trivial tasks, is to underrate his powers; that if Kant had not discredited the god of the rationalist theologians, Robespierre might not have beheaded the king. Heine warned the French among whom he was then living that the German Idealist metaphysicians—the followers of Fichte, Schelling and their kind—were fanatical believers, not to be deterred either by fear or by love of pleasure, and would one day rise in fury and raze to the ground the monuments of Western civilization. He declared that when this great metaphysical onslaught plunged Europe into war and destruction, the French Revolution would seem mere child's play. Heine was in no doubt, having experienced it himself, that the power of philosophical or metaphysical ideas (for instance those of Hegel, whose lectures he attended) can be very great—indirect, but far-reaching; that philosophers were not harmless word-spinners, but a great force for good and evil, among the most formidable unacknowledged legislators of mankind.

MAGEE And all because of words they write on paper or utter in lectures. The way language enmeshes with reality in and through philosophical activity is deeply problematical. Even with seemingly plain questions like "What is a right?", which you used just now as an example: is one enquiring into the meaning of a word, or is one enquiring into the nature of an abstract entity which exists in some way even though it's abstract? *What kind of a question* is the question "What is a right?"

BERLIN What you are doing, I think, is saying: "How do we discover what kind of arguments would lead you to accept the proposition that you have a certain right—say, a right to happiness —or, on the contrary, that you do not have it?" I seem to remember reading somewhere that when somebody said to Luther that men were entitled to happiness, or that the goal of life was happiness, he said: "Happiness? No! *Leiden*! *Leiden*! *Kreuz*! *Kreuz*!" ("Suffering, suffering; the Cross, the Cross".) This is at the heart of certain forms of Christian religion, one of the deepest beliefs, visions of reality, on which a very large number of exceedingly unshallow human beings have built their lives. This surely is not trivial. You can say that one is dealing with words—key words, but still words. You can say that we are merely asking "What does the word 'cross' mean? What does the word 'suffering' mean?" But that is not the point. We are not grammarians, we are not lexicographers. In order to find out what these words meant to Luther or others like him, what they mean in *this* sense of "mean", it is no use looking them up in the dictionary.

MAGEE But the question is still not entirely clear. If you are not trying to find out their meaning in *that* sense, what exactly is the nature of whatever it is you are trying to get at? After all, some of the greatest geniuses in the history of the human race have been thrashing out questions of this kind for two or three thousand years, yet without reaching any generally accepted answers. This suggests the peculiarity of the questions, at the very least. Perhaps they can't be answered. Perhaps what you're looking for isn't there.

BERLIN Well, let us ask ourselves: "What sort of questions can be answered?" At the cost of some over-simplification, one might say that there are two great classes of issues about which it can be said with a certain firmness that they can—at least in principle, if not always in practice—be settled. One is the class of ordinary empirical questions, questions about what there is in the world, the sort of thing ordinary observation or the sciences deal with. "Are there black swans in Australia?" "Yes, there are; they have been seen there." "What is water made of?" "It's made of certain types of molecules." "And the molecules?" "They consist of atoms." Here we are in the realm of verifiable, or at least falsifiable, assertions. Common sense works like this too: "Where is the cheese?" "The cheese is in the cupboard." "How do you know?" "I've looked." This is regarded as a perfectly sufficient answer to the question. In normal circumstances I would not doubt this, nor would you. These are called empirical questions, questions of fact which are settled either by ordinary common sense or, in more complicated cases, by controlled observation, by experiment, by the confirmation of hypotheses, and so on. That is one type of question.

Then there is another type of question—the sort of question which mathematicians or logicians ask. There you accept certain definitions, certain transformation rules about how to derive propositions from other propositions, and rules of entailment which enable you to deduce conclusions from premises. And there are also sets of rules in accordance with which logical relations of propositions can be checked. This gives you no information about the world at all. I am referring to formal disciplines which seem to be entirely divorced from questions of fact: mathematics, logic, game theories, heraldry. You don't discover the answer by looking out of the window, or at a dial, or through a telescope, or in the cupboard. If I tell you that the king in chess moves only one square at a time, it is no good your saying: "Well, you *say* it moves only one square at a time, but one evening I was looking at a chess board and I saw a king move two squares." This would not be regarded as a refutation of my proposition, because what I am really saying is that there is a rule in chess according to which the king is allowed to move only one square at a time, otherwise the rule is broken. And how do you know that the rule is true? Rules are not the kind of expressions that can be true or false, any more than commands or questions. They are simply rules: you either accept these rules or you accept other sets of rules. Whether such choices are free or not, and what the status of these rules is, are themselves philosophical questions, neither empirical nor formal. I shall try to explain what I mean in a moment.

One of the central properties of the two classes of question I've now mentioned is that there are clearly understood methods for finding the answers. You may not know the answer to an empirical question but you know what kind of answer is appropriate to this kind of question, what the range of possible answers is. If I say: "How long did Caesar live?", you may not know how many years he lived, but you know how to set about finding out. You know what kind of books to look up. You know what kind of evidence would be evidence for the answer. If I ask: "Are there flightless birds in Thailand?", you may not know the answer, but you would know what kind of observations or lack of them would provide it. The same is true of astronomy. You don't know what the other side of some distant planet looks like, because you have never seen it, but you know that if you could fly there, as you can now fly to the moon, perhaps you would see it. With formal disciplines, equally, there are unsolved problems, but equally there are accepted methods for solving them. You know that you cannot solve mathematical problems by looking or touching or listening. Equally, mere algebraic reasoning will not yield answers in the empirical sphere. The line I have drawn between these spheres is too sharp: the relations between descriptive statements and formal ones are, in fact, a good deal more complex: but this positivist way of putting it brings out the point I wish to stress. It is this: between these two great classes of questions there are other questions which cannot be answered in either fashion. There are many such questions, and they include philosophical questions. One of the *prima facie* hallmarks of a philosophical question seems to me to be this: that you do not know where to look for the answer. Someone says to you: "What is justice?", or "Is every event determined by antecedent events?", or "What are the ends of human life? Should we pursue happiness, or promote social equality, or justice or religious worship or knowledge—even if these do not lead to happiness?" How precisely do you set about answering these questions? Or suppose someone with an inclination to think about ideas says to you: "What do you mean by 'real'? How do you distinguish reality from appearance?" Or asks, "What is knowledge? What do we know? Can we know anything for certain? Apart from mathematical knowledge, is there anything we know, or could know, for certain? If we do, how do we know that we know it for certain?" What do you do to find out the answers to questions such as these, in the absence of any science or discipline such that you can say: "Well, now, there are experts. They will be able to tell you what good and right are, they will be able to tell you whether everything is causally determined, and also whether happiness is the right goal for human beings, and what rights and duties, knowledge and reality and truth are, and all such things; you just listen to them." A mathematician, of course, can answer mathematical questions. But you do not, do you, think that there are infallible moralists or metaphysicians who can give absolutely clear answers which any human being who could follow their reason is bound to accept? These questions seem to generate puzzles at the very beginning, problems about where to look. Nobody quite knows how to settle them. Ordinary men who put these questions to themselves persistently enough tend to get into a state of mental cramp, which lasts until they stop asking them and think about other things.

From
Men of Ideas

YING CHU

GERALD BRENAN

BERTRAND RUSSELL on his visit to China sought out Ying Chü to ask him his opinion of Western philosophy. "Most of your philosophizing," he said, "consists in trying to unravel the tangles that previous philosophers have made. Beating ones brains over such trivial matters is bad for the liver. Those who truly seek wisdom spend their days watching the river flow by and listening to the birds singing. Their nights they devote to love."

From
Thoughts in a Dry Season

IN THE HOURS OF DARKNESS
EDNA O'BRIEN

On a stretch of road far from London and not yet in sight of Cambridge, Lena suddenly remarked that it was like Australia. There was more than one reason for this: the physical loneliness was exactly like that she had experienced in the countryside above Sydney one warm intoxicating Saturday and the road itself, devoid of houses or tillage, suggested a depopulated land. Also the high grass on either side was tawny, bleached no doubt by the long phenomenal English summer. The bridges too that flanked the motorways were ugly and graceless and reminded her of that other time.

Her son Iain said that any minute they would see the spires of Cambridge and already her mind ran on to her first view of the old historic town, the various university complexes, the stout walls, the stained-glass windows and the overall atmosphere of studiousness. She was intrigued. She envisaged going into the hotel bedroom and drawing curtains—they would be dark red and once drawn she would click on a light and sit in an armchair to read some of Jane Austen in order to re-discover through that woman reserve and perseverance.

Her youngest son was going up to Cambridge and she was facing the predicament she had read about in novels—that of a divorced woman, bereft of her children, having to grow old without these beloved props, having in some indescribable way to take the first steps into loneliness as if she were a toddler again.

Two signposts read the same mileage for Cambridge even though they were miles apart and she said that was typical, then instantly decided that she was becoming a shrew. Soon maybe she would be questioning bills, talking to herself and finding fault with any services that were to be done to her house. To save face she remarked on the beauty of a fairly ordinary little village in which she noticed a post office, an ale house, whimsy-looking cottages and an antique shop.

The hotel at Cambridge was not what she had imagined. The entrance adjoined the car park and in the too huge lobby there were arrows pointing to several bars. Then hammering to testify that construction work was in progress. Would it stop at night?

She was obsessed with noise and could, she believed, be wakened by an air bubble in her water pipes at night. She followed the porter and was dismayed to find that he lost his way. It was a big ramshackle place with various flights of stairs leading to different quarters. Her bedroom was on the first floor and just outside was a child's cot and a single mattress standing on its end. The room was everything she dreaded—a single bed with a stained orange coverlet, matching curtains, plastic lampshade, wardrobe with three empty metal hangers that moved slightly as if propelled by some shiver. The one summoning bell brought no response—no buxom girl, no doddery old man, no housekeeper with motherly smile came in answer to the ringing of the green oblong button. In fact there was no way of telling if it was connected, or if in fact a bell had rung somewhere in the bowels of that place and was being ignored with a shrug. "Bad place to die", she thought, and as fervently as she had longed for the surprise and repose of that little room, she now longed to be out of it and safely at home.

She wanted tea. Her stockings were wet. She and Iain had had to walk the last bit of the journey carrying baskets, a record player, a drawing board and loose bits of lighting flex. He had parked the car outside the town because it was against university rules to own one. On their walk it had begun to drizzle and by now it was raining heavily. Lifting the curtain she looked at the spatters as they crawled down the windowpane and lodged on the frame beneath. The view was of a football field empty except for its goal posts. She would make the best of it.

In the lobby the guests were being served with tea and every-thing about them suggested not an academic life but a life of commerce. She had to step over bags bursting with shopping, and at first glance every mouth seemed to be allied to a piece of oily chocolate cake. She sat at one empty table waiting for service, and in her restlessness began to eat the bits of damp ribbony lettuce that served as decoration on the plate of sand-wiches that the previous occupant had devoured. The waiter strolled across and caught her in this nonsensical theft. She asked him to bring tea quickly as she was dining at seven. He spurned her to her face, he also spurned the entire human race and did both of these offices in broken English.

❋

Dinner was in one of the most esteemed of the colleges and they foregathered in a small overheated sitting room, that was full of furniture and pieces of china. Her host, a professor, had invited a younger professor and two freshmen. They sat and awkwardly sorted each other out, the young men laughing lightly at everything and constantly interjecting their remarks with bits of French as they bantered with each other about their sleeping habits and their taste for sherry or classical music. It was stiff. Her son should have had a different introduction, something much less formal, a bit of gaiety. The conversation centred for a long time on a professor who had the nickname of a woman and who received students in his long johns and thought nothing of it. Incongruously he was described as a hermit even though he seemed to be receiving students most mornings in his cluttered room. It was stifling hot. To calm herself, Lena thought of the beautiful mist like fine gauze sparkling on the courtyard outside, and above it a sky perfectly pictorial with its new moon and its thrilling stars.

They went down a short flight of stairs and then climbed some other steps to their early dinner. The host had done everything to make it perfect—smoked salmon, grouse, chantilly, different wines for each course and all this printed alongside each person's nameplace. The old servant was so nervous that he trembled as he stood over her and kept debating with his long hands whether to proffer the entrée dish or the gravy jug. It was touch and go. His master told him for God's sake to put the jug down. A movement that caused his neck to tremble like that of a half-dead cockerel's. Yes, "It was so" that students were sent down but they had to be awfully bad or else awfully unlucky and of course it was an awfully amusing thing. "I am in a modern English play," she thought, the kind of play that portrayed an intelligent man or woman going to seed and making stoical jokes about it. Academic life was not for her. She would rather be a barbarian. She sucked on the word as if it were sherbet. Barbarian.

The grouse was impossible to tackle. Everyone talked too much and tried too eagerly and this all-round determination to be considerate caused them instead to be distracted and noisy. Little bright jets of blood shot up as knives vainly attacked the game. To conceal his embarrassment the young professor said it was too delicious. The host said it was uneatable and if young Freddie's was delicious to give it to Lena since hers was like a brick. She demurred, said it was lovely, while at the same time resolved that she would eat the sprouts and would drink goblets of wine. A toast was raised to her son and he went scarlet as he heard himself being praised. Looking downwards she saw that the various plates contained a heap of little bones, decked with bits of torn pink flesh, and true to her domestic instinct she said they would make good broth, those leavings. A most tactless slip. Everyone raved over the nice raspberry chantilly and quite huge portions of it rested on the young men's dessert plates.

Having dined so early she felt it was appropriate to leave early. Earlier, her host had confessed to being tired and yet in his bedroom where she went to fetch her coat, she felt that he wanted to talk, that he was avid to tell some little thing. He simply said that he had never married because he could not stand the idea of a woman saying "we", organising his thought, his time, his suits of clothing and his money. It was a small, functional room with a washstand, an iron bed with a frayed paisley robe laid across it. Staring from the wall was a painting of a wolf with a man's eyes and she thought this professor is not as mild as he seems. On an impulse she kissed him and he seemed so childishly glad that she then became awkward and tripped over a footstool.

Out on the street they lingered, admiring the courtyard, the stone archways, and the beautiful formidable entrance. The town itself was just shops, and shut cafés, with cars whizzing up and down as on any high street. At the hotel she bade Iain goodnight and knew that the hour had come when they were parting more or less for ever. They made light of it and said they would cruise Cambridge on the morrow.

As she approached her bedroom she began to remonstrate with herself, began to laugh. The music she heard was surely phantom music because after all she had been insistent about securing a quiet room. But as she proceeded down the corridor the sound increased in volume and pitch and she wondered if anxiety could play such a thorough trick. When she put the key in her own door and entered, the furnishings were shaking from the implosion of the noise and she looked instinctively for men in white coats with hair oil, which was her outdated version of the members of a dance band. Yes, a dance was in progress. The metal hangers which she had forborne to use were almost doing a jig. The hotel telephonist could do nothing, was not even sympathetic.

She took her key and went down the stairs, then crossed the street to the college where her son was. The porter directed her and seemed to sense her dismay because he kept repeating the instructions, kept saying, "If you walk down now, towards the rectangular buildings, and take the first turning on the left you will find your son will be the fifth staircase along, and you will find him there." Walking along she thought only of the sleep that would "knit up the ravelled" day and hoped that in one of those buildings a bed awaited her, a bed, an eiderdown and total silence.

Coming towards her was a young man wearing a motor-cyclist's leather jacket that was too small for him. Something about the way he walked reminded her of restless youths that she had seen in an American film, of gangs who went out at night to have fights with other gangs, and inventing as a reason for murder their virility or their honour. This boy reminded her of that group. She wondered who he would be, thought that probably he had put on the jacket to give himself an image, was looking for friends. Four or five hundred young men were now installed in that college and she thought of the friendships that would ensue, of the indifferent meals they would all eat, the gowns they would buy, the loves and hatreds that would flourish as they became involved. She was glad not to be one of them. Just before the figure came level with her she realised that it was Iain and that obviously he was going in search of adventure. She lost heart then and could not tell him of her plan to find a bed in his house. She joked, pretended not to know him, walked past with her hips out and then in an affected voice said, "Haven't we met somewhere." Then she asked him if he was enjoying it and he said yes, but he always said yes at an awkward moment. They walked towards the gates and he said that his name was painted at the foot of the landing, his and three other names and how he had a little kitchen with a fridge and that there was a note informing him of a maid who would be at his services on the Monday. How she wanted to be that maid. They said goodnight again, this time a little more gamely since there was a mutual suspicion that they might meet a third time.

In the lobby some people had come out from the dance and a drunken woman was holding up a broken silver shoe asking if the heel could be mended. The dance would go on till two. Lena felt like crying. The manager asked if she would like another hotel and she said yes then ran to her room and packed things quickly, viciously. In the lobby yet again she felt herself to be conspicuous, what with half her belongings falling out of the bag and a look of madness. In the taxi she thought of warm milk laced with whisky. Vain thought. The porter in the new hotel was fast asleep and stirred himself only when the black Dalmatian dog bared his teeth at her legs which she quickly shielded with her suede bag. She had to pay there and then, and had to write the cheque by balancing the book against the wall as the counter space was taken up with various advertisement cards. Home, home, her heart begged. The last train for London had left an hour ago. She followed the porter down the corridor and herself let out a shriek when he admitted her to a room in which a shocked woman sat up in bed-jacket screaming. In fact the two women's screams coincided.

"Sorry about that, Madam." He had made a mistake. He made a similar mistake three times over, leaving some occupants of that wing in a state of anger and commotion. At last he

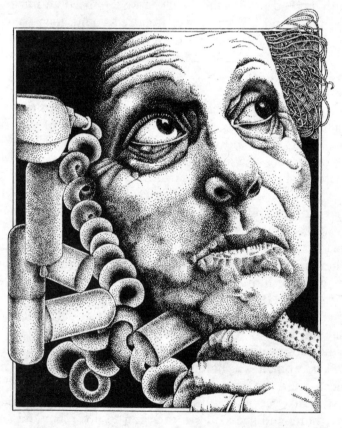

conducted her to an empty room, that was weirdly identical to the one she had just vacated. He said not to open the window in case of burglary.

Such nights are not remarkable for their sound sleeping, but this one had extra impediments. The single bed was so narrow that each time she tried to turn over she had to stop herself from falling onto the floor. The tap let out involuntary groans and now and then the Dalmatian gave a watchdog's moan. She put her black cardigan over the telephone to blot out its faint luminous glow. She was fighting for sleep. She took two large two-toned capsules that were filled with barbiturate. Her son at that same hour climbed up by means of scaffolding to the roof of Christ's College and with his friend was debating whether to pee on it or not, and make a statement that might result in their being rusticated. Up there they had brought the wine, the roast fillets of pork and the cheeses that she had given him for his first night's picnic. She could feel the sleeping pills starting to work as she put her hand out to assist herself in turning over. Nevertheless she tumbled, fell and conked her head on the bedside locker. It made her wide awake. The last sure little route to sleep was closed. It was a question of waiting till morning, so she dressed and then grappling with anger paced the room.

A hand-printed sign above the mirror caught her attention. It said, "In the hours of darkness, if a client has an urgent need will he or she please ring *and wait* because due to security the night porter may be prowling the building and not find himself adjacent to the switchboard." She took it down, re-read it with amazement, then wrote, "You must be joking", and signed her name in full. Then she sank into the gaping armchair and waited stoutly for morning.

Three Brothers
Joyce Grenfell

I had Three Brothers,
Harold and Robert and James,
All of them tall and handsome,
All of them good at games.
And I was allowed to field for them,
To bowl to them, to score:
I was allowed to slave for them
For ever and evermore.
Oh, I was allowed to fetch and carry for my Three Brothers,
Jim   and   Bob   and   Harry.

All of my brothers,
Harry and Jim and Bob,
Grew to be good and clever,
Each of them at his job.
And I was allowed to wait on them,
To be their slave complete,
I was allowed to work for them
And life for me was sweet,
For I was allowed to fetch and carry for my Three Brothers,
Jim   and   Bob   and   Harry.

Jim went out to South Africa,
Bob went out to Ceylon,
Harry went out to New Zealand
And settled in Wellington.
And the grass grew high on the cricket-pitch,
And the tennis-court went to hay,
And the place was too big and too silent
After they went away.

So I turned it into a Guest House,
After our parents died,
And I wrote to the boys every Sunday,
And once a year they replied.
All of them married eventually,
I wrote to their wives, of course,
And their wives wrote back on postcards—
Well . . . it might have been very much worse.

And now I have nine nieces
Most of them home at school.
I have them all to stay here
For the holidays, as a rule.
And I am allowed to slave for them,
To do odd jobs galore,
I am allowed to work for them
And life is sweet once more,
For I am allowed to fetch and carry for the children of
Jim   and   Bob   and   Harry.

WOMAN

JAMES THURBER

FOR centuries Woman has been quietly at work achieving her present identity. Not many years ago the Encyclopaedia Britannica listed nothing under "Woman", but merely said "See Man". The latest Oxford English Dictionary, however, gives woman twelve columns to man's fifteen. The development of her name from Old English through Middle English to Modern English is fascinating to trace in the O.E.D. She began as "wife", became "wifman" and underwent seventeen other changes until the word "woman" came into use about the year 1400. Most writers, glibly discussing the origin of the word over their brandy, contend that it derives from the derogatory phrase "with man" or the physiological "wombman". They don't know what they are talking about. Earlier male writers, equally mistaken, declared the word derived from "woe to man" or "wee man". Some of them were serious, others merely kidding, in the immemorial manner of the superior male.

I'm glad to report that the feminist Flecknor took a fairer view in 1653 when he wrote: "Say of Woman worst ye can, what prolongs their woe, but man?" In the past three hundred years the importance of women has often been derided by men, from J. Clarke's "A Woman, asse, and walnut-tree, the more you beat the better be" to Noel Coward's "A woman should be struck regularly like a gong". But there were wiser men who spoke of the female of the species with proper respect, and even fear. It was Congreve who wrote the almost invariably misquoted "Heav'n has no Rage, like Love to Hatred turn'd, Nor Hell a Fury, like a Woman scorned", and in 1835 Hook recognized the stature of the female with "A girl of seventeen is a woman, when a man of seventeen is a boy." Thirty-two years later, English law under Queen Victoria formally defined the female: "Woman shall mean a Female of the Age of Eighteen Years or Upwards", and twenty years after that, the British female legally became a woman at the age of sixteen, while males of the same age were still regarded as schoolchildren.

It was in the 1890's that the old-fashioned dependent woman was scornfully rejected by her own sex as the "cow-woman", and "new woman" and even "new womandom" came into common and spirited use. Ninety years before that decade of the self-assertive woman, J. Brown had arrogantly written, "No ecclesiastical power can reside in a heathen, a woman, or a child." Fortunately for his peace of mind, he didn't live to see the female become the residence of practically any power you can name. She is now definitely here to stay, whereas the decline of the male, even the actual decadence of the insecure sex, has been observed by alarmed scientists in a score of other species. A certain scorpion, for example, disappears with his mate after a ritualistic courtship dance, and is never seen again. The female, though, emerges from the honeymoon, fit as a fiddle and fresh as a daisy. And there is a certain female fish in the waters of the sea who has reduced the male to the status of a mere accessory. She actually

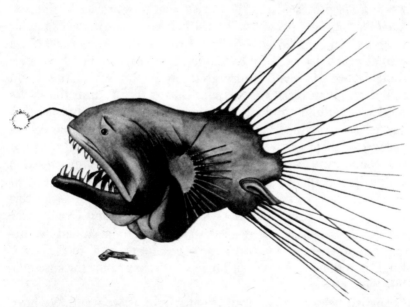

carries him about with her, for occasional biological use, in the casual way that a woman carries a compact or a cigarette lighter in her handbag. There are dozens of other significant instances of the dwindling of the male in the animal kingdom, but I am much too nervous to go into them here. Some twenty years ago, a gloomy scientist reported, "Man's day is done." Woman's day, on the other hand, is, by every sign and token, just beginning. It couldn't happen to a nicer sex.

From
"The Ladies of Orlon", *Alarms and Diversions*

DATA

PHILIP HOWARD

Data is not what they used to be

IN spite of protests from the purists that they are a Latin plural, *data* stubbornly persists in trying to become an English singular as *agenda* and *stamina* did before it/them. The *media* have/has a similar proclivity as in "the mass *media* is responsible" for something or other; usually and regrettably in the way of the world something that vexes the writer, who wants to lump the *media* together, without thinking of them as one *medium*, and another *medium*, and a third, and all the others. It is a notable recent *phenomena* that one *criteria* of education in an influential *strata* of the community is to be good at criticizing what the *media* is saying about all this *data* on the decay of English. Instead of crying barbarism, it is more constructive to investigate why this should be happening. Fewer people know Latin and Greek these days, and accordingly there are fewer around to be pained by outrages upon their methods of word-formation. And, in any case, English grammar evolves with majestic disregard for the susceptibilities of classical scholars.

English belongs to all of us, to change it as we want. We have made more fundamental changes to it in the past than altering the number of a few words from plural to singular. Think of the alarm that thoughtful Anglo-Saxons must have felt when they realized that the progressive simplification of Old English, particularly the loss of grammatical gender, was leading them away from mainland Europe and into an unpredictable grammatical isolation. Yet no whisper of such alarm comes down to us in their chronicles or linguistic laws. Perhaps they were less hypochondriac about their robust language than we are.

The distinction between singular and plural is not as clear-cut as it appears at first thought. It compels users of English to choose between one thing and any number from two to infinity, which are lumped together as plural. The old dual number, the inflected form expressing two or a pair, is the historic binary plural for referring to twos. It flourished in a number of languages, including Classical Greek and Gothic, and survives vestigially in English in "both", "either", and "whether", and the ease with which we can refer to a pair and a couple as compared with a trio and a foursome. Trousers, which customarily have two legs, are plural, though we refer to a pair of them. In French they are singular, *le pantalon*. But a bra, back in the dim days when such things were worn, was inescapably bipartite but invariably singular. Why should bathing-trunks, which have three openings of roughly equal size, be a pair of anything?

Professor Randolph Quirk, the Quain Professor of English Language and Literature at University College, London, is a brilliantly perceptive exegete of the quirks and quiddities of grammar. The Survey of English Usage at University College has since 1959 been fruitfully exploring and recording English grammar as it is spoken and written today. In November 1977 Randolph Quirk advanced a characteristically entertaining and persuasive explanation of why such plurals as *data* persist in changing number and turning singular. He describes *data* as an "aggregate" noun. And he defines such a noun as one in which the essential thing is choosing to ignore the individual components, and considering the collection as though it were a packaged unit. An aggregate noun is capable of being counted if it has to be, like sheep, but precise enumeration is not its point. We do not usually talk about three *data*, or 423 *data*, or of isolating one *datum* from the *data*. With the explosive increase in the quantities of *data* that modern science feels it necessary to handle, and (through computers) finds it possible to handle, the individual *datum* becomes decreasingly relevant. Small numbers of *data* become as embarrassing to enumerate as wild oats. We find it less obvious to conceive of *data* as consisting of *datum* upon *datum* upon *datum*. Above all, the word is used as a singular since it is merely the aggregates of *data*, considered as an indistinct mass like butter, that influence decision-making.

The same thing happened to *stamina*, another Latin plural. In English the singular *stamen* originally meant the warp of a textile fabric, a thread, and thence the supposed germinal principle or impulse in which the future characteristics of any nascent existence are implicit. *Stamina* became a singular aggregate noun because the individual "*stamens*" or fibres are irrelevant in considering the aggregate notion of vigour of bodily constitution. *Stamina* has gradually turned singular, but it was still plural at the time of Jonathan Swift. Similarly *media* are/is becoming an aggregate singular, because it is convenient in many contexts to think of the organs that influence public opinion as a single brass band, without separating it into its component instruments, as newspapers, magazines, television, and radio. The uneducated and impassioned often speak on television of the *media* and the press, so confining the word to broadcasting and giving it a new twist that spoils its usefulness.

The same thing happened to *news*. In the writings of such confident authorities as Queen Victoria and Benjamin Jowett the *news* are plural, like *les nouvelles* and *die informationen*. There is an agreeable legend at *The Times*, which may even have a basis of truth, though the manner of addressing the editor has evidently been brought up to date. During the Crimean War John Thaddeus Delane, the great editor of *The Times*, cabled William Howard Russell, the first war correspondent: "Are there any *news*?" Back down the wires the electric message came: "Not a damned *new*." Since those brave days we have come to think of *news* as an aggregate singular instead of a plural catalogue of items of *news*.

As we should expect, Professor Quirk's opinion is solidly rooted in the historical *data* of the word. *Data* started to change number in Computerese, the jargon of men who work with such vast quantities of *data* that the notion of enumerating them is as absurd as the notion of a farmer counting his wheat. No doubt it could be done, as scientists have calculated the number of atoms in the Universe, but it is not a calculation that one wants to do often.

The shift to thinking and speaking about *data* as an aggregate singular is recorded as occurring in the technical literature of computers from the 1960s. From there it spread into journalism and other general writing (*Science Journal*, 1970): "During each orbit *data* from the experiment is transmitted from the satellite to Fairbanks in Alaska, and from there to Oxford for initial processing." A dictionary of computers in the same year made an interesting distinction: "*Data* is sometimes contrasted with information, which is said to result from the processing of *data*."

The language and cast of mind of those who work with computers incline them to think of *data* as an aggregate singular. *Data* is put in a bank, like the singular money, handled, and transmitted over a *data link. Data* processing is an automatic and continuous process as innumerable as the barley being processed by a combine. A *data logger* records the successive values of a number of different physical quantities.

The computermen have got it into their noddles that *data* is an aggregate singular like English porridge. James Murray, the founding father of the *OED*, was reported by his granddaughter to have complained: "These porridge aren't properly cooked"; and some professional Scots still refer to their porridge as "they" or "them". There is evidently no future in outsiders protesting that they are wrong to say things like: "*Data* that is four to twelve years old is of limited use." Those of us whose atavistic Latinate sensibilities are outraged by the practice can avoid copying it, until perhaps usage drags us willy-nilly to conform, as it has with *stamina*. We certainly ought to refrain from adopting such Computerese as *data base* figuratively, when all that we mean is records, and to abstain from saying, or writing, the *media*, when all that we mean is the newspapers, or the telly.

And we can reflect with the tolerant but acute Randolph Quirk that the rise of the aggregate singular nastily illustrates the further relegation of the individual. If we start talking about a *strata* of society as a singular, as the sociologists do, we may forget that inside each homogeneous group large numbers of people, each one an individual, are struggling to get out. Is this the direction of English 1984? Professor Quirk comes to no firm conclusion, but his *data* are/is stimulating.

From
Weasel Words

BELOW STAIRS

MARK GIROUARD

THE peculiar character of Victorian servants' wings was the result of early-nineteenth-century arrangements being revised to make them more moral and more efficient. Efficiency involved analyzing the different functions performed by different servants, giving each function its own area and often its own room, and grouping the related functions into territories accessible to the gentry part of the house which they serviced. Morality meant—in addition to compulsory attendance at daily prayers and Sunday church—separation of the sexes except when they were under supervision. The organisation of related jobs into territories achieved this fairly efficiently in the daytime. At night, infinite care was taken to see that men and women slept in different parts of the house, without access one to the other. Within the male and female sleeping quarters it was normal for the servants to sleep one, or at most two, to a room. Servants' dormitories had survived into the early Victorian period, but were regarded with suspicion and soon got rid of.

The results of organisation and morality in terms of the plan can be seen in its most elaborate and carefully worked out form in houses designed by William Burn in the 1840s and '50s. Burn (who worked, incidentally, more for old families than for the new rich) was regarded at the time as providing houses that were the last word in organisation and efficiency. The servants' wing at Lynford in Norfolk, designed by him in 1856 for Mr Lyne Stephens, was a typical example of his work. It was divided into four zones—the butler's, the cook's, the housekeeper's and the laundry-maid's. The butler's zone was entirely male, the other three entirely female, except, possibly, for a male chef at the head of the cook's department. Male and female zones were kept separate, each with its own staircase to its own bedrooms. The servants' hall and steward's room occupied the neutral ground between them.

In grand houses the steward, housekeeper and head cook ate in the steward's room, along with the head gardener, the senior lady's maids and valets, the coachman, and visiting servants of the same rank. A footman or steward's-room boy waited on them. The other servants ate in the servants' hall, usually looked after by the odd man. In less grand houses the upper servants had breakfast and tea in the housekeeper's room, ate the main courses of dinner and supper in the servants' hall, and retired to the housekeeper's room to eat their pudding—just as their betters had retired to the drawing room to eat their dessert in the seventeenth and eighteenth centuries.

The housekeeper was in command of the housemaids and one or more still-room maids. She was responsible for cleaning the house, looking after the linen, and providing, storing, and where necessary preparing tea, coffee, sugar, groceries, preserves, cakes and biscuits. The institution of afternoon tea in the 1840s added to her responsibilities. Her central territory consisted of her own housekeeper's room, the still-room and sometimes a separate store-room and closet. Her own room was usually lined with china-cupboards and linen-presses but was also furnished as a comfortable parlour; it had the agreeable atmosphere of a room used for both business and gossip.

There was a similar atmosphere in the butler's pantry, with its

cupboards for storage, sinks and table for cleaning, and comfortable chair by the fire. The butler ruled over the footmen and any other indoor men-servants, except for the valets. He was in charge of the plate, drink and table linen, and his many responsibilities included (by way of footmen or groom of the chambers) furnishing all writing-tables and, in some houses, polishing the mirrors. In a big house like Lynford his pantry was the centre of a little kingdom of satellite rooms, including a safe or storage room for plate, a scullery to clean it in, cellars for wine and beer, and separate little cells in which the footmen or odd man brushed the clothes, cleaned the shoes, cleaned the knives, and trimmed, cleaned and filled the oil lamps. In some houses a footman, or even the butler himself, had a bedroom next to the safe, for security. Some pantries had a view of the front of the house from their windows, so that visitors could be seen in advance, and the front door open magically as their carriages drew up at the front steps.

The butler's pantry was often close to the dining room, as at Lynford; the kitchen almost never was. The Victorians, like earlier generations, thought it more important to keep kitchen smells out of the gentry end of the house. Although the closed range had been pioneered at the beginning of the century, in most houses roasting was still conducted at open fires; the bigger the house the greater the smell. In houses the size of Lynford the kitchen was usually a considerable distance from the dining room and had its own louvered roof, for ventilation. One or more kinks in the connecting corridor helped to keep smells from travelling, and a hot plate in the serving-room warmed the food up again.

The grandeur of a house could be measured by the number of chefs in the kitchen. Less grand houses had a single chef presiding over female under-cooks, kitchen-maids and scullery-maids; in many houses all the kitchen staff were women. A big country-house kitchen, bustling with chefs and kitchen-maids and lined with all that the latest Victorian technology had to offer, was an impressive sight; Robert Kerr in his invaluable contemporary book *The Gentleman's House* described it as "having the character of a complicated laboratory". The Victorians were proud of their kitchens, and of their complex equipment of roasting-ranges, stewing-stoves, boiling-stoves, turnspits, hotplates and hot closets. The kitchen was usually the only servants' room which owners or architects bothered to have photographed. By present-day standards its technology was, of course, cumbersome and limited.

There were no washing-machines, no extractors, no refrigeration, except what was provided by a marble slab or a box cooled with ice brought up from the ice house. Larders were kept cool by natural ventilation. Most big country houses had a game larder, planned for ventilation as a free-standing and often rather decorative building in the kitchen courtyard. Larder accommodation could be further subdivided into a pantry or dry larder, for cooked materials, and separate meat and fish larders for uncooked ones—in addition to the inevitable scullery, and occasional rooms for baking, salting, and smoking.

The laundry department was in a unique position, the result both of history and of the process of laundering. Laundry-maids had been working in country houses for many centuries before housekeepers and housemaids; they formed an independent group and were not always under the control of the housekeeper. Before the invention of washing-machines and tumble-driers laundering produced a great deal of steam and smell, and had to be accessible to a drying-ground; so laundering was usually on the periphery of the servants' quarters. The independence of the job tended to

bring pretty girls into it, and the position of the laundry to make it easily accessible to outside workers—especially to the grooms in the stable. As far as sexual segregation was concerned, the laundry was the Achilles' heel of the Victorian country house.

From
Life in the English Country House

AN ENGLISH COUNTRY HOUSE

HENRY JAMES

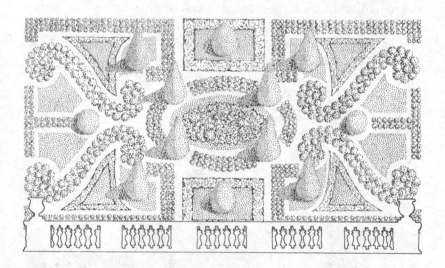

HYACINTH got up early—an operation attended with very little effort, as he had scarce closed his eyes all night. What he saw from his window made him dress as quickly as a young man might who desired more than ever that his appearance shouldn't give strange ideas about him: an old garden with parterres in curious figures and little intervals of lawn that seemed to our hero's cockney vision fantastically green. At one end of the garden was a parapet of mossy brick which looked down on the other side into a canal, a moat, a quaint old pond (he hardly knew what to call it) and from the same standpoint showed a considerable part of the main body of the house—Hyacinth's room

belonging to a wing that commanded the extensive irregular back
—which was richly grey wherever clear of the ivy and the other
dense creepers, and everywhere infinitely a picture: with a high-
piled ancient russet roof broken by huge chimneys and queer
peep-holes and all manner of odd gables and windows on different
lines, with all manner of antique patches and protrusions and
with a particularly fascinating architectural excrescence where a
wonderful clock-face was lodged, a clock-face covered with gilding
and blazonry but showing many traces of the years and the
weather. He had never in his life been in the country—the real
country, as he called it, the country which was not the mere
ravelled fringe of London—and there entered through his open
casement the breath of a world enchantingly new and after his
recent feverish hours unspeakably refreshing; a sense of sweet
sunny air and mingled odours, all strangely pure and agreeable,
and of a musical silence that consisted for the greater part of the
voices of many birds. There were tall quiet trees near by and afar
off and everywhere; and the group of objects that greeted his eyes
evidently formed only a corner of larger spaces and of a more
complicated scene. There was a world to be revealed to him: it
lay waiting with the dew on it under his windows, and he must go
down and take of it such possession as he might.

He rambled an hour in breathless ecstasy, brushing the dew
from the deep fern and bracken and the rich borders of the
garden, tasting the fragrant air and stopping everywhere, in
murmuring rapture, at the touch of some exquisite impression.
His whole walk was peopled with recognitions; he had been
dreaming all his life of just such a place and such objects, such a
morning and such a chance. It was the last of April and everything
was fresh and vivid; the great trees in the early air, were a blur of
tender shoots. Round the admirable house he revolved repeatedly,
catching every aspect and feeling every value, feasting on the
whole expression. . . . There was something in the way the grey
walls rose from the green lawn that brought tears to his eyes; the
spectacle of long duration unassociated with some sordid infirmity
or poverty was new to him; he had lived with people among whom
old age meant for the most part a grudged and degraded survival.
In the favoured resistance of Medley was a serenity of success, an
accumulation of dignity and honour.

From
The Princess Casamassima

THE LANDLADY
ROALD DAHL

BILLY WEAVER had travelled down from London on the slow afternoon train, with a change at Swindon on the way, and by the time he got to Bath it was about nine o'clock in the evening and the moon was coming up out of a clear starry sky over the houses opposite the station entrance. But the air was deadly cold and the wind was like a flat blade of ice on his cheeks.

"Excuse me," he said, "but is there a fairly cheap hotel not too far away from here?"

"Try The Bell and Dragon," the porter answered, pointing down the road. "They might take you in. It's about a quarter of a mile along on the other side."

Billy thanked him and picked up his suitcase and set out to walk the quarter-mile to The Bell and Dragon. He had never been to Bath before. He didn't know anyone who lived there. But Mr Greenslade at the Head Office in London had told him it was a splendid city. "Find your own lodgings," he had said, "and then go along and report to the Branch Manager as soon as you've got yourself settled."

Billy was seventeen years old. He was wearing a new navy-blue overcoat, a new brown trilby hat, and a new brown suit, and he was feeling fine. He walked briskly down the street. He was trying to do everything briskly these days. Briskness, he had decided, was *the* one common characteristic of all successful businessmen. The big shots up at Head Office were absolutely fantastically brisk all the time. They were amazing.

There were no shops on this wide street that he was walking along, only a line of tall houses on each side, all of them identical. They had porches and pillars and four or five steps going up to their front doors, and it was obvious that once upon a time they had been very swanky residences. But now, even in the darkness, he could see that the paint was peeling from the woodwork on their doors and windows, and that the handsome white façades were cracked and blotchy from neglect.

Suddenly, in a downstairs window that was brilliantly illuminated by a street-lamp not six yards away, Billy caught sight of a printed notice propped up against the glass in one of the upper panes. It said BED AND BREAKFAST. There was a vase of pussy-willows, tall and beautiful, standing just underneath the notice.

He stopped walking. He moved a bit closer. Green curtains (some sort of velvety material) were hanging down on either side of the window. The pussy-willows looked wonderful beside them. He went right up and peered through the glass into the room, and the first thing he saw was a bright fire burning in the hearth. On the carpet in front of the fire, a pretty little dachshund was curled up asleep with its nose tucked into its belly. The room itself, so far as he could see in the half-darkness, was filled with pleasant furniture. There was a baby-grand piano and a big sofa and several plump armchairs; and in one corner he spotted a large parrot in a cage. Animals were usually a good sign in a place like this, Billy told himself; and all in all, it looked to him as though it would be a pretty decent house to stay in. Certainly it would be more comfortable than The Bell and Dragon.

On the other hand, a pub would be more congenial than a boarding-house. There would be beer and darts in the evenings, and lots of people to talk to, and it would probably be a good bit cheaper, too. He had stayed a couple of nights in a pub once before and he had liked it. He had never stayed in any boarding-houses, and, to be perfectly honest, he was a tiny bit frightened of them. The name itself conjured up images of watery cabbage, rapacious landladies, and a powerful smell of kippers in the living-room.

After dithering about like this in the cold for two or three minutes, Billy decided that he would walk on and take a look at The Bell and Dragon before making up his mind. He turned to go.

And now a queer thing happened to him. He was in the act of stepping back and turning away from the window when all at once his eye was caught and held in the most peculiar manner by the small notice that was there. BED AND BREAKFAST, it said. BED AND BREAKFAST, BED AND BREAKFAST, BED AND BREAKFAST. Each word was like a large black eye staring at him through the glass, holding him, compelling him, forcing him to stay where he was and not to walk away from that house, and the next thing he knew, he was actually moving across from the window to the front door of the house, climbing the steps that led up to it, and reaching for the bell.

He pressed the bell. Far away in a back room he heard it ringing, and then *at once*—it must have been at once because he hadn't even had time to take his finger from the bell-button—the door swung open and a woman was standing there.

Normally you ring the bell and you have at least a half-minute's wait before the door opens. But this dame was like a jack-in-the-box. He pressed the bell—and out she popped! It made him jump.

She was about forty-five or fifty years old, and the moment she saw him, she gave him a warm welcoming smile.

"*Please* come in," she said pleasantly. She stepped aside, holding the door wide open, and Billy found himself automatically starting forward into the house. The compulsion or, more accurately, the desire to follow after her into that house was extraordinarily strong.

"I saw the notice in the window," he said, holding himself back.

"Yes, I know."

"I was wondering about a room."

"It's *all* ready for you, my dear," she said. She had a round pink face and very gentle blue eyes.

"I was on my way to The Bell and Dragon," Billy told her. "But the notice in your window just happened to catch my eye."

"My dear boy," she said, "why don't you come in out of the cold?"

"How much do you charge?"

"Five and sixpence a night, including breakfast."

It was fantastically cheap. It was less than half of what he had been willing to pay.

"If that is too much," she added, "then perhaps I can reduce it just a tiny bit. Do you desire an egg for breakfast? Eggs are expensive at the moment. It would be sixpence less without the egg."

"Five and sixpence is fine," he answered. "I should like very much to stay here."

"I knew you would. Do come in."

She seemed terribly nice. She looked exactly like the mother of one's best school-friend welcoming one into the house to stay for the Christmas holidays. Billy took off his hat, and stepped over the threshold.

"Just hang it there," she said, "and let me help you with your coat."

There were no other hats or coats in the hall. There were no umbrellas, no walking-sticks—nothing.

"We have it *all* to ourselves," she said, smiling at him over her shoulder as she led the way upstairs. "You see, it isn't very often I have the pleasure of taking a visitor into my little nest."

The old girl is slightly dotty, Billy told himself. But at five and sixpence a night, who gives a damn about that? "I should've thought you'd be simply swamped with applicants," he said politely.

"Oh, I am, my dear, I am, of course I am. But the trouble is that I'm inclined to be just a teeny weeny bit choosy and particular —if you see what I mean."

"Ah, yes."

"But I'm always ready. Everything is always ready day and night in this house just on the off-chance that an acceptable young gentleman will come along. And it is such a pleasure, my dear, such a very great pleasure when now and again I open the door and I see someone standing there who is just *exactly* right." She was halfway up the stairs, and she paused with one hand on the stair-rail, turning her head and smiling down at him with pale lips. "Like you," she added, and her blue eyes travelled slowly all the way down the length of Billy's body, to his feet, and then up again.

On the first-floor landing she said to him, "This floor is mine."

They climbed up a second flight. "And this one is *all* yours," she said. "Here's your room. I do hope you'll like it." She took him into a small charming front bedroom, switching on the light as she went in.

"The morning sun comes right in the window, Mr Perkins. It *is* Mr Perkins, isn't it?"

"No," he said. "It's Weaver."

"Mr Weaver. How nice. I've put a water-bottle between the sheets to air them out, Mr Weaver. It's such a comfort to have a hot water-bottle in a strange bed with clean sheets, don't you agree? And you may light the gas fire at any time if you feel chilly."

"Thank you," Billy said. "Thank you ever so much." He noticed that the bedspread had been taken off the bed, and that the bedclothes had been neatly turned back on one side, all ready for someone to get in.

"I'm so glad you appeared," she said, looking earnestly into his face. "I was beginning to get worried."

"That's all right," Billy answered brightly. "You mustn't worry about me." He put his suitcase on the chair and started to open it.

"And what about supper, my dear? Did you manage to get anything to eat before you came here?"

"I'm not a bit hungry, thank you," he said. "I think I'll just go to bed as soon as possible because tomorrow I've got to get up rather early and report to the office."

"Very well, then. I'll leave you now so that you can unpack. But before you go to bed, would you be kind enough to pop into the sitting-room on the ground floor and sign the book? Everyone has to do that because it's the law of the land, and we don't want to go breaking any laws at *this* stage in the proceedings, do we?" She gave him a little wave of the hand and went quickly out of the room and closed the door.

Now, the fact that this landlady appeared to be slightly off her rocker didn't worry Billy in the least. After all, she was not only harmless—there was no question about that—but she was also quite obviously a kind and generous soul. He guessed that she had probably lost a son in the war, or something like that, and had never got over it.

So a few minutes later, after unpacking his suitcase and washing his hands, he trotted downstairs to the ground floor and entered the living-room. His landlady wasn't there, but the fire was glowing in the hearth, and the little dachshund was still sleeping in front of it. The room was wonderfully warm and cosy. I'm a lucky fellow, he thought, rubbing his hands. This is a bit of all right.

He found the guest-book lying open on the piano, so he took out his pen and wrote down his name and address. There were only two other entries above his on the page, and, as one always does with guest-books, he started to read them. One was a Christopher Mulholland from Cardiff. The other was Gregory W. Temple from Bristol.

That's funny, he thought suddenly. Christopher Mulholland. It rings a bell.

Now where on earth had he heard that rather unusual name before?

Was he a boy at school? No. Was it one of his sister's numerous young men, perhaps, or a friend of his father's? No, no, it wasn't any of those. He glanced down again at the book.

Christopher Mulholland   231 Cathedral Road, Cardiff
Gregory W. Temple   27 Sycamore Drive, Bristol

As a matter of fact, now he came to think of it, he wasn't at all sure that the second name didn't have almost as much of a familiar ring about it as the first.

"Gregory Temple?" he said aloud, searching his memory. "Christopher Mulholland? . . ."

"Such charming boys," a voice behind him answered, and he turned and saw his landlady sailing into the room with a large silver tea-tray in her hands. She was holding it well out in front of her, and rather high up, as though the tray were a pair of reins on a frisky horse.

"They sound somehow familiar," he said.

"They do? How interesting."

"I'm almost positive I've heard those names before somewhere. Isn't that queer? Maybe it was in the newspapers. They weren't famous in any way, were they? I mean famous cricketers or footballers or something like that?"

"Famous," she said, setting the tea-tray down on the low table in front of the sofa. "Oh no, I don't think they were famous. But they were extraordinarily handsome, both of them, I can promise you that. They were tall and young and handsome, my dear, just exactly like you."

Once more, Billy glanced down at the book. "Look here," he said, noticing the dates. "Ths last entry is over two years old."

"It is?"

"Yes, indeed. And Christopher Mulholland's is nearly a year before that—more than *three years ago*."

"Dear me," she said, shaking her head and heaving a dainty

little sigh. "I would never have thought it. How time does fly away from us all, doesn't it, Mr Wilkins?"

"It's Weaver," Billy said. "W-e-a-v-e-r."

"Oh, of course it is!" she cried, sitting down on the sofa. "How silly of me. I do apologise. In one ear and out the other, that's me, Mr Weaver."

"You know something?" Billy said. "Something that's really quite extraordinary about all this?"

"No, dear, I don't."

"Well, you see—both of these names, Mulholland and Temple, I not only seem to remember each one of them separately, so to speak, but somehow or other, in some peculiar way, they both appear to be sort of connected together as well. As though they were both famous for the same sort of thing, if you see what I mean—like . . . well . . . like Dempsey and Tunney, for example, or Churchill and Roosevelt."

"How amusing," she said. "But come over here now, dear, and sit down beside me on the sofa and I'll give you a nice cup of tea and a ginger biscuit before you go to bed."

"You really shouldn't bother," Billy said. "I didn't mean you to do anything like that." He stood by the piano, watching her as she fussed about with the cups and saucers. He noticed that she had small, white, quickly moving hands, and red fingernails.

"I'm almost positive it was in the newspapers I saw them," Billy said. "I'll think of it in a second. I'm sure I will."

There is nothing more tantalising than a thing like this which lingers just outside the borders of one's memory. He hated to give up.

"Now wait a minute," he said. "Wait just a minute. Mulholland . . . Christopher Mulholland . . . wasn't *that* the name of the Eton schoolboy who was on a walking-tour through the West Country, and then all of a sudden . . ."

"Milk?" she said. "And sugar?"

"Yes, please. And then all of a sudden . . ."

"Eton schoolboy?" she said. "Oh no, my dear, that can't possibly be right because *my* Mr Mulholland was certainly not an Eton schoolboy when he came to me. He was a Cambridge undergraduate. Come over here now and sit next to me and warm yourself in front of this lovely fire. Come on. Your tea's all ready for you." She patted the empty place beside her on the sofa, and she sat there smiling at Billy and waiting for him to come over.

He crossed the room slowly, and sat down on the edge of the

sofa. She placed his teacup on the table in front of him.

"*There* we are," she said. "How nice and cosy this is, isn't it?"

Billy started sipping his tea. She did the same. For half a minute or so, neither of them spoke. But Billy knew that she was looking at him. Her body was half turned towards him, and he could feel her eyes resting on his face, watching him over the rim of her teacup. Now and again, he caught a whiff of a peculiar smell that seemed to emanate directly from her person. It was not in the least unpleasant, and it reminded him—well, he wasn't quite sure what it reminded him of. Pickled walnuts? New leather? Or was it the corridors of a hospital?

"Mr Mulholland was a great one for his tea," she said at length. "Never in my life have I seen anyone drink as much tea as dear, sweet Mr Mulholland."

"I suppose he left fairly recently," Billy said. He was still puzzling his head about the two names. He was positive now that he had seen them in the newspapers—in the headlines.

"Left?" she said, arching her brows. "But my dear boy, he never left. He's still here. Mr Temple is also here. They're on the third floor, both of them together."

Billy set down his cup slowly on the table, and stared at his landlady. She smiled back at him, and then she put out one of her white hands and patted him comfortingly on the knee. "How old are you, my dear?" she asked.

"Seventeen."

"Seventeen!" she cried. "Oh, it's the perfect age! Mr Mulholland was also seventeen. But I think he was a trifle shorter than you are, in fact I'm sure he was, and his teeth weren't *quite* so white. You have the most beautiful teeth, Mr Weaver, did you know that?"

"They're not as good as they look," Billy said. "They've got simply masses of fillings in them at the back."

"Mr Temple, of course, was a little older," she said, ignoring his remark. "He was actually twenty-eight. And yet I never would have guessed it if he hadn't told me, never in my whole life. There wasn't a *blemish* on his body."

"A what?" Billy said.

"His skin was *just* like a baby's."

There was a pause. Billy picked up his teacup and took another sip of his tea, then he set it down again gently in its saucer. He waited for her to say something else, but she seemed to have lapsed into another of her silences. He sat there staring straight ahead of him into the far corner of the room, biting his lower lip.

"That parrot," he said at last. "You know something? It had me completely fooled when I first saw it through the window from the street. I could have sworn it was alive."

"Alas, no longer."

"It's most terribly clever the way it's been done," he said. "It doesn't look in the least bit dead. Who did it?"

"I did."

"*You* did?"

"Of course," she said. "And have you met my little Basil as well?" She nodded towards the dachshund curled up so comfortably in front of the fire. Billy looked at it. And suddenly, he realised that this animal had all the time been just as silent and motionless as the parrot. He put out a hand and touched it gently on the top of its back. The back was hard and cold, and when he pushed the hair to one side with his fingers, he could see the skin underneath, greyish-black and dry and perfectly preserved.

"Good gracious me," he said. "How absolutely fascinating." He turned away from the dog and stared with deep admiration at the little woman beside him on the sofa. "It must be most awfully difficult to do a thing like that."

"Not in the least," she said. "I stuff *all* my little pets myself when they pass away. Will you have another cup of tea?"

"No, thank you," Billy said. The tea tasted faintly of bitter almonds, and he didn't much care for it.

"You did sign the book, didn't you?"

"Oh, yes."

"That's good. Because later on, if I happen to forget what you were called, then I can always come down here and look it up. I still do that almost every day with Mr Mulholland and Mr . . . Mr . . ."

"Temple," Billy said. "Gregory Temple. Excuse my asking, but haven't there been *any* other guests here except them in the last two or three years?"

Holding her teacup high in one hand, inclining her head slightly to the left, she looked up at him out of the corners of her eyes and gave him another gentle little smile.

"No, my dear," she said. "Only you."

From
Tales of the Unexpected

A STAY IN COLOGNE

PATRICK LEIGH FERMOR

In 1933, at the age of eighteen, Patrick Leigh Fermor decided to walk across Europe from the Hook of Holland to Constantinople. He carried only a borrowed rucksack, and the journey took him a year and a half. After crossing the German border into Westphalia, he followed the course of the Rhine to Cologne.

I woke up in a bargemen's lodging house above a cluster of masts and determined to stay another day in this marvellous town.

It had occurred to me that I might learn German quicker by reading Shakespeare in the famous German translation. The young man in the bookshop spoke some English. Was it *really* so good, I asked him. He was enthusiastic: Schlegel and Tieck's version, he said, was *almost* as good as the original; so I bought *Hamlet, Prinz von Dänemark*, in a paperbound pocket edition. He was so helpful that I asked him if there were any way of travelling up the Rhine by barge. He called a friend into consultation who was more fluent in English: I explained I was a student, travelling to Constantinople on foot with not much money, and that I didn't mind how uncomfortable I was. The newcomer asked: student of what? Well—literature: I wanted to write a book. "*So!* You are travelling about Europe like Childe Harold?", he said. "Yes, *yes*! Absolutely like Childe Harold!" Where was I staying? I told them. "Pfui!" They were horrified, and amused. Both were delightful and, as the upshot of all this, I was asked to stay with one of them. We were to meet in the evening.

The day passed in exploring churches and picture galleries and looking at old buildings, with a borrowed guidebook.

Hans, who was my host, had been a fellow-student at Cologne University with Karl, the bookseller. He told me at dinner that he had fixed up a free lift for me next day on a string of barges heading upstream, all the way to the Black Forest if I wanted. We drank delicious Rhine wine and talked about English literature. The key figures in Germany I gathered, were Shakespeare, Byron, Poe, Galsworthy, Wilde, Maugham, Virginia Woolf, Charles Morgan and, very recently, Rosamund Lehmann. What about Priestley, they asked: *The Good Companions?*—and *The Story of San Michele?*

It was my first venture inside a German house. The interior was composed of Victorian furniture, bobbled curtains, a stove with green china tiles and many books with characteristic German bindings. Hans's cheerful landlady, who was the widow of a don at the University, joined us over tea with brandy in it. I answered many earnest questions about England: how lucky and enviable I was, they said, to belong to that fortunate kingdom where all was so just and sensible! The allied occupation of the Rhineland had come to an end less than ten years before, and the British, she said, had left an excellent impression. The life she described revolved round football, boxing matches, fox-hunts and theatricals. The Tommies got drunk, of course, and boxed each other in the street—she lifted her hands in the posture of squaring up—but they scarcely ever set about the locals. As for the colonel who had been billeted on her for years, with his pipe and his fox terriers— what a gentleman! What kindness and tact and humour! "Ein Gentleman durch und durch!" And his soldier servant—an angel!—had married a German girl. This idyllic world of cheery Tommies and Colonel Brambles sounded almost too good to be true and I basked vicariously in their lustre. But the French, they all agreed, were a different story. There had, it seems, been much friction, bloodshed even, and the ill-feeling still lingered. It sprang mainly from the presence of Senegalese units among the occupying troops; their inclusion had been interpreted as an act of calculated vengeance. The collapse of the Reichsmark was touched on, and Reparations; Hitler cropped up. The professor's widow couldn't bear him: such a mean face! "So ein gemeines Gesicht!"—and that voice! Both the others were against him too, and the whole Nazi movement: it was no solution to Germany's problems; and wrong . . . the conversation slid into a trough of depression. (I divined that it was a theme of constant discussion and that they were all against it, but in different ways and for different reasons. It was a time when friendships and families were breaking up all over Germany.) The conversation revived over German literature: apart from Remarque, the only German book I had read was a translation of *Zarathustra*. Neither of them cared much for Nietzsche, "But he understood us Germans," Hans said in an ambiguous tone. The Erasmian pronunciation of Latin cropped up, followed by the reciting of rival passages from the ancient tongues: innocent showing off all round with no time for any of us to run dry. We grew excited and noisy, and our hostess was delighted. How her husband would have enjoyed it! The evening ended with a third round of handshakes. (The first had

taken place on arrival and the second at the beginning of dinner, when the word *Mahlzeit* was ritually pronounced. German days are scanned by a number of such formalities.)

The evening ended for me with the crowning delight of a bath, the first since London. I wondered if the tall copper boiler had been covertly lit as a result of a lively account of my potentially verminous night in the workhouse . . . "My husband's study," my hostess had said with a sigh, when she showed me my room. And here, under another of those giant meringue eiderdowns, I lay at last between clean sheets on an enormous leather sofa with a shaded light beside me beneath row upon row of Greek and Latin classics. The works of Lessing, Mommsen, Kant, Ranke, Niebuhr and Gregorovius soared to a ceiling decoratively stencilled with sphinxes and muses. There were plaster busts of Pericles and Cicero, a Victorian view of the Bay of Naples behind a massive desk and round the walls, faded and enlarged, in clearings among the volumes, huge photographs of Paestum, Syracuse, Agrigento, Selinunte and Segesta. I began to understand that German middle-class life held charms that I had never heard of.

From
A Time of Gifts

WALKING BARE
TED HUGHES

What is left is just what my life bought me
The gem of myself.
A bare certainty, without confection.
Through this blowtorch light little enough

But enough.
The stones do not cease to support me.
Valleys unfold their invitations.
A progress beyond assay, breath by breath.

I rest just at my weight.
Movement is still patient with me—
Lightness beyond lightness releasing me further.

And the mountains of torment and mica
Pass me by.

And new skylines lift wider wings
Of simpler light.

The blood wrapped cries have hardened
To moisteners for my mouth.

Hurrying worlds of voices, on other errands,
Traffic through me, ignore me.

A one gravity keeps touching me.

For I am the appointed planet
Extinct in an emptiness

But a spark in the breath
Of the corolla that sweeps me.

From
Cave Birds

STORM FORCE

CLARE FRANCIS

In their 65-foot yacht ADC Accutrac *Clare
Francis and her crew took part in the 1977–78
Whitbread Round the World Race, competing with
fourteen other ships of various sizes and types. The
journey covered some 27,000 miles, and took seven
months. In the passage which follows, the boat is
sailing westwards across the south-western Pacific
through the Roaring Forties, and is at least 2,000
miles from the nearest landfall.*

THE next day it began to blow from the south—just off the
starboard bow. In one way we were quite pleased about this,
for we reckoned to do well against the lighter boats in heavy
weather. We were lying in a good position—as on the second leg,
we had managed to do well in the first few days—and we expected
to consolidate our position in a hard windward blow. *Disque d'Or*
was a little to the north and behind, and that was where we
wanted her to stay. By the second New Year's Eve night, it was
blowing Force 7 from the south and the barometer was still low.
All thoughts of a second celebration vanished as we battened
down the hatches for a wet, windward slog. We had not had a
hard windward blow since the first leg and we had almost forgotten what it was like. Now we began to remember with burning
clarity. Someone wrote in the deck log, "Pretty shitty, eh, Folks?"
and that about summed it up. As a reply I wrote "Think . . . it
could be dead calm or blowing 125 knots. You lot just don't know
when you're well off!" This impressed no-one. As the wind
steadily increased through the night to Force 9, the boat became
wetter and more uncomfortable, until it was difficult to sleep for
the noise and hullabaloo. We shortened sail down to treble-reefed
main and small jib topsail, but the boat was still going too fast.
She was jumping off waves and landing with such a crash that
those in the forward cabins were having a hard time staying in
their bunks. After one spectacular crash, Sam was heard to say,
"Another mile gone. Sounds like we're backing over them now."
Every time the bows shuddered into a wave we feared that something would break and we decided we would have to shorten sail
again, putting up the previously unused storm jib. This was one

of the few sails we had kept from the original wardrobe. It looked good and strong and brand-new and we put it up with confidence.

Half an hour later, it ripped. My views on the sail loft that had made it were not very charitable. Storm jibs just do not rip—they should be built like fortresses. Yet this had proved to be as flimsy as a piece of silk.

We were now in a spot. There were no other sails we could put up. We were carrying a staysail and a reefed main, but our speed had fallen drastically. We put the staysail onto the main forestay and settled down to repairing the storm jib. Sam told me it would be no easy matter. Each layer of the sail cloth would have to be peeled back, fitted into place and resewn. It would take hours. There was nothing we could do but sit back and wait.

For the next eight hours we sat it out, our speed reduced to five or six knots, and the conditions getting worse as the seas built up. Everyone began to feel a little ill and even Jacques could not face his pipe. Eve sweated away at the sewing machine, handing over to Sam or Bumble when sickness overwhelmed her and she had to shoot up on deck. More comments appeared in the deck log; "I think it might clear up and get wet", "Still dry enough for a fag!" and "I feel sorry for the next watch." A tin of milk powder flew across the galley and exploded in a white sticky mess everywhere, finding its way behind the cooker, and into the lockers until it glued up the hinges.

Those of us who had been up on the foredeck were soaked and, on going below, found our bunks were little better. A tiny deck leak dripped straight on to the bunk where Jacques and I tried to grab the odd hour's sleep, wetting the pillows and the mattress. We rigged up an elaborate plastic sheet arrangement to deflect the drips, and it proved to be moderately successful—the moisture slid down the bulkhead and soaked the mattress from underneath instead of on top.

The wind showed no signs of moderating. On Chat Hour we heard that *Disque d'Or*'s leak had started again, which was not entirely surprising in view of the cursory repairs carried out in Auckland. *Condor* were worried about their mast which was too slim and flimsy for the boat. It was whipping back and forth so violently that they were frightened of losing it and had been forced to slow down. *GB II*'s mainsail track had been pulled out of the mast and they were unable to raise much mainsail. We did not hear from two of the boats at all, the beginning of a widespread attack of radio failures that would break out during the leg.

Not for the last time I blessed our Marconi transmitter which was standing up to the punishment so well.

When steering we were forced to wear goggles and face masks to protect ourselves from the spray which flew across the deck like thousands of sharp hailstones. To prevent the whole deck crew from becoming wet and cold, only two would stay on deck, while the other two went below to dry out for a while. The sky was deep grey and the seas were high, with foaming white crests. It was exhilarating to steer, letting the boat climb the waves then flicking her nose up into a crest, to prevent her from being knocked sideways. Up and over, riding the great waves in the powerful machine, feeling the strength of the wind against the sails—I loved it, just as I have always loved bad weather. I was only sorry we couldn't go faster still.

Whenever I was about to go on deck in this kind of weather Jacques would give me a critical look to make sure I was wearing a safety harness. I found harnesses a blessed nuisance and hated wearing the things but, quite rightly, Jacques would often insist. It was not a matter of setting a good example—the others were extremely diligent about wearing theirs—but of fear. Jacques and I had a deep and horrifying terror of losing each other at sea. Falling overboard is not a very nice way to go and the possibility of it happening made our blood run cold. It was bad enough for one of us to imagine losing the other, but the manner in which it would happen, the desperate feeling of helplessness as we would try to turn the boat around and search in the large, grey seas was extremely painful to contemplate. It was over the wearing of harnesses that Jacques and I had our only disagreements. I always feel as safe as houses on the deck of a boat and, while I could concede that a harness was necessary in really bad weather, it was difficult to agree as to where good weather ended and bad began!

It was difficult to sleep while the gale was blowing and when I went below for a rest I read Chris Bonington's account of his successful Everest expedition. It impressed me very much, not only because it was a good story well told, but because of the many and various difficulties the expedition had encountered—in organisation, in the climbing itself and in the leadership of such a mixed group of strong and varied personalities. It was interesting to read how Chris Bonington had solved all these complex problems and I was particularly fascinated by his solutions to the difficulties of leadership. The rest of the crew read the book over the next few weeks and were all equally impressed. The next time someone went up the mast, the first spreaders were referred to as Camp One and the deck as Base Camp.

The weather had gone from what Tony described as "very average" to "below average". Now the barometer was falling further and I kept calling up from the chart table to ask if there was a visible change in the conditions. "A marginal change," Tony replied, "but I'm not sure in which direction."

I wrote in the deck log, "The barometer's falling again—you ain't seen nothing yet!"

But I was wrong. A few hours later the barometer levelled off and at long last the wind began to moderate. The reply in the log —it was Sam's writing, of course—read, "The barometer's fallen and we ain't seen nothing!"

Later he added the observation that it was "an impudent little morning", and indeed it was. In the usual way of the sea we had only just put up the repaired storm jib when the wind moderated sufficiently to raise the Number Two topsail. However, it stayed at a lively Force 7 for a long time and water and spray continued to cover the decks. Below, the cabins were still running with condensation and damp and, to add to the feeling of discomfort, we slept in our wet clothes to avoid getting yet another set of dry clothes wet when we next went on deck. It was easier to sleep in wet clothes and dry them out a little in the process than to take wet clothes off and attempt to put them on again when going on deck. There are few things more unpleasant than donning wet clothes when they are cold and clammy.

Finally, the wind moderated to Force 4 and veered to the west and then to the north. With a sigh of relief we opened the hatches and aired our clothes. A watery sun came through the cloud and, although we were now at 54° south, it was warm enough to dry the boat out and take the worst of the moisture from our clothes. There is something wonderful about the aftermath of a gale, a feeling of contentment and relief that makes the simplest things particularly pleasurable. The tiny shafts of sunlight and the splashes of colour on the waves were a beautiful sight.

From
Come Wind or Weather

ALONE ON A WIDE SEA

NAOMI JAMES

*A few weeks later, as the Whitbread fleet sailed up
the Southern Ocean on the homeward journey,
Naomi James had reached a similar point on the
route from New Zealand to Cape Horn. Alone in
her 53-foot yacht* Express Crusader *she was
attempting to circumnavigate the world. In the
event she achieved a triumphant success: she was
the first woman to sail single-handed round the
world via Cape Horn, and she did so in the fastest
time ever. Here she begins with a quotation from
her log.*

26 February (Day 172)

6 p.m.: Goodness how I ache! I can feel every muscle and
bruise acutely. Priorities now are: 1) to survive this weather;
2) to rig better shrouds; 3) to head north.

Fierce squalls pass every ten minutes or so, fifty-knotters
at least. Each one builds up its own nasty waves and one of
them has just broken right over *Crusader*. I saw it coming as
I was looking out of the window, and I hung on. Luckily she
didn't heel too far over. If only the barometer would rise.
I've been lying-a-hull or just creeping forward with the
storm jib for almost three days now, and I know that it could
last a lot longer. I wish I had a way of cheering myself up.
I've started re-reading one of the books in my library but
haven't been able to concentrate at all.

Sometimes I lie in my bunk for an hour at a time, and to
stop myself from staring at the barometer I gaze through the
skylight at the rigging and sky, which doesn't make me feel
any better. I can't sleep.

8 p.m. I'm soon going to be faced with the decision as to
whether I should stay lying-a-hull and risk capsize, or steer
down wind and risk personal injury from waves breaking over
the stern. The thought of the way that wave bent the self-
steering rudder gives me the shudders. There's a good force
eight now with horrible squalls, and every now and again a
wave bangs into *Crusader* with a shocking thud. I am running
the engine in order to charge the batteries in case Radio

Wellington try to contact me tonight. At least the diesel drowns the noise outside, and with the cabin light switched on the world seems quite friendly—so long as I don't look out.

I've made some re-arrangements down below and put the heavy things like boxes of tinned margarine and bags of sugar into empty lockers which can be fastened shut. Until now they have lain secured by lee-cloths on the top bunk: safe now, but hardly so in the event of a capsize.

Just before it got dark, I watched the effect of a squall coming over the sea. The waves were flattened, but the surface boiled under the furious wind. When a squall hits it shakes the mast and yet there isn't a shred of sail up. To drown the noise I am now playing the cassette, in place of the engine, and trying to deaden my mind with a glass of port.

On the 27th, that which I had always dreaded happened. Hours later I wrote in my log:

I capsized at 0.500 this morning. I was only half awake at the time, but suddenly aware that the wind had increased even beyond the prevailing force ten. It was just daylight, and I was trying to make up my mind whether to get up and try steering when I heard the deafening roar of an approaching wave. I felt the shock, a mountain of water crashed against *Crusader*'s hull, and over she went. An avalanche of bits and pieces descended on me as she went under, and I put up my arms to protect my face. After a long and agonizing pause she lurched up again. I don't recall the act of climbing out of my

bunk or even my sleeping bag, but I found myself well and truly free of them both.

As far as I remember, my first move was to look through the skylight at the rigging. It scarcely registered that the mast was still standing. I could hear water running into the bilges, so I quickly started to pump. For a terrible moment I felt that she was sinking, but as I pumped I could see the level going down. I pumped in a frenzy for a few minutes and then jumped on deck to see if the mast and rigging were really all right.

I noticed one spinnaker pole had gone and the other was broken. The sails which had been lashed along the guard rails were dragging in the water. I hauled them aboard somehow and re-tied them to the rails. The radio aerial was flying loose, and the deck fitting from which it had been torn was now letting in water. As a temporary measure I plugged it with an old T-shirt and returned below to continue pumping the bilges. There was a strong smell of paraffin and milk. All the stores on the top bunk had been hurled out and the lee-cloth hung in shreds. My main concern was that she might go over again, so I left things below as they were, dug out some thick socks, gloves, hat and oilskins (all wet) and went to the helm to steer.

I secured my safety harness to the compass binnacle and faced the waves so that I could see them coming. The vision scared me stiff. The waves were gigantic, a combination of twenty-foot swells with twenty- to thirty-foot waves on top. One crashed near by, and it didn't need any imagination to realize what would happen if one of these monsters fell on me.

Suddenly *Crusader* started to surf, and I gripped the wheel desperately to keep the stern directly on to the wave and hold her straight. The next wave picked her up like a toy and wrenched all control from me. There was nothing but mountains of water everywhere, like waterfalls. The speed was impossible to gauge as there was nothing to judge it by, and the water all round me was at deck level, seething and hissing as if on the boil. Finally, the wave passed and she slowed down. I started to cry from a feeling of helplessness at being out of control and caught at the mercy of one of those awful waves. But I still had to leave the wheel to pump the bilges. When I got back to the wheel a wave broke over the stern, and I threw my arms round the binnacle as the water cascaded over me and filled the cockpit. Fortunately the volume of water wasn't too alarming. What was the lesser evil, I wondered: capsizing or being crushed by a wave? What would

Rob do? Keep on top of the situation and trust to luck. I had to accept the dismal thought that there was only me here with my quota of luck; I steered numbly onwards and hoped that my luck would last.

On the fourth occasion that I went below to pump I saw the barometer was 1003 and rising slowly. I was confronted by a terrible mess, but the biggest things had held in place; there was no actual damage except for odd dents and scars on the roof of the saloon. My neck was very sore—somehow I must have pulled a muscle at the moment of capsize because I was aware of aches as soon as I reached the deck.

I steered on devoid of thought and incapable of feeling. At 10.30 a.m. I detected a lull, followed half an hour later by another. At last I began to feel better, and when on a trip below I saw a bottle of port rolling in a corner and took a swig. I also grabbed some water biscuits and ate them at the wheel.

At 11.30 the wind was down to force eight, but I kept steering until 2 p.m., by which time the wind had reduced to intermittent heavy squalls. It now seemed safe, so I left her lying-a-hull. The radio was drenched but it worked, and after an hour of concentrated cleaning up the interior was almost back to normal. However, there seemed to be a curious itinerary of missing items, including my fountain pen, the can opener, hairbrush and kettle. Most of my crockery was broken. A bad moment was finding my Salalite transistor quite dead; that meant no more time signals to check the error of my chronometer. Still, the clock was quartz and kept very good time, and there was no reason to think it might suddenly become erratic.

My bed was sopping wet, but fortunately I had a spare sleeping bag stowed away in a plastic bag. I hauled it out in triumph—bone dry! The cabin heater soon dried out my pillow. I had no dry footwear and on the floor was a slippery mixture of milk, paraffin and bilge water.

After clearing up I made myself a cup of tea and heated some tomato soup. I then slept for an hour but only fitfully as I could hear water dripping into the bilges. I finally stirred myself and found that the water was coming from the hole in the deck where the insulator had been. The best I could do was to fill it with more rags until the weather improved.

From
At One With the Sea

THE HIGHEST POINT IN THE WORLD

PETER HABELER

*In May 1978 two Austrian mountaineers, Peter
Habeler and Reinhold Messner, achieved the
astounding feat of climbing Mount Everest relying
entirely upon their own bodily resources, and
without any form of artificial oxygen. They set out
to do so in the face of almost unanimous medical
advice that such a course was suicidal: that in the
thin air above 8,000 metres the lack of sufficient
oxygen supplies to the brain will quickly begin to
destroy its cells, leading to the impairment of vision,
hearing and other faculties, followed within a few
minutes by unconsciousness.*

REINHOLD signified to me with a movement of his hand that
he wanted to go on ahead. He wanted to film me climbing up
over the ridge, with the bubbling sea of clouds below.

To do this he had to take off his snow goggles in order to focus
the camera better. It occurred to me that his eyes looked inflamed,
but I thought nothing more of it, no more than he did. Our
altitude was now 8,700 metres, and we had obviously reached a
point in which normal brain functions had broken down, or at
least were severely limited. Our attentiveness and concentration
declined; our instinct no longer reacted as reliably as before; the

capacity for clear logical thinking had also apparently been lost. I only thought in sensations and loose associations, and slowly I was overcome by the feeling that this threatening fearful mountain could, in fact, be a friend, if only I could understand him properly.

Today I am certain that it is in these positive and friendly sensations that the real danger on Everest lies. When one approaches the summit, one no longer perceives the hostile, the absolutely deadly atmosphere which has penetrated before. I have probably never been so close to death as I was during this last hour before reaching the summit, not even that time on the Wilder Kaiser mountain when I fell thirty metres down the rope in a free fall, and miraculously survived unhurt. Then, at least, I was still aware of the danger of death, but now I was not. The urgent compulsion to descend again, to give in to fatigue, which had overcome me already in Camp V, and with which body and soul had rebelled against, this deadly and threatening adventure, had disappeared. I was now feeling the complete opposite. I had been seized by a real sense of euphoria. I felt somehow light and relaxed, and believed that nothing could happen to me. Undoubtedly, many of the men who have disappeared for ever in the summit region of Everest had also fallen victim to this treacherous euphoria. I can well imagine Mick Burke sitting happily smiling on the summit, and thinking to himself, "How beautiful it all is up here; I'd like to stay here." And then his life was snuffed out like the flame of a candle. It must have been exactly the same with him. At this altitude the boundaries between life and death are fluid. I wandered along this narrow ridge, and perhaps for a few seconds I had indeed gone beyond the frontier which divides life from death. By a piece of good fortune I was allowed to return. I would not risk it a second time, my reason forbids me to gamble with my life in such a way again.

After our return, Reinhold and I were hailed as victors over Everest, but this is false. Everest was neither conquered nor overcome by us—it simply tolerated us. And if we can talk about a victory at all, then it is at the most a victory over our own bodies, over fear.

It was a very personal, lonely victory in a struggle which each of us fought alone, and the victory was not achieved on the last metres which still lay before us. It had already been achieved at the moment when we took the first step out into the unknown. And it was secured and documented when we returned alive from the kingdom of the dead.

In spite of all my euphoria, I was physically completely finished. I was no longer walking of my own free will, but mechanically, like an automaton. I seemed to step outside myself, and had the illusion that another person was walking in my place. This other person arrived at the Hillary Step, that perilous 25 metres high ridge gradient, and then climbed and pulled himself up in the footsteps of his predecessors. He had one foot in Tibet and the other in Nepal. On the left side there was a 2,000 metre descent to Nepal; on the right the wall dropped 4,000 metres down towards China. We were alone, this other person and myself. Although he was connected to me by the short piece of rope, Reinhold no longer existed.

This feeling of being outside myself was interrupted for only a few moments. Cramp in my right hand bent my fingers together, and tore me violently back to reality. I was attacked by a suffocating fear of death. "Now I've had it." This thought went through my head, "Now the lack of oxygen is beginning its deadly work."

I could see the sherpa in front of me who, a few days ago, had been brought down to the base camp. With him, too, it had started this way, and by the time the doctors had attended to him, he was already paralysed on one side. Presumably he would never recover again properly. Nevertheless—he was alive; he was rescued. But up here that was impossible. I massaged my right forearm and bent my fingers, and then the cramp eased.

From then on I prayed, "Lord God, let me go up right to the top. Give me the power to remain alive, don't let me die up here." I crawled on my elbows and knees and prayed uninterruptedly, more fervently than I have ever done in my life before. It was like a dialogue with a higher being. And again I saw myself crawling up, below me, beside me, higher and higher. I was being pushed up to the heights, and then suddenly I was up again on my own two feet: I was standing on the summit.

It was 1.15 on the afternoon of 8 May 1978.

And then suddenly Reinhold was with me too, still carrying his camera and the three-legged Chinese surveying instrument. We had arrived. We embraced each other. We sobbed and stammered, and could not keep calm. The tears poured from under my goggles into my beard, frozen on my cheeks. We embraced each other again and again. We pressed each other close. We stepped back at arm's length and again fell round each other's necks, laughing and crying at the same time. We were redeemed and liberated, freed at last from the inhuman compulsion to climb on.

After the crying and the sense of redemption, came the emptiness and the sadness, the disappointment. Something had been taken from me; something that had been very important to me. Something which had suffused my whole being had evaporated, and I now felt exhausted and hollow. There was no feeling of triumph or victory. I saw the surrounding summits, the Lhotse, the Cho Oyu. The view towards Tibet was obscured by clouds. I knew that I was standing now on the highest point in the whole world. But, somehow, it was all a matter of indifference to me. I just wanted to get home now, back to that world from which I had come, and as fast as possible.

From
Everest, Impossible Victory

CRETE

LAWRENCE DURRELL

To the Greeks Crete seems the most authentically Greek of all the islands because of the length of its history and its relative remoteness from the ancient centres of war and diplomacy.

Crete, for example, played no part in the Persian or the Pelo-
ponnesian wars, during which the rest of the Greek dependencies
were almost bled to death; with her crack fleet, she had time to
take stock of things from the neutrality of her perch in the main
deep of the Aegean.

"The big island" Crete is always called in the colloquial
tongue; and big it is, spacious and full of the brooding presence of
its four groups of mountains, which have more or less divided it
into four countries with four chief towns. The mountains are high
enough to be snow-tipped throughout the dour winter, and very
often the traveller in the lowlands will have the feeling he is
crossing a continent rather than an island. In almost any direction
his eye turns, it is halted, not by a sea-line as in the smaller islands,
but by a land skyline, often massive and forbidding. It is
sumptuously rocky, though the verdant and bounteous valleys
that open everywhere offer no lack of water or shade or greenery;
indeed Crete has quite a lot of high mountain pasture, unlike
many islands of the same size.

Once you round the broad butt of the Peloponnesus and enter
the Aegean, you have turned a new page in the strange, variegated
album of Greek landscapes—quite different from those of the
romantic Ionian islands. The Aegean is pure, vertical, and
dramatic. Crete is like a leviathan, pushed up by successive
geological explosions. It is also like the buckle in a slender belt of
islands which shelter the inner Cyclades from the force of the
deep sea, and which once formed an unbroken range of mountains
joining the Peloponnesus to the south-west Turkish ranges. The
valleys are the deep faults between eminences. After Sicily,
Sardinia, Corsica and Cyprus, it is the largest island in the
Mediterranean. In continuity of history and purity of bloodstock,
it is probably true to say, as the Greeks do, that it is "the most
Greek" of the islands.

Though beautiful in its spacious style, its ruggedness and its
sudden changes of weather make it a disquieting place for the
visitor. It strikes a minatory note, which is echoed in all the
enigmatic and somewhat vexatious folklore it has accumulated
around figures like Zeus, Minos and others—not to mention the
famous Minotaur which must still lurk somewhere underground
today, like the Loch Ness Monster, waiting to be discovered by
television. Yes, it is a strange place, full of echoing wind-haunted
valleys and grand glades, of plains full of secret villages which lie
baking in the noonday sun, of mountains with holm-oak forests

where the charcoal burners stand, like black demons, over their fuming pits.

Its shape is rugged as well, for Crete has been sculpted by a conflict of tides which forever range and gnaw at its cliffs. From the air, it looks something like the case of a violin that has been absent-mindedly cut about with a hacksaw by a retarded child; the whole northern part is heavily indented, yet poor in big harbours. Suda Bay, next to Chanea, is to some extent an exception, but even that is not a really fine commercial harbour. However, smaller craft and yachts will generally find a lay-by, though it is more difficult on the southern coast, for there the mountains rise iron-bound from the deep sea and form great walls against which the sea pounds and shocks and explodes all the year long. The best way into the island and the mood of the island is, as always in Greece, by sea, which gives the pace and the dimension necessary for the traveller to take in what he sees.

But today the traveller who harbours romantic notions of a sort of Greek Tibet, will find himself in for a shock. The air-time from Athens is under an hour, and tourism has swamped the island with summer sun-lovers—which has had an inevitable effect on prices, urbanization, and morals. The whole of the northern coast—or a good two-thirds of it—is turning itself into a playground, a place of summer habitation, for sun-hungry Nordics. However, we must make the best of what is left. The Cretans remain dour and gay, which makes one feel slightly better about it; and who could say they are wrong to pine for a higher standard of living—as we all so quaintly call it? In the thirties, when we stayed in a village or camped, we managed without such indispensable things as washing-machines and fridges. Our fridge was the nearest well, or the sea even, into which we lowered bottles and perishables; the village granny was our washing-machine, an excellent one (and glad of the money), even if sometimes we caught trifling children's illnesses like ringworm or Dobie's itch from badly washed clothes. All Cretan housewives would agree that among modern amenities there are real godsends like Buta-gas, insect spray, and washing soaps (it is odd to realize how recently these have appeared on the scene: and even DDT, penicillin and the sulfa group of drugs only date from the end of World War II). Life was quite different without them in remote places like Greek islands. For my part, I would cite the island telephone as a worthwhile modern amenity; today you can ring now from one island to another, from one hotel to another. You never could before; even pre-paid telegrams did not work. You just had to hope you would find a room when you arrived at your destination.

The Cretans have seen everything—the collapse of the Minoan Empire, the rise of Venice, the slave markets of Turkey, Nazi parachutists and American hippies—nothing has been spared them. If they remain a trifle sceptical and shy, brusque and censorious, it is hardly surprising. One must also realize that they have only belonged to Greece since 1913, though the last Turkish soldier left the island in 1896. The intervening years were years of fragmentation and neglect; they were pawns of the great powers and Crete was split up, as Berlin is now, into sectors and sections. The transition was abrupt, and today one sees new and old rubbing shoulders everywhere. The costumes in the market, at the airport, in the harbour, are a wild mixture of ancient and modern; the music of the juke-boxes is similar, pouring out *bouzouki* music and modern jazz.

Four mountain clumps loom around if one comes by plane into the modern airport. ("Bones of the elephant and the pygmy hippopotamus have been found in geologically recent cave-deposits while deer only became extinct in historic times.") What must it have been like in Homer's day? About this we know a little from the way he doffs his hat to the island in the *Odyssey*, hailing it as a land famous for its hundred cities, its rich and numberless buildings. But the feeling he conveys is that he had not personally touched down here, that he was citing a ready-made descriptive compliment: a tourist handout of the day perhaps?

On the other hand, St Paul (who got into trouble almost wherever he went) had a particularly hard time in Crete, for he told Titus (the first Bishop of Crete) that, to quote a poet, the islanders were "always liars, evil beasts, and slow bellies". It is clear that he had gone into a bar in Chanea for an *ouzo*, with a mass of contentious epistles under his arm, and had naturally received what the New York bartenders would call "the bum's rush". Much the same thing happened in Cyprus. As for the phrase "slow bellies", this needs checking with the original; it surely must be a bad translation. How could the saint so assail the digestive tract of the Cretans? Cretans eat faster and more than most islanders. I suspect the passage means something different—perhaps that they were slow to kindle to the faith. At any rate, it is clear St Paul thought the Cretans had not been sent

on earth to charm; which suggests he must have been badly treated. The truth is that the Cretans are the Scots of Greece; they have lived through countless crises to emerge always just as truly themselves—indomitable friends or deadly enemies. If their hospitality wavered under the scandalous begging of the hippies, it soon reasserted itself. And even today it is dangerous to express admiration for something, for you will certainly find it in your baggage as a farewell gift when you leave. You cannot refuse.

They are adamant. I knew a lady who got a baby this way.

From
The Greek Islands

THE GENTLEMAN ABROAD

DOUGLAS SUTHERLAND

THE English gentleman invented abroad.

Edward VII, who was not quite a gentleman but let that pass, was among the first to spread around the rumour that the young ladies of Paris threw off their clothes more readily than their English sisters and the French named a boulevard after him in recognition of his researches on that subject.

Let it be understood that gentlemen do not take holidays in the same way that other people do. That is to say that if they go up to

London they do so for a definite and stated purpose, whether it be to buy a suit, see their solicitors or merely to change their watch strap. The fact that they take advantage of the situation to have a few nights out on the tiles is nothing to do with the main business in hand. In this way, if in no other, they resemble businessmen attending a sales convention.

Gentlemen in Europe

The gentleman adventured into Europe not to rest from the onerous business of being a gentleman but to find new outlets for his energy. He had to find something to do between the end of the foxhunting season and the beginning of the shooting season. Thus it came about that he pioneered golf at Le Touquet, gambling at Deauville and boar shooting in the Ardennes. It was because the hard weather made hunting impossible after Christmas that he invented the improbable sport of sliding down Swiss mountains, precariously balanced on two narrow boards. It was because his doctor ordered it that he made it fashionable to sit up to his neck in hot mud at Baden-Baden and to drink the unpleasant-tasting waters of Vichy in the belief that he could then ruin his liver for the rest of the year drinking brandy.

Grateful foreigners

Foreigners have a lot to be grateful to the English gentleman for and, during the last century the French in particular showed their gratitude with their hotels Prince de Galles and Reine Victoria and their Place des Anglais. Admittedly they also christened venereal disease the Pox Britannica and its preventive "*un capot Anglais*", but that is beside the point.

Competition

All that is changed now. The Americans started the rot with their lavish tipping and their eccentric habits like not changing for dinner which has had the effect of both raising the price and lowering the tone so far as the English gentleman is concerned. Of course that is not the end of it all. It was not long before Greek shipping magnates were being bowed over the threshold of the best casinos, moving-picture stars were being given the best suites in hotels and German industrialists were queueing up to be the first into the dining-room of the most expensive restaurants. It all goes to show that one cannot trust foreigners to know their place any longer.

The Final Thrust

Perhaps the final dagger thrust to the gentleman's flirtation with Europe has been the influx of his own countrymen who have deserted the delights of Wigan Pier and Blackpool illuminations to crowd the beaches of the once fashionable resorts, showing their braces and demanding chips with everything. The English gentleman never smothered himself with sun tan oil or wore dark glasses or flowered shirts and he finds himself a figure of fun being jostled on the promenade in his white ducks and straw boater.

A few gentlemen still go abroad to stay in some beleaguered château in France, to shoot partridges in Spain or to complain that there is no horse-radish sauce with the roast beef in Reid's Hotel in Madeira but now, on the whole, he prefers to stay at home for the Chelsea Flower Show.

There are, however, just a few occupations which still attract the gentleman away from his home shores. It has already been pointed out that it was the English gentleman who invented skiing and, by and large, he has remained an ardent adherent to winter sports. On no account, however, will he be found as a member of a packaged tour taking instructions from some damned fellow in a red jersey. Most gentlemen are very good skiiers indeed, having been taught from a very early age by their fathers or a private tutor. They tend to return year after year to the same resort which their forebears made fashionable, partly because of the respectful treatment they receive from the Swiss hoteliers who, in spite of their reputation for avarice, still prefer to have an English milord as a guest to a German industrialist, and partly because it is in the larger resorts that they can enjoy other aspects of winter sporting which are largely ignored by the proletariat. Skating is one and curling, a very gentlemanly game, is another. So, too, is bobsleighing which appeals to the liking certain gentlemen have of living dangerously and has so few British adherents who can afford the necessary time or practice that an otherwise idle gentleman has a good chance of making the international team. The peak attraction of all for the gentleman is the Cresta Run which is so designed that the competitor on his sled (correctly *luge*) hurtles down a precipitous and tortuous course at approximately a hundred miles an hour with his nose only inches from the ice. It used to be almost entirely an English form of torture but now, rather to their chagrin, other nations are going in for it, particularly Americans who do rather well at it.

There are still a few gentlemen who preserve the tradition of the 1930s, made fashionable by the Prince of Wales, of spending Easter golfing at Le Touquet and immersing themselves in mud at Baden-Baden but, of late, there has developed an even more gentlemanly activity abroad—visiting old battlefields. Expeditions are still being fitted out for incredibly old gentlemen of Great War vintage to visit the once blood-soaked beaches of Gallipoli in the Dardanelles, but the battlefields of the last war all over Europe have an increasing annual quota of bristly moustached ex-officers with walking sticks, binoculars and map cases pointing out to each other the exact spot where "poor old Bertie caught his" or where "we blew up that damned Kraut tank".

Like the common tripper who boasts of his exploits in his Spanish resort for the rest of the year, visiting battlefields provides the gentleman with a party monologue for many a dinner party through the long winter months ahead.

From
The English Gentleman

9 MAY 1956

HAROLD NICOLSON

British Embassy, Paris

I lunch at the Embassy with Cynthia [Jebb], Nancy Mitford and Antonia Pakenham. Then we get into the huge car and drive to Port Royal. It is, as usual, a holiday, and the museum at Port Royal is closed. One should always visit these places, as no description suffices. The valley is sharper and steeper than I imagined, and the monastery more hidden in the depths. There are some remains of the chapel and a tomb-stone marking the place more or less where Racine was buried before being transferred. The line of the cloister is marked by a row of trees. The hill slopes up rapidly to Les Granges at the top. The nightingale sings. Antonia, being a Jansenist, is rather moved. So am I.

Then off we go to Versailles. We draw up in front of the château, but are not allowed in, as Tito is there. We then go round hoping to see the Trianon, but that also is barred by gendarmes. I ask Nancy to show us the Parc aux Cerfs. Again a surprise. I had envisaged a pavilion somewhere attached to the park. But not at all. It was in the Rue St Médéric, in the middle of the town, a small eighteenth-century house in the street, which might have belonged to the local doctor. "You admit," says Nancy, "that my King had simple tastes." She says that often he was in such a hurry to get there, that he did not bother to change and arrived wearing the Order of the Saint-Esprit. They explained to the prostitutes in the Rue St Médéric that he was a Polish cousin of the Queen.

We drive back through the park at St Cloud which is looking superb with its clipped avenues and its vast chestnuts. The whole route through the Bois and up the Avenue Foch is stiff with police lining the pavements for Tito. But there is no crowd at all.

Gladwyn [Jebb] returns very late from a party at the Czech Embassy. We do not dine till 9, but Gladwyn gives me a bottle of Mouton Rothschild 1948 which is the best claret I have ever drunk. He tells me that the French communist party are in a fix about Stalin. They recently expelled one of their members for writing an article suggesting that Stalinism was not quite so wonderful as all that. If they are now to toe the Moscow line, they will prove to the world that they are a satellite party. Gladwyn says that we are wrong to think that France is a poor, distraught country. We never realise that France may be badly governed but it is excellently administered. Moreover, people are rich and prosperous. Wages and employment are high. If they lose Algeria, it will be a severe blow to them. They may then seek for a strong government in the person of de Gaulle.

What an odd man Gladwyn is! Had I not known him so well for so many years, I might think him rude and disagreeable. He gives me the impression of intellectual strength.

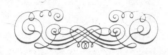

JUNE 1967

CECIL BEATON

HAVE been reading Volume II of Harold Nicolson's *Diaries* with as much pleasure as I read his first. I wonder why, in spite of being told again and again by his friends, James Pope-Hennessy and others, what a fine fellow he is, I've never liked the man.

Once more he shows himself to be an honest, good character, sensitive to others, candid about himself. He is never vulgar, and always has an eye for the comic. Often he is able in the written word to move me; in fact I finished this book in a blur of tears.

But when scrutinizing the photographs I again see that I am as put off by his physical appearance there, as I am in life. How unfair this is. But the Kewpie-doll mouth, the paradoxical moustache, the corpulence of hands and stomach all give me a *frisson* and there is no getting over the fact that I could never get to know him well enough to become a close friend. Sad, because he could have been a help and guide and an influence for the better.

Oysters
in Green Waistcoats

MICHEL GUERARD

For four people

Main ingredients
24 plump oysters—native *or* Portuguese
Ingredients for the accompanying sauce
5¼ oz *150g* butter, softened to room temperature
Pepper
1 tablespoon lemon juice
Ingredients for the garnish of vegetables
2½ oz *70g* carrots
2¾ oz *80g* white part of leeks
¾ oz *20g* butter
1¾ pints *1 litre* water and 2 teaspoons coarse salt
24 lettuce leaves
Salt and pepper
Equipment
4 oyster plates *or* 4 plates covered with coarse salt
1 shallow saucepan
1 large saucepan
1 small saucepan

Clean and wash the carrots and leeks, and cut them into fine julienne strips.

Heat the butter in a shallow pan and cook the julienne briskly, seasoned with salt and pepper, for 2 minutes. Keep hot.

Bring the water and salt to the boil in a large pan. Blanch the lettuce leaves in it for 1 minute and drain them on a cloth.

*

If the oysters have not been opened by the fishmonger, open them with an oyster knife. Using a teaspoon, remove the oysters from their shells and put them in a sieve, placed over a small saucepan so that the juice is caught.

*

Wash the concave halves of the shells and place them in the hollows of the oyster plates or on the salt-covered plates, making sure they are firm and won't tip over. Keep them hot in a low oven with the door open.

*

Heat the oyster juices to simmering point in the small saucepan and poach the oysters for 30 seconds in the simmering liquid. Remove the oysters with a slotted spoon. Reserve the cooking liquid.

*

Wrap the oysters in the lettuce leaves, making them into little parcels. Put them back in the shells and keep hot.

Bring the oyster cooking liquid to the boil and reduce by half, (*don't* add salt!). Add the 5¼ oz *150 g* butter in pieces over a lowered heat, shaking the pan with a swirling circular motion to blend the butter sauce. It will become thick and rich. (You can whisk the sauce instead of shaking the pan.) Season with two turns of the pepper-mill and add the tablespoon of lemon juice. Cover each individual oyster with a tablespoon of butter sauce and strew with a few of the julienne vegetables. Serve immediately.

*

The oysters can be cooked, wrapped in their lettuce leaves and replaced in their shells the day beforehand, and stored in the refrigerator overnight. When you need them, let them return to room temperature then give them 1 minute in a very hot oven (470°F/Mark 9/240°C). Take them out of the oven, and pour over the butter sauce, which *must* be made the same day.

For a special dinner, Christmas for instance, the vegetable julienne could be replaced with half a teaspoon of chilled caviar per oyster.

From
Cuisine Gourmande

FOOD IS A PROFOUND SUBJECT

IRIS MURDOCH

The central character in Iris Murdoch's novel
The Sea, The Sea *(which won the Booker Prize in*
1978) is Charles Arrowby, a well-known theatre
director, over sixty and a bachelor, who has come to
live in a lonely house beside the sea, "to repent of a
life of egoism".

IT is after lunch and I shall now described the house. For lunch, I may say, I ate and greatly enjoyed the following: anchovy paste on hot buttered toast, then baked beans and kidney beans with chopped celery, tomatoes, lemon juice and olive oil. (Really good olive oil is essential, the kind with a taste, I have brought a supply from London.) Green peppers would have been a happy addition only the village shop (about two miles pleasant walk) could not provide them. (No one delivers to far-off Shruff End, so I fetch everything, including milk, from the village.) Then bananas and cream with white sugar. (Bananas should be cut, *never* mashed, and the cream should be thin.) Then hard water biscuits with New Zealand butter and Wensleydale cheese. Of course I never touch foreign cheeses. Our cheeses are the best in the world. With this feast I drank most of a bottle of Muscadet out of my modest "cellar". I ate and drank slowly as one should (cook fast, eat slowly) and without distractions such as (thank heavens) conversation or reading. Indeed eating is so pleasant one should even try to suppress thought. Of course reading and thinking are important but, my God, food is important too. How fortunate we are to be food-consuming animals. Every meal should be a treat and one ought to bless every day which brings with it a good digestion and the precious gift of hunger.

I wonder if I shall ever write my *Charles Arrowby Four Minute Cookbook*? The "four minutes" of course refer to the active time of preparation, and do not include unsupervised cooking time. I have looked at several so-called "short order" cookery books, but these works tend to deceive, their "fifteen minutes" really in practice means thirty, and they contain instructions such as "make a light batter". The sturdy honest persons to whom my book would be addressed would not necessarily be able to make a light batter or even to know what it was. But they would be hedonists. In food and drink, as in many (not all) other matters, simple joys are best, as any intelligent self-lover knows. Sidney Ashe once offered to initiate me into the pleasures of vintage wine. I refused with scorn. Sidney hates ordinary wine and is unhappy unless he is drinking some expensive stuff with a date on it. Why wantonly destroy one's palate for cheap wine? (And by that I do not of course mean the brew that tastes of bananas.) One of the secrets of a happy life is continuous small treats, and if some of these can be inexpensive and quickly procured so much the better. Life in the theatre often precluded serious meals and I have not always in the past been able to eat slowly, but I have certainly learnt how to cook quickly. Of course my methods (especially a liberal use of the tin opener) may scandalize fools, and the various people (mainly the girls: Jeanne, Doris, Rosemary, Lizzie) who urged me to publish my recipes did so with an air of amused condescension. Your name will sell the book, they tactlessly insisted. "Charles's meals are just picnics", Rita Gibbons once remarked. Yes, good, even great, picnics. And let me say here that *of course* my guests *always* sit squarely at tables, never balance plates on their knees, and *always* have proper table napkins, *never* paper ones.

Food is a profound subject and one, incidentally, about which no writer lies. I wonder whence I derived my felicitous gastronomic intelligence? A thrifty childhood gave me a horror of wasted food. I thoroughly enjoyed the modest fare we had at home. My mother was a "good plain cook", but she lacked the inspired simplicity which is for me the essence of good eating. I think my illumination came, like that of Saint Augustine, from a disgust with excesses. When I was a young director I was idiotic and conventional enough to think that I had to entertain people at well-known restaurants. It gradually became clear to me that guzzling large quantities of expensive, pretentious, often mediocre food in public places was not only immoral, unhealthy and un-aesthetic, but also unpleasurable. Later my guests were offered simple joys *chez moi*. What is more delicious than fresh hot buttered toast, with or without the addition of bloater paste? Or plain boiled onions with a little cold corned beef if desired? And well-made porridge with brown sugar and cream is a dish fit for a king. Even then some people, so sadly corrupt was their taste, took my intelligent hedonism for an affected eccentricity, a mere gimmick. (*Wind in the Willows* food a journalist called it.) And some were actually offended.

However, it may be that what really made me see through the false mythology of *haute cuisine* was not so much restaurants as dinner parties. I have long, and usually vainly, tried to persuade my friends not to cook grandly. The waste of time alone is an absurdity; though I suppose it is true that some unfortunate women have nothing to do but cook. There is also the illusion that very elaborate cooking is more "creative" than simple cooking.

Of course (let me make it clear) I am not a barbarian. French country food, such as one can still occasionally find in that blessed land, is very good; but its goodness belongs to a tradition and an instinct which cannot be aped. The pretentious English hostess not only mistakes elaboration and ritual for virtue; she is also very often exercising her deluded art for the benefit of those who, though they would certainly not admit it, do not really enjoy food at all. Most of my friends in the theatre were usually so sozzled when they came to eat a serious meal that they had no appetite and in any case scarcely knew what was set before them. Why spend nearly all day preparing food for people who eat it (or rather toy with it and leave it) in this condition? A serious eater is a moderate drinker. Food is also spoilt at dinner parties by enforced conversation. One's best hope is to get into one of those "holes" where one's two neighbours are eagerly engaged elsewhere, so that one can concentrate upon one's plate. No, I am no friend to these "formal" scenes which often have more to do with vanity and prestige and a mistaken sense of social "propriety" than with the true instincts of hospitality. *Haute cuisine* even inhibits hospitality, since those who cannot or will not practise it hesitate to invite its devotees for fear of seeming rude or a failure. Food is best eaten among friends who are unmoved by such "social considerations", or of course best of all alone. I hate the falsity of "grand" dinner parties where, amid much kissing, there is the appearance of intimacy where there is really none.

After this tirade it looks as if the description of the house will have to wait until another day. I might add here that (as will already be evident) I am not a vegetarian. In fact I eat very little meat, and hold in horror the "steak house carnivore". But there are certain items (such as anchovy paste, liver, sausages, fish) which hold as it were strategic positions in my diet, and which I should be sorry to do without; here hedonism triumphs over a peevish baffled moral sense. Perhaps I ought to give up eating meat, but by now, when the argument has gone on so long, I doubt if I ever will.

I will *now* describe the house. . . .

From
The Sea, The Sea

THE RESTAURANT
NOEL BLAKISTON

THE *Madame Bovary* had not been open many months when Catherine went to work there. It was kept by two young men, Pat and Steve, helped in the kitchen by two other young men, Freddie and Bertie. Besides Catherine there was a second waitress, Lesley. There were only ten tables to be served, for the restaurant was small and intimate. Its atmosphere was more that of a night club than of an ordinary restaurant and it was indeed only open for dinners and suppers. A mural at the end of the room depicted a four-wheeler, with the blinds down, perambulating the streets of Rouen.

The food was exceedingly good and not expensive. An important actor had discovered the place and talked about it to his friends. Suddenly the *Madame Bovary* had become the rage. Those who did not book a table stood little chance of finding room. The restaurant was patronized not only by actors, intellectuals and upper Bohemia, but by the smart and the grand. It was in the company of some of the latter that Catherine had been taken there. At the end of the dinner she had spoken to the waitress who was clearing the table and laying the coffee-cups.

"Jolly good dinner! Will you tell the chef how much we've enjoyed it?"

"Certainly, Madame, thank you."

"Yes," said Stacy Ferminjoy, "it's been excellent. We'll be seeing you again."

"Not me, sir. I'm leaving in a few days."

"Oh, I'm sorry. You'll be hard to replace."

"Thank you, sir."

"As a matter of fact," asked Catherine, "do you know if they have got anyone to take your place?"

"I don't believe anything's actually settled yet."

"Which of those two—" Catherine looked at Pat and Steve, who were busy behind a counter, "which is the boss?"

"Both. They're equal."

"They look it," murmured Stacy.

Catherine got up and walked over to them, watched by her companions. The conversation that took place across the counter appeared to be extremely gay. The teeth of the young men in their bronze, sailor-boys' faces glistened as they laughed.

"Ever seen anyone exercising her charm?" muttered the Hon. Derek Harbottle.

Now Catherine was writing something on a pad. Presently she walked back, beaming, to her table.

"I've got the job!" she said. "They're bliss! I'm mad about them!"

"The job!" said the other girl at the table. "Honestly, Cathy, you don't mean it really, do you? Are you mad?"

"Perhaps I'm mad. I mean it, anyhow."

"What's the idea?" said Stacy.

"I want a change. One can't just go on being a deb."

"But—why, you'll never be able to come out again in the evenings! Honestly, Cathy, what's the idea?"

"I want to see life."

"This! Life! Aren't we life?"

Catherine looked at last year's President of Pop, at the heir to the Harbottle millions and at the daughter of the Lord Privy Seal.

"Perhaps not absolutely the whole of life," she said slowly.

There was a silence at the table.

"I'm sorry," she said, "that was frightfully rude. I didn't mean to be unpleasant. Promise, you'll come and dine here often, won't you? And I have one night a week off. Oh, I forgot, I wonder what my parents will have to say!"

The fact that she had forgotten to wonder what her parents would have to say was evidence not of any indifference to their opinion but rather of the trust that existed between them and herself.

"Cathy's head is screwed on the right way," said Lord Westfield to his wife, "I'm sure she'd never do anything irrevocably foolish."

"So am I, absolutely. It's just sometimes her taste that. I'm a teeny weeny bit doubtful about in the present phase she's going through. Those jeans she's now wearing—they are so terribly tight!"

"It would be insincere of me to say I disapproved of them. Do you know, when I was her age, *I* used to be thought rather loud. It's hard to believe, isn't it?" It was indeed.

The job in the restaurant, after some moments of surprise, received full parental sanction, tempered only with regret that they would now be seeing so little of her in the evenings.

"Not that we can say we've seen much of her in the evenings lately!"

"True enough! How long will you be doing it for do you suppose, Cathy?"

"At least until I've saved up enough to buy a portable radiogram."

The idea of getting a job had been establishing itself in Catherine's mind some weeks before that evening at the restaurant. Partly, she wanted the gramophone and was not going to ask her father for it after all he had lately coughed up on her behalf. Then, she did indeed want a change. She was sick of the Dereks and Stacys. She had seen enough of them during this crowded summer, in which, though she had taken a prominent part in all the fun which is offered to a lovely and exuberant girl of her position, she had not once felt her heart go pit-a-pat. She had refused five proposals without a second thought. It was a little boring that her affections should have remained so completely unmoved through these months of exposure in the Marriage Market, though she told herself that she was in no hurry whatever to meet her fate. She had not been six weeks in the *Madame Bovary* when she met it.

The hour was about nine o'clock. Things were in full swing in the restaurant. There was a babble of voices. Catherine, by the counter, drawing a cork, glanced towards the door.

"Look, Lesley, look what's just coming in! Isn't that rather bliss?"

Two men had just entered the restaurant and were taking off their coats, one of them elderly and prosperous-looking, the other still perhaps in his thirties, thin, pale, with an interesting face, or so Catherine at once thought it.

"That's a Mr. Rutherford," said Lesley. "He comes fairly often."

Catherine moved towards them. Steve, too, advanced.

"Good evening, Mr. Rutherford," he said, "this is your table."

"Thank you, Steve," said the fat man, taking his seat and motioning his guest to the place in front.

"A new young lady I see."

"Yes," said Steve, "this is Cathy."

Catherine smiled entrancingly.

"Now what do you recommend this evening, Steve?" said Mr. Rutherford, taking up the menu.

"The *Bœuf Stroganov* is very good."

After some discussion *Oeufs Bovary* were ordered, followed by *Bœuf Stroganov*, and a bottle of Burgundy. Cathy wrote down the order, then hurried away to attend to it.

"Isn't he bliss?" she said to Lesley, busy at the counter.

"Him? Isn't he rather fat?"

"Not the old one, silly."

"I hadn't noticed the other." She looked over her shoulder. "A bit washed out, isn't he?"

"He has suffered, you see. I am sure there is much to reclaim. Those sensitive eyes—he keeps lowering them. Bertie," she called into the kitchen "are those eggs ready, yet?"

The restaurant, as always, was full. For the next hour the waitresses were continuously on the move. There was no chance for what Catherine described as "hovering". She learned little about the new client to whom she had taken such a fancy. The elderly man was doing all the talking, mostly about books, it seemed.

"Cathy," he said, as she put a Stilton cheese on the table, "will you please get us another bottle of this excellent Burgundy. And, Cathy, do I yet know you well enough to ask where Steve gets his waitresses?"

Cathy glanced at the other man to see if he shared Mr. Rutherford's curiosity on this point. He looked down.

"I mean," Mr. Rutherford went on, "where does he find such remarkably pretty young ladies?"

"The highways and hedges," said Catherine, with a smile of glittering gaiety, as she turned on her heel. In the mirror towards which she walked she noticed that they were both, yes both, looking after her.

As Mr. Rutherford plied his guest with wine the latter became more animated. Catherine removed the cheese, cleared the table and brought them cups of coffee.

"They're getting fundamental," she said to Lesley. This was another of Cathy's words, descriptive of the talk generated in some clients by a good dinner. Lesley giggled. She found Catherine extremely funny. Indeed, she admired and adored her without reserve. What Catherine could find so wonderful in that young, or not so young, man was, however, beyond her.

"I'm going to hover," said Cathy.

The conversation of the two men, much of which she was able to overhear, had indeed become rather fundamental.

"The consolations of religion," the younger man was saying, "what are they? The promise of eternal life. What does that mean? The survival of my ego for ever and ever. Do I want that? Absolutely not. Just the opposite. I want to be relieved of the thing. It simply isn't interesting enough. I don't exactly hate or despise it. I just don't love it, in the way that one can love things."

"Or people?"

"No doubt. All I am saying is that when the magic ends and one returns to the common light of day, there again is the inevitable companion, whom one had forgotten about for a full hour perhaps, that old fellow the self, quite a nice fellow in his way, sometimes rather amusing, but not very gifted or very interesting, and, oh dear, *connu*. And you are offered this eternal companionship as a prize! People who make such an offer must be quite ignorant of rapture. Is a death-wish the sin against the Holy Ghost?"

"Cathy," said Mr. Rutherford, "would you get us two brandies?" He looked at his companion. The time had come to broach a matter of business.

"Let's get back to Charles Braid," he said.

"One always gets back to Charles Braid."

"Why do you say that?"

"Because on almost every subject you can think of he said something decisive."

"True enough. You do honestly hold a very high opinion of him?"

"Of course. He is balm. He was unquestionably the dominant writer of our time."

"You adored him?"

"Of course, on this side—no, on the other side idolatry. Why do you ask such obvious questions?"

"I just wanted to be absolutely sure before making my proposition. You see, I am, as you know, his literary executor. Will you write his life?"

"Me? Charles Braid's life? My hat!"

"You look surprised. Before we go any further, let me say that you were his choice for the job."

"You don't say? Good heavens! But why me?"

"He had a high opinion of you. It was only about a fortnight before the end that I got him to talk about this matter of his biography. He wasn't, as you know, terribly keen on thinking about his own death. Perhaps he had an inkling how dreary the place was going to seem after his departure. Anyhow, that day he was quite willing to talk. He admitted that he would prefer that the life was not written by just anyone. We are talking about the official life. There will, no doubt, be various other lives by various admirers or by those of his less-successful rivals or imitators who have scores to pay off and those who want to put themselves right with posterity. I know of one or two such already brewing. And there will of course be a spate of effusive female books. What I am talking about is the life that will be written with access to the three suitcases of papers I have at home. Well, there we were talking over luncheon in that restaurant on the terrace that he was so fond of. You know the place, of course. There is a trellis of vines over the tables. It was May and the vines were in flower—one of the sweetest and headiest of Mediterranean smells, almost as good as that of a hot fig-tree. We were going through the names of possible biographers. He was keen on it not being anyone of his own generation or near it. 'I can't stick anyone over forty,' he said. 'They're so busy trying to make names for themselves.' Then he insisted that the person should be a gentleman. Also it would be desirable that he should show some evidence of being able to write. So, at length, we came to your name. 'By God,' he said, after only a moment's thought, 'the very man.' He looked out to sea, picking his teeth. 'I like him,' he said, 'I like him very much. My heart goes out to the un-ambitious. What a feeling of civilization it gives one to see fine talents being put to no use whatever! Yes, he's our man. He'd do it excellently, I believe. But look here, it mustn't be forced on him. He has far better things to do. I'd hate to interfere with his young life.' "

Rutherford paused.

"He said all that, did he? How beautiful! How lovely! I'm overwhelmed." The young man did indeed look much moved.

"You needn't decide at once," said Rutherford. 'I'll give you, say, a fortnight, to think it over. You realize of course that there will be a good deal of research to be done. There are various veils one ought to lift, if only to prevent anybody else lifting them. The Oxford period, for instance. He once told me that the three letters he wrote to the Master of his college at the time of his being sent down were the best things he ever wrote. I don't imagine they were quite the kind of letter the recipient would want to keep. Still, what a scoop if they did happen to survive! Anyhow, the whole incident needs a good deal of clearing up. Then there are various memories that should be tapped while they are still with us, both here and out there. Old Mirella, for instance. Cathy, may I have the bill, please?"

"Pat," said Cathy at the counter, "the bill for number four, please. Lesley, you're quite wrong about him being washed out. He's on fire, behind those lids. Have you ever thought of a honeymoon, Lesley, an interesting man opposite you in a restaurant-car, pouring out ideas, and it is all yours? I love him to distraction. Thank you, Pat."

She took the bill to her clients, whom she found writing in their engagement books. They were meeting again for dinner at the

Madame Bovary that day fortnight.

Catherine's passion survived a night's rest. Indeed, next morning she realized, somewhat to her astonishment, that her whole life had suddenly become dedicated to a single end. It was simply a question of waiting—weeks, months, years?—until he should come to a similar realization. What hope? There had been hardly an indication of any hope, had there? The fourteen empty days ahead of her seemed unbearably long. Still, she was not a person to waste her time.

"Papa."

"Yes, my love."

"Have we got any of Charles Braid's books in the house?"

"I've got *Lotus Land* in the study, and one or two others, and that collection of apophthegms from his works that somebody made. Why do you ask?"

"I was reading him in a friend's house the other day. He's balm."

"I shouldn't have thought he was terribly suitable for a maiden of tender years."

"Still, can you lend me one? I need it to be *au fait* with the people I meet at my work."

"Do you indeed?"

"Be an angel and let me have the apo-whatnots?"

Then there came one of her nights off and she went with a friend to a concert and there, as they were moving across the *foyer* at the end of the interval, she had seen him. He had passed quite close, coming towards her, and had he or hadn't he recognised her and faintly smiled? It was exasperating not to know. She turned to look after him. He, too, had turned to look. An indication—surely this was an indication?

"Papa," she said next day, "don't you think that Charles Braid is the dominant writer of our time?"

"I advise you not to pay too much attention to him, my treasure."

"He says, 'Those who give advice generally have nothing else to give.'"

"Does he? Does he indeed!"

"Papa."

"Yes, my love."

"Would you say it's tartish to take a bull by the horns?"

"No, I wouldn't say so, not necessarily by any means. Though it was never your mother's technique. She—no."

"Oh, come on. She what?"

"No."

"Oh yes, come on. You began. That's not fair."

"Very well, then. Perhaps you've reached years of discretion. Well, when I popped the question. what do you think she said?"

"I can't wait."

"It was by the Serpentine. She was looking at a duck. She simply said 'What?' "

Catherine screamed.

" 'What'! 'What'! By the Serpentine! Oh, my aunt! Looking at a duck!" She shrieked convulsively and ran along the passage to her mother's room to laugh at, and with, her. For some minutes her ecstatic screams pealed through the house as she reconstructed the scene of her parents' engagement.

At length the fortnight passed. The evening had arrived. Catherine as usual was at the restaurant at about six o'clock. For half an hour she and Lesley were busy laying the tables. Then, when all was set, and before any clients had arrived, Steve, as usual, poured out a glass of Burgundy for each member of the staff.

"Hear me, Lesley," said Catherine. " 'It is a function of art to draw off the melancholy from life.' 'Hope yes, Faith yes——' No! As you were, try again. 'Hope yes, Charity yes—but what has a scholar to do with Faith?' "

"Cathy, what on earth are you talking about?"

Catherine explained.

"It's just a question of what openings they give me. Oh, Lesley, don't you think he's balm?"

"What's that?"

"I'm not absolutely sure, but I think it's the same sort of thing as bliss, only more so."

Customers began to come in and dinners to be served. At length, after more than an hour and a half Catherine was taking the money at the table that was reserved, at half-past eight, for Mr. Rutherford. And then—there they were.

"Good evening, Cathy."

"Good evening, Cathy."

"Good evening."

"Well now," said Mr. Rutherford, looking down the menu, "what shall it be this evening? What do you feel like? *Homard Homais?* How's that done, Cathy?"

"Cooked in butter, with prawns and *Calvados*."

"Sounds all right. Should we try that?"

"I'd like just what I had the other time."

"The eggs, yes," said Catherine, "but *Bœuf Stroganov* is not on tonight, though of course I can get it if you specially want it."

"So you remembered," he said, looking up at her for the merest fraction of a second. "Yes," he went on, "I'd like it to be just like the first time."

"And I'll have the *Homard* and after that a *Tournedos*," said Mr. Rutherford.

"And the Burgundy as before?" said Catherine.

Mr. Rutherford glanced at his companion, who nodded, and Catherine left them.

"Freddie, precious," she called into the kitchen, "could you manage a *Strog*? Yes, I know it's not on the list, but this is a matter of the heart, *vouz savez*. Oh, that's angelic of you, I'll never forget it."

"Well?" said Lesley, at her shoulder.

"An I mistake not, there may be indications, just the faintest indications. If only I could hold his eyes for four seconds I believe that'd do the trick."

Meanwhile a gay young party of six was coming into the restaurant, friends of Catherine. She and Steve moved two small tables together to accommodate them. Derek Harbottle was among them. Before sitting down he pinned an orchid on to the front of Catherine's dress.

"Be making up your minds what you're going to eat," she said, "and I'll be back in a minute."

She moved swiftly, ravishingly.

"*Homard Homais*," she said as she put the hot plates in front of her two male customers, "and *Oeufs Bovary*."

"I like the orchid," said Mr. Rutherford. "Lucky Cathy!"

"Luck? 'It is a principle of mine (my only one) to regard whatever good fortune may come my way as deserved.'"

The two men looked at her in astonishment as she moved away to take the orders of the large table.

"My God," said the younger of them suddenly, "that's Charles Braid! Those are the opening words of *Lotus Land*!"

"Are they indeed? I'd forgotten. I say, what an extraordinary young lady she is, our Cathy! And, by the way, that brings us to business. How do you feel about it? Will you do the job?"

"Of course I will. Try, that is."

"I'm delighted." And Mr. Rutherford plunged into certain

financial matters. Presently Catherine was setting the next course before them.

"Cathy, you brilliant girl," said Mr. Rutherford, "I gather you're a Braid fan. Do you know his works by heart?"

"Nearly."

"I believe he is not generally thought a very suitable author for a young lady."

"My father keeps pressing him on me."

"You must have a most enlightened father."

"He's all right." She gave a rippling laugh.

"Well, you're among friends. This gentleman," he indicated his companion, "is no less than Charles Braid's biographer-to-be."

Well, look up properly, for heaven's sake! That's not the way to be won by a fair lady!

"Cathy! Lady Catherine!" Her friends called.

"Excuse me," she said moving away to attend to them. It was a busy night for her. There was no time for hovering. She was rushed off her feet, and when Mr. Rutherford and his friend had left, she found herself in possession of little new information about the latter. She did not even know his name and she knew of no assignation to look forward to. Perhaps they would never come to the restaurant again. Perhaps this was the end, the whole episode was finished. Yet, surely, surely she had made some impression?

The days passed and nothing happened. On her evening out she went again with a friend to the concert hall, the only place she knew where hope might flower. Blank. Another blank week then followed. On the next evening out she went again to the concert, this time alone. Again blank. She was getting angry.

Returning home that night, she found a note on the hall table in her mother's hand to the effect that the restaurant had telephoned. It was nothing important. No message left. Unusual, thought Catherine. What could that be about? She learned the next evening from Lesley. *He* had been to the restaurant, himself, alone, to dine.

"I thought you'd like to know he was here, so I telephoned."

"Lesley, you angel, how blissful of you! Tell me everything. Did you talk to him? What did he say?"

"He didn't say a lot. He seemed very disappointed that you weren't here."

"Oh, did he? More."

"He asked questions about you, who you were, etcetera. I hope

I got it right."

"More."

"Well, there wasn't any more really. He's going away to the country for some days, then he booked a table for himself and fatty for Tuesday week. He seemed all sort of worked up."

"Hm. I see. Yes. What's happened you see, Lesley, is that he doesn't know whether he's coming or going. It's proving too strong for him and he's struggling against it and he feels he's slipping. He's absolutely *déconcertato*."

She pirouetted among the empty tables, then stopped before the wall painting and, with an operatic gesture, stretched her arms towards Rouen cathedral. "I know that my," she yelled with a full-throated and vulgarly tremulous gust of song, "I know that my Redeemer liveth."

Bertie's face appeared at the kitchen door.

"Has she laid an egg or something?"

"Here," said Steve, passing her a glass of Burgundy," I expect that's made you thirsty."

With a fixed date ahead the days passed to some purpose. There was something restful, too, about the knowledge that he was out of London. It ruled out the daily hope and disappointment that lay in the possibility of meeting. On three mornings a week now she was having Italian lessons.

"All her own idea, these lessons. Paid for by herself too. The child has some gumption," said Lord Westfield proudly to Catherine's godfather. More gumption perhaps than he supposed. Might not she assist at those confabulations with old Mirella. . . .?

Then, there they were again one evening at the usual table.

"Defence, Lesley," said Catherine. "You watch. That's the order for tonight. Defence in depth. Each position to be defended to the last cartridge!"

The young man had much to say this evening. He was describing his visit to Oxford and his efforts, at Braid's college, to run to earth some priceless Braidiana. He had obtained interviews with the Master, the Dean and various of the fellows. He had the impression that they were ready for him, that he was not by any means the first of such inquirers. They were uniformly polite. Suavely, smilingly, they met him with an unequivocal *non possumus*. They knew of nothing that the college could tell him about Charles Braid.

"But, good heavens!" he said at length to the youngest of the fellows. "Isn't the college proud of having harboured, even if only for a year, the greatest prose writer of our time? Univ. has a monument to Shelley."

"I know. Personally I admire him very much."

"Well, then. All I am asking is this. The letters that Braid wrote to the Master, Weatherall—he once told a friend of mine that they were the best things he ever wrote. It occurs to me that as the great Weatherall had such a feeling for literature and as he is known to have been such a humorous and large-minded man, there is just a chance that he kept those letters."

The other hesitated.

"Yes," he said. "I may as well tell you. There is in the college archives a little packet of papers about Braid and his expulsion. It includes the letters."

"Ah! And you have seen the letters?"

"Yes."

"What are they like?"

"Superb."

Catherine stood by the table uncorking a second bottle of Burgundy.

"So they survive," said Mr. Rutherford. "How fascinating! But why won't they let us see them?"

"Apparently the fellows have decided that at least another generation should pass before they are released. Silly old dodderers!"

"Who looks after them?"

"The Dean acts as college archivist."

"Is there no way round him? Is he——?"

"No, apparently quite the reverse. I became rather chummy with one of the porters, who told me a lot of scandal about the Dean and undergraduettes."

"Cathy," said Mr. Rutherford, "do you think you could find us some of that French mustard?"

Catherine's policy of defence showed itself sadly ineffective during the evening. Though she could not doubt that the enemy was fully mobilised, nothing in the nature of an attack took place. And the evening was slipping away, and already they were having their coffee, and, oh dear, they would go away leaving her nothing to look forward to but just that terrible blank, and already she was making out the bill and—damn defence!

"Would you like a table reserved for another night?" she said.

"Should we?" said Mr. Rutherford. "Or are you sick of this place?"

The younger man looked up at Catherine for nearly two continuous seconds. "I couldn't bear to go anywhere else," he said, but did not follow up the attack, and, two minutes later, they were gone.

"Papa," said Catherine a few mornings afterwards.

"Yes, my treasure."

"Should one strike while the iron is hot?"

"Of course, every time."

"And if it's cold?"

"Strike all the same. What's the suitcase for?"

"I'm going away for the night. It's my night off. I'm going to Oxford."

"Don't get into mischief."

"How singular that you should say that, when it's precisely for that purpose that I am going."

The days were getting noticeably longer. It was light now as Catherine walked to her work through the square off which the *Madame Bovary* was situated. A blackbird each evening was singing in a plane tree. Catherine, too, was singing as, some days later, she passed under the tree.

"Steve," she said, taking off her coat, "your teeth are flawless pearls. It is conceivable that I might like to leave a little early tonight. Could I, just this once?"

"Of course."

"Grazie infinitissime!"

The evening proved a particularly strenuous one, at least in the early part. It was difficult to know quite why, for almost all the seats were occupied all the time every night. There just were some customers some nights who had the knack of running the waitresses off their feet. Catherine had little opportunity of hearing the conversation of her adored one, though she was conscious of his eyes continually upon her. Anyhow, what did she care about their conversation? She was swift, indifferent, remote, this evening, immortal, the archer goddess. Now she was taking their money.

"Cathy," he began, in a new sort of voice. A declaration? Far too late, my fine fellow!

"Excuse me," she said turning away.

She brought the change and, as she put it on the table, put also in front of him a paper packet tied in string. He undid the string and looked at the little file of papers in the packet. Taking out a letter, he unfolded it. It was headed "The Bullingdon Club.

3 November 1891." "My dear Master," it began. He read a few lines, then looked up, pushing the packet towards Mr. Rutherford.

"My God!" he said.

Catherine at that moment, in coat and hat, was leaving the restaurant. He got up and hurried after her. "Cathy," he called in the street. "Cathy!" She did not look round. He began to run. She, too, began to run. "Cathy, stop! I adore you. I absolutely worship you. You are my life. Cathy, don't you see? I love you! I love you!" She turned into the square, dark and empty at this time of night, and ran along beside the railings. "Cathy, stop! Don't you see, I love you! I adore you! I've known it from the first moment!"

She stopped suddenly.

"You've known it from the first moment," she panted. "Then why in heaven's name? All these weeks! Oh, it makes me wild!" She stamped with fury, then began to run again. She ran as fast as she could. But he could run faster.

THE BEGINNING
LORD ROTHSCHILD

MOST people associate the name Rothschild with banking, in spite of the 1976 London Telephone Directory containing Rothschilds who are Dental Surgeons, Accountants, Physicians, "Furn Fabrics, Linen", and one who just calls himself Trading Co. There are one hundred and thirty-eight different varieties in the Manhattan Telephone Directory. Though my father went each day to what is always known as "Rothschilds," in the City of London, he somehow found time to be a scientist as well—quite impossible today—with the result that my sisters and I grew up in an atmosphere of undiluted natural history. My earliest recollection, when I was about four years old, was of being sent into the garden by my father to try to catch a very rare butterfly, a gynandromorph Orange Tip: one which is half male and half

female, with its orange tip, therefore, on only one wing. I remember being punished a few years later for going into the long grass without wearing my galoshes (rubbers) to catch another very rare butterfly, an albino Meadow Brown. The sentence was terribly severe: I had to give the white Meadow Brown to my eldest sister. She gave it back to me, beautifully mounted, as a twenty-first birthday present. I have it still, some forty-five years later. It seems a little faded, but of course I now don't know if it is or not.

Rare varieties of common butterflies occupied a special place in our lives, alongside more mundane entomological activities: for example, keeping dug-up bumble bee nests, covered by inverted flower pots, on our bedroom windowsills. That most dedicated of collectors, my uncle the late Lord Rothschild, was, certainly, not immune to the thrill of the chase; and I think I can remember all twenty stone of him lumbering with his butterfly net after the silver variety of the Small Copper. It got away.

My parents, though Liberal in politics, seemed to me severe. Looking back, I do not remember much of what one might expect in a Rothschild house from reading recently published accounts of my family. We were simultaneously spoilt and regimented; and we had little human contact with our parents. In retrospect they were like policemen on traffic duty—stop, go, filter: but they could also endorse one's licence, and did. I remember having spinach for tea because I would not eat it for lunch. I also remember my sister Miriam and myself being coached by a cricket professional who told us wistfully that when he bowled to the great Ranjitsinjhi in the nets at Cambridge there was a gold watch on each stump; he never got one.

Our house seemed full of governesses and tutors. Miss Joyce taught me Latin grammar so mercilessly and efficiently that when, aged eight, I was sent to my preparatory school, Stanmore Park, I was put straight into the top form, only to be demoted after a week to a level more suitable to my age and relative ignorance of everything except Latin grammar. Stanmore Park, I am convinced, was a hell hole. Vernon Royle, the headmaster, was known as 'the Reverend' although not in Holy Orders. He was a famous cricketer. We were told that while he was dozing at cover point one day, a black object hurtled towards him and he caught it. His catch turned out to be a swallow. Under his captaincy the Stanmore Park masters beat the South Africans on tour and one of them, W. N. Roe, who published some quite well-known logarithm tables, made more than four hundred runs in one innings of a first-class match. R. F. Reynolds was a superb shot with a piece of chalk when a boy in his form annoyed him. Nose, cheek, forehead were his three preferred targets, in that order; he never hit a boy in the eye. His classroom was on the second floor and he dangled a boy called Openshaw outside the window, by his hair. Openshaw was not too popular so we were amused. Another master, D. W. Carr, who was said to have invented the googlie before Bosanquet, got drunk one evening and tried to remove the appendix of a boy called Cremer with a penknife.

Cremer, who had other difficulties at Stanmore Park, became a good poet later. I was upset when the classics master, J. M. Quinton, who was nice to me, committed suicide in the lavatory of a train; upset by two boys called Schilizzi who were very good at games and bullied many of the small boys; and also upset by one master who used to humiliate me in front of the other boys. There were, of course, some memorable moments of the pleasanter kind at Stanmore Park. I played "In the Hall of the Mountain King" (Greig's Peer Gynt Suite) alone on the piano on parents' day, which was said to be a great honour; and the school was given a half holiday when I won a scholarship to Harrow school.

I became painfully aware of being a Jew when a boy called Michel kicked my shins shortly after I arrived at Stanmore Park and called me a dirty little Jew. My father and mother were, I suppose, atheists or agnostics. At any rate there was no religious indoctrination at home, though we had to say our prayers, kneeling at our mother's bed, each morning and evening. As far as I can remember, these prayers consisted of asking God to bless all and sundry, including *kind* friends. They ended with a request to make me a good little boy amen. At the time I did not feel there was any detectable response to these injunctions, intoned twice daily under the supervision of my mother or, in her absence, of one or other of the army of nurses and governesses who tried to control us.

Eleven boys were fired from my house at Harrow school in my first term. I did not know why at the time, there having been no indoctrination on such matters either at home or at Stanmore. This lacuna in my education was, however, soon filled: just a fact or a way of life according to inclination or particular circumstances. Being intellectually precocious, no doubt unpleasantly so, I was frequently punished. This usually took the form of a beating—often by the Schilizzis who also went from Stanmore to Harrow—for being cheeky or for "lip" as it was then called at Harrow. I was frightened of the beatings because they were so painful. A boy called Stilwell knew this and threatened to report me for lip to the head of the house unless I agreed to have a homosexual relationship with him. I was sufficiently unnerved by this blackmail to take the unpardonable step of reporting Stilwell to my house-master, C. G. Pope. Stilwell got into terrible trouble or so it seemed at the time. Until then Mr Pope had disliked me; but after my astonishing behaviour I became one of his favourites and was quite often let off the hateful early morning school. He helped me with a thank-you letter to my Austrian cousin Alphonse

—in Greek because my German was not good enough. (Alphonse, who had one of the best stamp collections in the world outside the British Royal family, read only a Latin-Greek dictionary when travelling by train.)

One of the many hideous aspects of life at Harrow school (which is, no doubt, much more civilized now) concerned "Privileges". It was a three-year privilege to wear bedroom slippers. The icy stone steps in our house therefore produced very painful chilblains: according to matron, it was through lack of calcium. It was a three-year privilege to whistle (as if one wanted to), to have a hot bath, or to close the lavatory door. A boy called Usborne did not go to the lavatory for a whole term as a result. We were much mystified by this feat of endurance but I suspected he secretly relieved himself at the Music School which, because of its cellular construction, was also the headquarters for homosexual activities. A boy called Whidborne minor, whom I thought particularly beautiful, behaved very badly to an older boy, Hewlett, in the Music School. Whidborne told Hewlett that he could do whatever he liked to him. Hewlett complied with alacrity and imagination, upon which Whidborne screamed and shouted, asserting that he had been indecently assaulted. Hewlett left Harrow on the 4 p.m. train to London the next day. Beautiful as he was Whidborne minor was treated with some reserve and caution from then onwards.

Boredom with the Punic Wars (or the way we were taught about them), and the imbecile behaviour evoked by this boredom, made Mr Pope append a curt note to one of my end of term reports: "Must do better if he wishes to stay". The day after this thunderbolt arrived at home I detected some change, which I could not immediately identify, in my mother's study. She quickly solved the puzzle. "You will see", she said, "that there are now two desks. The one on the left is my usual one, that on the right is for you. There is a copy of your Roman History textbook and writing paper on yours. Each morning during the holidays you will read about the Punic Wars and write essays which I shall set and correct. If the marks for any particular essay are not high enough, the question will be reset for the next morning." How did she know about the Punic Wars? When did she mug them up? In the evenings, instead of playing double dummy bridge, which she often did? I could not find out, but the results the next term were electrifying. My essays on Hamilcar Barca and Massinissa were specially singled out for praise. "A much better effort and performance this term", and, after that, Mr Pope became even more friendly. The amazing thing to me now, more than fifty years and a number of children later, was my blind obedience to my mother. "No way", "Get lost", "You must be joking", or even "Get stuffed" were not at that time part of the vocabulary of a boy aged fifteen enjoying a normal, happy relationship with his parents.

Religious instruction of Jewish boys at Harrow was a continual source of discussion and dissension. The parents of some Jewish boys, like my own, were indifferent; others felt that their children should know something about Judaism. The headmaster, on the other hand, said that Chapel was not an exercise in proselytization, but more in the nature of a general address: no more divisive than a discourse on Britain's coal industry. To begin with, therefore, non-Christian boys went to Chapel and to Chapel only. But in the middle of one service, a Persian boy produced a gong from underneath his tails, hit it three times, then lay down on the floor of the Chapel with his head facing east. After this episode the headmaster felt that although attendance at Chapel was still desirable for infidels, they should also have the benefit of some other system of instruction more appropriate to their own religions. Accordingly, each Saturday the Jewish boys were herded into a classroom known as the Tin Tabernacle, where a distinguished Shakespearean scholar, Sir Israel Gollancz, attempted to teach them the principles of Judaism. This turned out to be quite boring and after two Saturdays one very clever Jewish boy, Tony Goldschmidt (killed in World War II) put a question to Sir Israel: "What does the word 'Ducdame' mean in *As You Like It*?" Sir Israel, who seemed as bored by religious indoctrination as we were, reacted with alacrity, erudition and enthusiasm. So all the Jewish boys got top marks in their papers on *As You Like It*. Sir Israel was plied with further questions about Shakespeare's plays and sonnets, to his evident enjoyment, but some of the boys reported to their parents that all religious teaching had ceased and that the Tin Tabernacle had become a second wooden O. As a result, Sir Israel left and was replaced by a mediocrity whose name I have forgotten.

Towards the end of my time at Harrow I became good, better, or difficult to ignore at cricket: an automatic passport to popularity which until then had eluded me. I was even allowed to stop re-reading the first chapter of our biology textbook and to progress from *Amoeba* to a higher organism. I had not been permitted to press on before because my friend Pleydell-Bouverie experienced difficulty with or distaste for *Amoeba*; and it was not thought right for one of the two boys studying biology in the top form to get too far ahead of the other. Clearly such a state of affairs would have meant more work for the biology master, D. M. Reid, who, like his pupil, published a classification of the animal kingdom. But being in the cricket eleven and a member of the Harrovian analogue of Pop, called Phil, changed all that. I was given the privilege of abandoning Pleydell-Bouverie to his *Amoeba* and

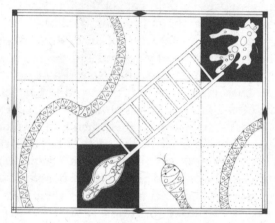

passing on to *Paramoecium*. About that time a nice old boy with a twinkling eye and a frock coat came to Harrow and gave me a *viva* for a scholarship to Cambridge, which I won. He was called Harold Hartley and later became a great friend of mine. I much admired him.

When I arrived home for the vacation after my first term at Cambridge my mother asked me if I had made any new friends (apart from the Harrovians who went to Cambridge at the same time). I had to say I had not, something of which I was very ashamed. She asked the same question each vacation. After a year or so of shame, I was able to announce, and from time to time produce, Garrett Moore (now Lord Drogheda), Dick· Sheepshanks (killed in the Spanish Civil War), Sammy Hood, Gerald Cuthbert (killed in World War II), Anthony Blunt and a clever, dissolute young man called Guy Burgess with whom my mother got on very well. Perhaps he was a Soviet agent even then. As a matter of fact, I thought Burgess might have fascist or pro-Nazi inclinations because of his friendship with a good-looking, fair-haired undergraduate of Trinity College called Micky Burn, who was inordinately interested in the Hitler Youth. I now suspect that the friendship between Burgess and Burn was not political.

Having been brought up with butterflies, birds, bees and insects instead of with human beings, I inevitably had a scientific albeit anti-entomological bent (in spite of being made to do classics until the age of sixteen, something for which I am now very grateful). So it came as rather a shock at the age of twenty-one to learn that I was expected at least to try the life of a banker in the City of London. This I did, but the moment was unfortunate. In 1931 there was a world recession; the City seemed moribund, boring, rather painful. I did not like banking which consists essentially of facilitating the movement of money from Point A, where it is, to Point B where it is needed; nor did I like it any more, forty-five years later when, as a temporary expedient, I tried to run Rothschilds for fifteen months. After my first six months in the City I returned to Cambridge University to be a scientist. Except for the war years I lived there until I was forty-eight in a relaxed and, perhaps, somewhat unworldly atmosphere.

From
Meditations of a Broomstick

THE KING'S DEPARTURE

FRANCES DONALDSON

ON Saturday afternoon, 5 December [1936], Monckton formally told Baldwin of the King's decision to abdicate. Thus the crisis was over. On Monday 7 December it could be seen to be over, the King and his subjects having separately reached a decision which coincided too closely for any further disruption or interruption of their intentions to be possible. When members of parliament returned from their constituencies after the weekend, they were in a mood of solid agreement. Whether or not there had been any real danger of a constitutional crisis the week before, it quickly became clear that, once the situation was fully understood, the country as a whole felt quite strongly that the King could not marry and remain on the throne.

The House of Commons showed their solidarity by turning on Winston Churchill. His press release had made him unpopular, and when he attempted to ask the Prime Minister for an assurance that no irrevocable step would be taken, he was actually howled down. It is an appalling thing to have several hundred men unexpectedly turn and yell at one, and Churchill was horrified and suitably chastened.

A new diarist had now appeared on the scene, Blanche Dugdale, who gives us an unsurpassable account of the King's mood on the same day:

> Lunched at the Club with Walter [Elliot] who explains the King's *one* idea is Mrs Simpson. Nothing that stands between him and her will meet his approval. The Crown is only valuable if it would interest *her*. He must have marriage because then she can be with him always. Therefore he has no wish to form a "Party" who would keep him on the Throne and let her be his mistress. Therefore he has no animosity against Ministers who are not opposing his abdication. . . . He is very upset by the newspapers, never having seen anything but fulsome adulation in all his forty years!

The last week of the King's reign was not uneventful. Both his own advisers and the government had for some time been increasingly worried by his vulnerability, if he abdicated, to an intervention by the King's Proctor in Mrs Simpson's divorce suit. Monckton says: "I was desperately afraid that the King might give up his throne and yet be deprived of his chance to marry Mrs Simpson." On Saturday 5 December he suggested a solution to Baldwin when the Prime Minister visited the King at the Fort. His proposal was that there should be two bills—one giving effect to the King's wish to renounce the throne and the other making Mrs Simpson's decree nisi absolute immediately. And he wrote: "This would finally have cleared up a grave constitutional position affecting the whole world and have left no ragged ends or possibilities of further scandal."

Describing the scene at Fort Belvedere when Monckton made his suggestion to Baldwin, the Duke of Windsor wrote that Baldwin himself thought it a just accommodation but said that some opposition must be expected from his colleagues. He promised his own support and then said that in the event of the Cabinet refusing the second bill he would resign.

On Sunday morning there was a meeting of senior ministers at which Baldwin did what he could to urge his colleagues to accept Monckton's suggestion. However, the others feared an outcry of one law for the rich and one for the poor, and thought that to rush the decree through would publicly confirm the worst about Mrs Simpson and give the appearance of a bargain. Neville Chamberlain put the reasons against it as follows: (1) it could not be denied that the King regarded the bill as a condition of abdication, and it would therefore be denounced as an unholy bargain; (2) it would irretrievably damage the moral authority of the government at home and in the Empire; (3) it would be looked on as an injury to the marriage law in general; (4) it would injure the respect for the monarchy.

By this time, too, the Cabinet were anxious to get the whole matter wound up. It was hurting the Christmas trade (incredibly this seems to have been true), "holding up business" and "paralysing our foreign policy". And Chamberlain at least was also tired of the continued opportunity given to the "Simpson Press" to misrepresent what was happening. He complained:

> The public is being told that we are engaged in a fight with the King, because we have advised him to abdicate and he has refused. That is quite untrue, and we must say so. He asked us to examine the morganatic marriage proposal, we told him we could have nothing to do with it, and he has accepted that view. The public is also being told that we are trying to rush the King into a decision that he has not time to think over. That is equally untrue. He has been thinking it over for weeks, though he has been unwilling to face up to realities.

When Monckton was called in to be told that the Cabinet could not agree to the second bill he said that the decision would greatly disappoint the King who, in the light of it, would undoubtedly ask for additional time for thought. But Monckton's response had come from the depths of his deep disappointment, for at Fort Belvedere preparations for the Abdication went on. (When asked directly by the 3rd Earl Baldwin whether his father had promised to resign if he could not persuade the Cabinet, but had not kept his word, Monckton made it plain that the Prime Minister had offered his resignation but he had assured him that "he was perfectly certain that the King would permit no such action, and persuaded S.B. not to consider it further." And he said he confirmed this with the King immediately after.)

The events of Monday 7 December are obscure and likely to remain so because everyone gives a different account.

In Cannes, under the influence of Lord Brownlow, Mrs Simpson prepared a statement for the press, which read: "Mrs Simpson, throughout the last few weeks, has invariably wished to avoid any action or proposal which would hurt or damage His Majesty or the Throne. Today her attitude is unchanged, and she is willing, if such action would solve the problem, to withdraw from a situation that has been rendered both unhappy and untenable." Lord Brownlow doubted that this statement was sufficiently strong, and wished for a forthright declaration that Mrs Simpson had no intention of marrying the King. But she shrank from dealing him so cruel a blow. She also telephoned the King to tell him of her decision and to read him the statement. "After I finished there was a long silence. I thought that David in his anger had hung up. Then he said slowly, 'Go ahead, if you wish; it won't make any difference.'"

The Duke of Windsor's account is not very different, although he leaves out the anger. "It did not occur to me that she was asking to be released. Yet that was what she meant. And others read into her statement the same thing."

However, according to both Monckton and Sir Edward Peacock, the King was a party to this statement and it was given to the press with his approval. Monckton says:

> Meantime he was most anxious that Mrs Simpson's position should be improved in the eyes of the public, and it was with his full approval that she made her statement on Tuesday, December 8, from Cannes that she was willing to give up a position that had become both unhappy and untenable. This, when published, was looked upon as being perhaps the end of the crisis, but we at the Fort knew of the statement before its publication, and that his intention was quite unchanged.

And Sir Edward Peacock commented: "She apparently began to think of her own unpopularity, and a statement was suggested, which she issued from Cannes. The King approved, well realizing that this would to some extent divert criticism from her to him, the very thing he wanted."

On the same day that this statement was circulated to the press,

Theodore Goddard learned that another affidavit was about to be served on the King's Proctor by a private individual, to the effect that the intervener was in a position to show why the decree should not be made absolute "by reason of material facts not having been brought before the court and/or by reason of the divorce having been obtained by collusion". Goddard felt that he ought to see his client (some say because of the intervention, others because she had begun to issue statements to the press) and he told Monckton that he proposed to go to Cannes. However, when Monckton told the King, he sent for Goddard and forbade him to go. On hearing this, Baldwin then also sent for Goddard and encouraged him to go. His reasons for wanting Goddard to go to see Mrs Simpson are obscure and have been given different interpretations. His biographers believe that he "made a last and almost certainly genuine attempt to get Mrs Simpson to give up the King" by withdrawing her divorce action. Other motives have been attributed to him, although only Lord Beaverbrook managed to think of one that was discreditable. (He believed that Baldwin did it because, if Mrs Simpson could have been persuaded to withdraw, he would have been absolved without shame from his promise to resign—a likely motive for someone who, according to Beaverbrook, had been plotting for weeks to bring about the Abdication of the King.)

Another solution which has had quite a wide circulation is that when Mrs Simpson left England she took with her the emeralds which Queen Alexandra brought from Denmark at the time of her marriage, and Goddard was sent over simply to get them back. For obvious reasons it is not possible to find corroboration for this. All one can say is that Lord Davidson believed it, and told it to more than one person.

And certainly without some explanation of this kind Baldwin's action seems incomprehensible. When, after weeks of negotiation, he had reached an agreement which, even if it was not entirely satisfactory, brought a much-needed end to the crisis, and done this without putting pressure on the King or dividing the country, why should he try to re-open the whole thing by sending Goddard on this errand? Two things give weight to the idea that this was, nevertheless, what he did. The first is that the Duchess of Windsor's account confirms it. The other is the rest of Baldwin's conduct at the time.

In many ways a humorous man, Baldwin had great areas of unsophistication, one might even say insensitivity, and he invariably over-rated his influence with the King. On the day Goddard left for Cannes he decided that Edward must consult his conscience and that he was the man to make him do it. "He must wrestle with himself in a way he has never done before," he is reported to have said, "and, if he will let me, I will help him. We may even have to see the night through together." And packing his bag and accompanied by Dugdale, he set off for Fort Belvedere.

The King was surprised when Monckton told him of the Prime Minister's proposed visit, remarking that he thought everything had already been said, but he agreed to receive him.

On arrival at Fort Belvedere, Walter Monckton, who travelled down with the Prime Minister, saw at once that the King was in a state of utter exhaustion and "seemed worn out". He also showed obvious signs of distress at the sight of Baldwin's suitcase. Monckton then went to Sir Edward Peacock, who was in the house, and arranged for him to ask the Prime Minister to stay with him at his own house, Bodens Ride, nearby. However, as soon as this suggestion was made to Baldwin, he said it would be better for him to return to London.

In recounting this episode in *A King's Story*, the Duke of Windsor is at his most hostile to Baldwin, charging him with paying this visit merely because it would make his own part in the crisis sound better if he could claim to have made a "humble and sincere" effort to get the King to change his mind. And he goes on to say that he went to Sir Edward Peacock and asked him to take Baldwin away. This account gives a good deal of interest to the notes Sir Edward made at the time:

> He [the King] said to me that at the moment he felt unable to have people about & seemed completely done. I suggested that I take the Prime Minister & Dugdale away & give them dinner at Bodens Ride, but he said immediately: "I could not do that. The Prime Minister has been so kind as to come here to help me, I could not let him leave without giving him dinner. He must stay." I finally secured his assent to arrange with the Prime Minister that he & Dugdale should go home after dinner, but he was urgent that I should not do so unless I was sure that it would not hurt the PM's feelings.

Here is Monckton's account of the interview that took place between Baldwin and the King:

Once again when the audience took place I was present with the Prime Minister and the King. The Prime Minister was a little deaf when he was tired, and on this occasion it had a curious result, as when the Prime Minister had urged once again all that he could do to dissuade the King, for the sake of the country and all that the King stood for, from his decision to marry, the King wearily said that his mind was made up and he asked to be spared any more advice on the subject. To my astonishment, Mr Baldwin returned to the charge with renewed vigour and, I thought, put the position even better than before. He asked me immediately afterwards if I thought he had said all that he could, and when I explained that I thought he had done even more, it was plain that he had not heard the King's request to him to desist.

The audience took place in the drawing-room. . . . I can see them sitting there now, the King in his chair in front of the fire, Mr Baldwin at right angles to him on the sofa, and myself on a chair between them. It was the room in which the Abdication was to be signed in three days' time.

That night there were nine to dinner, the King, the Dukes of York and Kent, Monckton, Peacock, Allen, Ulick Alexander, Baldwin and Dugdale. The King was as jolly as a lark. Monckton wrote:

> This dinner party was, I think, his *tour de force*. In that quiet pannelled room he sat at the head of the table with his boyish face and smile, with a good fresh colour while the rest of us were pale as sheets, rippling over with bright conversation, and with a careful eye to see that his guests were being looked after. . . . As the dinner went on the Duke [of York] turned to me and said: "Look at him. We simply cannot let him go." But we both knew there was nothing we could say or do to stop him.

In the meantime in Cannes it seems likely that Mrs Simpson understood for the first time the inevitable end of this affair and did indeed agree to do anything that might prevent the King from abdicating. She was ready to surrender everything, even to withdraw her divorce petition. Goddard telephoned to Baldwin the following message:

> I have today discussed the whole position with Mrs

Simpson—her own, the position of the King, the country, the Empire. Mrs Simpson tells me she was, and still is, perfectly willing to instruct me to withdraw her petition for divorce and willing to do anything to prevent the King from abdicating. I am satisfied that this is Mrs Simpson's genuine and honest desire. I read this note over to Mrs Simpson who in every way confirmed it.

(signed) *Theodore Goddard*

(counter-signed) *Brownlow*

But this whole absurd adventure had been begun days, even weeks, too late, and, if it had been successful, could only have resulted in the King losing both the throne and his future wife. By now the King was absolutely determined, and surely he was right to believe that, if he had given up Mrs Simpson for the Crown at this juncture, it would have rested on a head "forever bowed in shame". No one could alter his decision.

However, now it was the turn of the Cabinet, previously so anxious for an ultimatum, to have second thoughts, although this may have been the result of a wish to safeguard themselves. A formal message was sent to the King: "Ministers are reluctant to believe that Your Majesty's resolve is irrevocable and still venture to hope that before Your Majesty pronounces any formal decision, Your Majesty may be pleased to reconsider an intention which must so deeply distress and so vitally affect all Your Majesty's subjects." The King replied: "His Majesty has given the matter his further consideration but regrets he is unable to alter his decision."

Nothing remained but the formalities and the arrangements for the King's future rank and finance.

On 9 December Monckton and Peacock went to see the Duke of York and "secured his assent to His Majesty retaining Royal Rank & that if and when he is allowed to come to England he should have the Fort to live in. The Duke of York authorized Monkton to tell this to the King."

Later on the same day Monckton and Simon drafted the King's Message to Parliament. And later still Monckton went back to Downing Street where arrangements were made for the Instrument of Abdication and the Messages to be distributed throughout the Empire at the right time and place. He also had an interview with Queen Mary who said to him: "To give up all this for that!"

Monckton arrived at Fort Belvedere with the draft Message and the draft Instrument of Abdication at 1 a.m. the next morning. Sir Edward Peacock was already there and had told the King of a Cabinet decision that he should stay out of England for a period of not less than two years.

On Thursday morning, 10 December, the Instrument of Abdication was signed and witnessed by the King's three brothers, as was the King's Message to the House of Commons. That afternoon the Speaker to the House of Commons read the King's Message to a packed House and, speaking from notes, Baldwin then made one of the most famous speeches of his whole career. Here is Sir Harold Nicolson's account of it:

> The Prime Minister then rises. He tells the whole story. . . . His papers are in a confused state . . . and he hesitates somewhat. He confuses dates and turns to Simon, "It was Monday, was it not, the 27th?" The artifice of such asides is so effective that one imagines it to be deliberate. There is no moment when he overstates emotion or indulges in oratory. There is intense silence broken only by reporters in the gallery scuttling away to telephone the speech paragraph by paragraph. I suppose that in after-centuries men will read the words of that speech and exclaim. "What an opportunity wasted!" They will never know the tragic force of its simplicity. "I said to the King. . . ." "The King told me. . . ." It was Sophoclean and almost unbearable.

When *A King's Story* appeared it became clear nevertheless that the speech left the King with a grievance. That morning Baldwin had asked Walter Monckton whether there were any special points the King would like him to mention, and the King sent him two notes: one asking him to say that he and the Duke of York had always been on the best of terms as brothers and "the King is confident the Duke deserves and will receive the support of the whole Empire"; the other asking him to say that "the other person most intimately concerned had consistently tried to the last to dissuade the King from the decision which he had taken". Baldwin read out the first note but he did not mention the second. In the same way the first note was found among his papers, the second was not. To anyone who has studied what Baldwin felt, it seems obvious that, whereas the King would undoubtedly have sent such a request, Baldwin would have found it impossible to comply with it. How easy, if that were so, to crumple it up in one's pocket.

The financial arrangements for the future Duke of Windsor were initially discussed by the Cabinet, and Harding pressed the Prime Minister through Walter Monckton to combine in the Instrument of Abdication the provision for an income of £25,000 a year with an undertaking on the ex-King's part not to return to the country without the consent of the Monarch and the government of the day. And Monckton makes it plain that he believed that if the King had made up his mind earlier he would have negotiated from greater strength.

However, in the end the financial arrangements were made not with the government but with the Duke of York. Probably the chief reason for this was that any settlement had to take into account the peculiar position of Balmoral and Sandringham, of which, under the wills of Queen Victoria and King George V, Edward VIII was a life tenant. Any satisfactory financial settlement had to be based on the transfer of those to his brother. Naturally no one but their financial and legal advisers was a party to the settlement, but informed guesses put the figure for Sandringham and Balmoral at one million pounds and the yearly income paid by George VI to his brother at £60,000. Over and beyond this the Duke of Windsor is believed to have taken substantial sums out of the country from other sources.

At Fort Belvedere only one thing seriously upset the King. This was a message from Sir John Simon saying that in the changed circumstances he would feel bound to withdraw the detective who had been guarding Mrs Simpson at Cannes. The King was so greatly distressed that Monckton protested to Simon who, possibly as a result of this, decided to bear the brunt of any criticism himself, and reversed the order.

The day ended with what Lord Birkenhead has described as "an emotional and somewhat embarrassing evening". Mr and Mrs Hunter, who were friends of the King's, had been invited to dinner and Monckton, who was not present, received from Peacock the following account of what happened:

> In a short time the butler came in to say that Mrs Hunter was of the party at the Fort and wanted very much to see me. So I drove over and saw Kitty Hunter, who burst into tears and explained to me how Mrs S. had fooled her to the last, declaring that she would never marry the King. Her account of the dinner suggests that the poor King must have had a pretty difficult time, because apparently Kitty and George wept into their soup and everything else during the meal,

in spite of the King's heroic efforts to carry off the dinner cheerfully.

Once he had decided to abdicate, the King determined to fulfil his desire to broadcast to the nation. He tasted at once the joys of being a subject of the King because the government could no longer restrain him. However, he instructed Walter Monckton to inform Baldwin that as a matter of courtesy he would allow the Cabinet to see in advance what he intended to say. On the evening of 10 December he worked late into the night and he was up early the next day to finish his speech. Then he invited Winston Churchill to luncheon to wish him goodbye and to show him the draft. (During this luncheon he ceased to be King.) The Duke of Windsor has said that it is not true that Churchill wrote his broadcast speech—he wrote it himself—but he was responsible for one or two phrases which the student of Churchilliana should be able to spot.

As Churchill stood on the doorstep saying goodbye to the ex-monarch there were tears in his eyes and he gave a fresh association to Marvell's famous lines on the beheading of Charles I:

> *He nothing common did or mean*
> *Upon that memorable scene.*

The ex-King's decision to broadcast to the nation made urgent the question of his future rank and titles. "The pundits were confounded," Sir John Wheeler-Bennett writes, and they sought the counsel of the new King. In a memorandum annexed to his record of the Abdication crisis, George VI gives an account of an interview with Lord Wigram and Sir Claud Schuster (as representative of the Lord Chancellor), who came to ask his view on the matter. The question, the King was told, was urgent because Sir John Reith, the Director-General of the BBC, was proposing to introduce the ex-King on the air as Mr Edward Windsor. The King said that this would be quite wrong but that before going any further it was necessary to know what his brother had given up by the Abdication. Upon Schuster replying that he was not quite sure, King George, who is normally represented as being completely bowled over at this time by his sense of his own inadequacy, gave a convincing exhibition of regal testiness as well as the solution to the problem:

I said, it would be quite a good thing to find out before

coming to me. Now as to his name. I suggest HRH D[uke] of W[indsor]. He cannot be Mr E. W. as he was born the son of a Duke. That makes him L[or]d E. W. anyhow. If he ever comes back to this country, he can stand and be elected to the H. of C. Would you like that? S replied No. As D of W he can sit and vote in the H. of L. Would you like that? S replied No. Well if he becomes a Royal Duke he cannot speak or vote in the H. of L. and he is not being deprived of his rank in the Navy, Army or R. Air Force. This gave Schuster a new lease of life and he went off quite happy.

King George also gave instructions as to how his brother should be described on the radio that night, and it was on his specific command that the ex-King was introduced as His Royal Highness Prince Edward. That evening King George visited his brother to tell him that he had decided to create him a Duke as the first act of his reign. "How about the family name of Windsor?" And the following morning at his Accession Council he announced his intention to create him the Duke of Windsor, although it was not until after the Coronation that the style and title were given legal form.

During the day the ex-King received what he has described as "a hint" from the Prime Minister that he would be gratified if he would stress that he had at all times received every possible consideration from him; a hint about which the Duke of Windsor writes bitterly, after brooding for years on the fact that Baldwin had refused his own request to do justice to Mrs Simpson. And during the day it was arranged, through Mrs Simpson on the telephone, that he should go to Baron Eugene de Rothschild's house, Schloss Enzesfeld, near Vienna—the last stages of the Abdication having been conducted at such speed that not until now had any consideration been given to the ex-King's future.

That evening he dined with his assembled family at Royal Lodge, and after dinner Walter Monckton fetched him and drove him to Windsor Castle from where he was to broadcast. Mounting the Gothic staircase to a room in the Augusta Tower, he was met by Sir John Reith. So that his voice might be tested, he read a newspaper report of a reference to the fact that the new King was an ardent tennis player. Then Sir John Reith announced: "This is Windsor Castle, His Royal Highness Prince Edward," and he spoke to the listening world in a voice which, gradually gaining confidence, ended on a high note of courage:

At long last I am able to say a few words of my own.

I have never wanted to withhold anything, but until now it has been not constitutionally possible for me to speak.

A few hours ago I discharged my last duty as King and Emperor, and now that I have been succeeded by my brother, the Duke of York, my first words must be to declare my allegiance to him. This I do with all my heart.

You all know the reasons which have impelled me to renounce the throne. But I want you to understand that in making up my mind I did not forget the country or the Empire which as Prince of Wales, and lately as King, I have for twenty-five years tried to serve. But you must believe me when I tell you that I have found it impossible to carry the heavy burden of responsibility and to discharge my duties as King as I would wish to do without the help and support of the woman I love.

And I want you to know that the decision I have made has been mine and mine alone. This was a thing I had to judge entirely for myself. The other person most concerned has tried up to the last to persuade me to take a different course. I have made this, the most serious decision of my life, upon a single thought of what would in the end be the best for all.

This decision has been made less difficult for me by the sure knowledge that my brother, with his long training in the public affairs of this country and with his fine qualities, will be able to take my place forthwith, without interruption or injury to the life and progress of the Empire. And he has one matchless blessing, enjoyed by so many of you and not bestowed on me—a happy home with his wife and children.

During these hard days I have been comforted by my Mother and by my Family. The Ministers of the Crown, and in particular Mr Baldwin, the Prime Minister, have always treated me with full consideration. There has never been any constitutional difference between me and them and between me and Parliament. Bred in the constitutional tradition by my Father, I should never have allowed any such issue to arise.

Ever since I was Prince of Wales, and later on when I occupied the Throne, I have been treated with the greatest kindness by all classes, wherever I have lived or journeyed throughout the Empire. For that I am very grateful.

I now quit altogether public affairs, and I lay down my burden. It may be some time before I return to my native land, but I shall always follow the fortunes of the British race and Empire with profound interest, and if at any time in the future I can be found of service to His Majesty in a private station I shall not fail. And now we all have a new King, I wish him, and you, his people, happiness and prosperity with all my heart. God bless you all. God Save the King.

After the broadcast he returned to Royal Lodge to say goodbye to his family. It was late and his mother and his sister Mary left quite soon, but the four brothers and Walter Monckton sat on until midnight when the Duke of Windsor and Monckton left to drive to Portsmouth. As he took his leave of his brothers he bowed to the new King, a gesture which led the Duke of Kent to cry out: "It isn't possible. It isn't happening."

All the way down he talked quietly and composedly to Walter Monckton about their early friendship at Oxford and about the First World War.

At Portsmouth the ex-King had been expected for hours before he arrived, and a naval guard with rifles and fixed bayonets had been paraded, while the *Fury* waited alongside, ready for sea. On the dockside friends and members of his household waited to say goodbye. Admiral Sir William Fisher, Commander-in-Chief Portsmouth, was there to say goodbye for the Navy. There were tears in his eyes as he did so. The King seemed in the same good spirits he had shown all week, and, if he felt any emotion appropriate to the enormity of the occasion, he gave no sign of it. His friends escorted him down to his cabin to say goodbye. "Godfrey Thomas had served him for 17 years," Monckton wrote, "and felt that in some way he had failed in his duty, and that what was virtually his life's work had been shipwrecked."

Fury sailed immediately and anchored in St Helen's Roads for the night, proceeding in time to cross the Channel and arrive in France in the morning.

From
Edward VIII, The Road to Abdication

11 DECEMBER 1936

SIR HENRY CHANNON

"THE King is gone, Long Live the King." We woke in the reign of Edward VIII and went to bed in that of George VI. Honor and I were at the House of Commons by eleven o'clock, and as she stood for a time in the queue waiting to go to the Strangers Gallery, I talked with Mikey and David Lyon who were waiting to hear their sister made Queen of England. They were simple, charming and bored as ever. When the Bill came it was passed into Law with the minimum of time. Lord Halifax who moved it, and Lord Onslow who was on the Woolsack, are both Honor's uncles, and I realised how vested and what a close corporation the aristocracy of England still is. Then the Royal Commission was sent for, and the Lords Onslow, Denman and one other, filed out of the Chamber, and returned in full robes and wigs. Black Rod was sent to summon the Speaker, who, followed by his Commons, appeared at the bar. The Clerk read the Royal Commission. The three Lords bowed, and doffed their hats. The Bill was read. The King was still King Edward. The Clerk bowed "Le Roi le veult" and Edward, the beautiful boy King with his gaiety and honesty, his American accent and nervous twitching, his flair and glamour was part of history. It was 1.52.

We went sadly home, and in the street we heard a woman selling newspapers saying "The Church held a pistol to his head". In the evening we dined at the Stanleys' cheerless, characterless house, and at ten o'clock turned on the wireless to hear "His Royal Highness, Prince Edward" speak his farewell words in his unmistakable slightly Long Island voice. It was a manly, sincere farewell, saying that he could not carry on the responsibilities of Kingship without the support of the woman he loved. There was a stillness in the Stanleys' room. I wept, and I murmured a prayer for he who had once been King Edward VIII.

Then we played bridge.

From
Chips, The Diaries of Sir Henry Channon

28 JANUARY 1937

MARIE BELLOC LOWNDES

I shall always believe that had Mrs Simpson stayed in England instead of going to France, it is probable that Edward VIII would never have abdicated. It is a very different thing to advise a man over the telephone to do this or that, and to beg him to do what you wish to be done when you are actually with him. There seems little doubt that Mrs Simpson was kept in complete ignorance of what was really going on during those crucial ten days, for I have heard that the news of the Abdication came on her as a terrible shock and made her very angry. She is said to have rung up the King and cried "Call out the soldiers!"

I also believe that had Mrs Simpson had one sensible, intelligent friend of either sex who knew something of the world or of human nature, she and the King might actually have carried through their scheme of marriage. Had she, for instance, been content to wait her turn for a quiet divorce in London, while nothing could have prevented the American Press making the most of it, there would have been no crowds, no local gossip, no scandal such as was caused by the case being heard at Ipswich.

If she had then lived in retirement, even close to London, for the six months, seeing only a few people and giving out that it was her intention in time to return to America—and had the King meanwhile contented himself with not seeing her under his own roof—there would have been very little talk. Of course the King would have had to force himself to be courteous to the Archbishop of Canterbury, and the more old-fashioned of his parents' friends, with regard to the Coronation Ceremony. Then, had he been crowned and so became "the Lord's Anointed", when the divorce decree was made absolute, he could have married her and Mrs Simpson would then have become Queen of England, and I cannot believe, great as would have been the shock and anger of the British, that there would have been any serious effort made to compel him to abdicate. At every point of the story the two behaved with extraordinary folly and lack of ordinary good sense.

I spent this New Year at Trent. Among the guests was Winston Churchill. On the last day of the week the party had become much smaller. We were all going away on Monday. Churchill said to Philip that he would like to sit next to me at dinner, as he had not yet done so. After a little while I said to him, "We have heard everything you had to say concerning the King and all that has happened; but you have never once mentioned the person who seems to me to be all-important in the matter". He exclaimed: "Who do you mean?" I replied "I mean Mrs Simpson". He answered: "That——." I said "Yes, that——. You have never mentioned her yet. Surely she is playing a great part in this melancholy business." He turned on me and observed in a scoffing tone, "I suppose you know very little of the King and his ways?"

As a matter of fact, I knew a great deal, partly owing to my friendship with one of the ladies with whom the King had believed himself to be in love. Also because I was on terms of friendship with one of the King's gentlemen. However, I remained silent. He went on, "If you knew much about the King, you would know that women play only a transient part in his life. He falls constantly in and out of love. His present attachment will follow the course of all the others."

During the fearful and what may even be called terrible weeks which preceded the Abdication, Churchill was passionately anxious that Edward VIII should remain King. He was constantly at Belvedere, and I remember someone telling me that Winston had said in a despairing tone: "There is about him an eel-like quality. He slips through one's fingers. In the morning he makes up his mind to stay: by the evening he had decided to go and give up everything."

Churchill undoubtedly did his very best to persuade the King to "stick it out". At the time there were people who meanly said that this advice was owing to the fact that because the then King's character was weak and irresolute, if he remained on the throne, Churchill would be the "power behind it" and really rule the country. This I regard as a wicked libel. Churchill had a great sense of the value of continuity in history and he believed that the Abdication would shake the country to its foundation.

VISIT TO THE DUKE AND DUCHESS OF WINDSOR
CECIL BEATON
September 1970

WENT to the house in the beautiful Bois de Boulogne to have tea with the Duchess. On arrival in this rather sprawling, pretentious house full of good and bad, the Duchess appeared at the end of a garden vista, in a crowd of yapping pug dogs. She seems to have suddenly aged, to have become a little old woman. Her figure and legs are as trim as ever, and she is as energetic as she always was, putting servants and things to rights. But Wallis had the sad, haunted eyes of the ill. In hospital they had found she had something wrong with her liver and that condition made her very depressed. When she got up to fetch something, she said: "Don't look at me. I haven't even had the coiffeur come out to do my hair," and her hair did appear somewhat straggly. This again gave her a rather pathetic look. She loves rich food and drink but she is now on a strict diet and must not drink any alcohol.

Wallis tottered to a sofa against the light in a small, over-crowded drawing-room. Masses of royal souvenirs, gold boxes, sealing wax, stamps and seals; small pictures, a great array of flowers in obelisk-shaped baskets. These had been sent up from the Mill, which will be sold now the Duke is not able to bend down for his gardening.

We talked as easily as only old friends do. Nothing much except health, mutual friends and the young generation was discussed. Then an even greater shock; amid the barking of the pugs, the Duke of Windsor, in a cedar-rose-coloured velvet golf-suit, appeared. His walk with a stick makes him into an old man. He sat, legs spread, and talked and laughed with greater ease than I have ever known. At last, after all these years, he called me by my Christian name and treated me as one of his old "cronies". He has less and less of these; in fact it is difficult for him to find someone to play golf with. There were moments when the Prince of Wales' charm came back, and what a charm it was! I noticed a sort of stutter, a hissing of the speech when he hesitated in mid-sentence. Wallis did not seem unduly worried about this and said: "Well, you see, we're old! It's awful how many years have gone by and one doesn't have them back!"

We talked of the current trends in clothes, hippies, nudity, pornography, "filthy" postcards, etc. The thought struck me that had it not been for the sex urges of their youth, these two would not be here together today. But they are a happy couple. They are both apt to talk at once, but their attitudes do not clash and they didn't seem to have any regrets. The Duke still talks of his investiture as Prince of Wales, and asked me to find out where the crown is that he wore at Caernarvon. He got to his feet (with stick) to look out some illustration in a book and talked of the old "characters"—Fruity, Ali Mackintosh, Freddie Cripps, Eric Dudley.

An hour passed quickly enough, but I felt we were perhaps running out of small talk when I looked at my watch and realized I must leave for an Ionesco play. The leave-taking was lengthy, due to many red herrings on the way. The Duchess leaning forward on tiny legs, looked rather blind, and when an enormous bouquet of white flowers and plants arrived, she did not seem able to see it. She leant myopically towards it and asked, "What's that? A tuberose? An arum lily?" The man corrected her—"An auratum"—"Ah yes, will you tell them how beautifully they have done them." I watched her try to open the card to see who this incredibly expensive "tribute" had come from. I'm sure it cost all of £75! "Who is it from?" asked the Duke. "Don't be so full of curiosity," said his wife trying to read without glasses. "It's from Jane Englehard!"

The two old people, very bent, but full of spirit and still both dandies, stood at the door as I went off in Lilianne's smart car. Through the passage of years I had become one of their entourage, an old friend, and the Duke even said to me "Well, between these four walls. . . ."

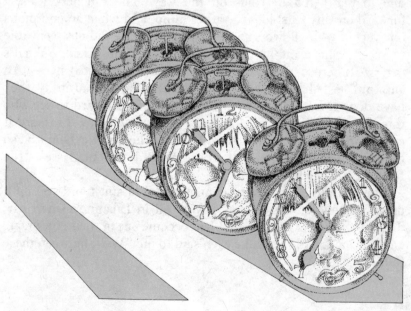

DREAMING

J. Z. YOUNG

THE fact that we need active sleep and that it is associated with dreaming has been considered to support the idea that the benefits of sleep come from dreams. It is interesting that dreaming is initiated by the monoamine systems of the locus coeruleus, which also influence the reward centres of the hypothalamus. This may be a significant connection, since dreams are so much concerned with wish-fulfilment. The stereotyped behaviour of cats that is released during dreaming after lesions is highly organized, it is not a set of epileptic discharges, but indicates that the brain activity evoked by the sleep program is itself following some program. This suggests the idea that dreaming fulfils some special function in relation to instinctive behaviour. The active sleep in infants before and after birth might be connected with the fact that their "instinctive" neural mechanisms are actively maturing, with but a minimum of external influence. Dreams could thus be regarded as providing for better building of the memory model by continued operation of the mechanism for memorizing during the night, even when no further information from external sources is available. The newborn rat, which has a very immature brain, has much active sleep, but the baby guinea-pig, whose brain is mature at birth, has little. The function of dreaming may thus be to stimulate the unfolding of the genetically programmed patterns of the neurons, linking this with the information that has come in during the previous day.

A dream is a sort of extension and fantasy of life, often expressing urges that are suppressed or disguised during the day. Can it be that fulfilling our wishes in dreams is in some way beneficial? We live out our fears in dreams too, and perhaps we get over them in this way. I do not think that anyone can give a sure answer to these questions. Nor is it really known what determines the elaborate symbolism that is used in dreams. If they are in some way an attempt to act out what we desire or fear, why should the hopes or anxieties be disguised in symbols? Is it because the implications of our fears are too traumatic to be fully faced? As a small example—when I was about to retire from University College I dreamed with dread of having to give a lecture in Helsinki. "Why in Finland?" I asked my wife. She saw the symbolism at once, "Its the finish of life!" People who have lived through battles or other terrifying experiences certainly relive them in dreams for long afterwards, but it is not clear whether this somehow relieves their pain.

The subject-matter of dreams is influenced by sounds heard during sleep. The ring of the alarm clock often enters into a dream. In an experiment by Berger (1963), names were introduced from a tape recorder during active sleep and the sleeper then awakened and a report of his dream recorded. There were many associations, some only by the sound or rhyme—thus with the name Robert the dream was of a "distorted rabbit". Jung has called these "clang responses". Other associations were more complicated; thus to "Naomi"—"We travelled north with an aim to ski". The theory that dreams are wish-fulfilments is not borne out by hungry or thirsty people, they do not have obviously relevant dreams. Psychoanalysts will find symbolic references in all such situations, but it is hard to establish their validity.

From
Programs of the Brain

PSYCHOBABBLE

R. D. ROSEN

ONCE upon a time, you sought out a psychotherapist because you hadn't slept well in three years, because every time you entered an elevator you almost blacked out from fright, because for some medically inexplicable reason your right arm kept going numb on you, because you couldn't keep the thought out of your mind that Bert Parks was sleeping with your wife, because you couldn't stand it if the vegetables were touching the potatoes on your dinner plate, because there was some impolite secret whispering itself in your ear, because you had this feeling, something not quite specific, yet—well, in fact, to be honest, you hadn't left your house in six months. Eager to remove these obstacles so that you could get on with your life, you spent some time with a therapist and, if you were at all lucky, you found that symptoms began to disappear and all kinds of awful feelings got their chance to be heard, and you tried to talk them out and find your way back into the grim past, and it was a very messy business for a while, you kept blacking out in elevators—though less often now—and new symptoms intruded like uninvited guests, and then you stopped blacking out in elevators altogether—and you hadn't even been discussing elevators!—but other anxieties mounted and you had to adjust to new conceptions of yourself and talk *that* out, and things improved—gradually—and you perhaps came to understand that your life was not as bad as you had thought—the world was not modeled on your family after all—but neither were things ever going to be as good as you would like; yet, in the course of your therapy you had acquired new compassion for yourself and others and at the same time sharpened your critical perspective, and you felt sadder but wiser and you had bought some time to enjoy life without having your right arm go numb in the middle of the day. You had exchanged some of that old neurotic misery for some ordinary human suffering.

These days, fewer seem willing to settle for anything so quaint as ordinary human suffering. Consumer expectations have risen, demanding the "permanent and uninterrupted bliss" offered by Theta, Primal Therapy's post-Primaldom, the you you never thought you could be, a total eclipse of anxiety. The idea of being "cured" has been fetishized; mental health is thought of less and less as the capacity to confront, explore, and transmute the sometimes irreducible contradictions of living, and more and more as a total triumph over all that threatens the autonomy of the individual.

From
Psychobabble

PSYCHOLOGY

KATHERINE MANSFIELD

WHEN she opened the door and saw him standing there she was more pleased than ever before, and he, too, as he followed her into the studio, seemed very, very happy to have come.

"Not busy?"

"No. Just going to have tea."

"And you are not expecting anybody?"

"Nobody at all."

"Ah! That's good."

He laid aside his coat and hat gently, lingeringly, as though he had time and to spare for everything, or as though he were taking leave of them for ever, and came over to the fire and held out his hands to the quick, leaping flame.

Just for a moment both of them stood silent in that leaping light. Still, as it were, they tasted on their smiling lips the sweet shock of their greeting. Their secret selves whispered:

"Why should we speak? Isn't this enough?"

"More than enough. I never realised until this moment . . ."

"How good it is just to be with you. . . ."

"Like this. . . ."

"It's more than enough."

But suddenly he turned and looked at her and she moved quickly away.

"Have a cigarette? I'll put the kettle on. Are you longing for tea?"

"No. Not longing."

"Well, I am."

"Oh, you." He thumped the Armenian cushion and flung on to the *sommier*. "You're a perfect little Chinee."

"Yes, I am," she laughed. "I long for tea as strong men long for wine."

She lighted the lamp under its broad orange shade, pulled the curtains and drew up the tea-table. Two birds sang in the kettle; the fire fluttered. He sat up clasping his knees. It was delightful—this business of having tea—and she always had delicious things to eat—little sharp sandwiches, short sweet almond fingers, and a dark, rich cake tasting of rum—but it was an interruption. He wanted it over, the table pushed away, their two chairs drawn up to the light, and the moment come when he took out his pipe, filled it, and said, pressing the tobacco tight into the bowl: "I have been thinking over what you said last time and it seems to me . . ."

Yes, that was what he waited for and so did she. Yes, while she shook the teapot hot and dry over the spirit flame she saw those other two: him, leaning back, taking his ease among the cushions, and her, curled up *en escargot* in the blue shell armchair. The picture was so clear and so minute it might have been painted on the blue teapot lid. And yet she couldn't hurry. She could almost have cried: "Give me time." She must have time in which to grow calm. She wanted time in which to free herself from all these

familiar things with which she lived so vividly. For all these gay things round her were part of her—her offspring—and they knew it and made the largest, most vehement claims. But now they must go. They must be swept away, shooed away—like children, sent up the shadowy stairs, packed into bed and commanded to go to sleep—at once—without a murmur!

For the special thrilling quality of their friendship was in their complete surrender. Like two open cities in the midst of some vast plain their two minds lay open to each other. And it wasn't as if he rode into hers like a conqueror, armed to the eyebrows and seeing nothing but a gay silken flutter—nor did she enter his like a queen walking soft on petals. No, they were eager, serious travellers, absorbed in understanding what was to be seen and discovering what was hidden—making the most of this extra-ordinary absolute chance which made it possible for him to be utterly truthful to her and for her to be utterly sincere with him.

And the best of it was they were both of them old enough to enjoy their adventure to the full without any stupid emotional complication. Passion would have ruined everything; they quite saw that. Besides, all that sort of thing was over and done with for both of them—he was thirty-one, she was thirty—they had had their experiences, and very rich and varied they had been, but now was the time for harvest—harvest. Weren't his novels to be very big novels indeed? And her plays. Who else had her exquisite sense of real English Comedy? . . .

Carefully she cut the cake into thick little wads and he reached across for a piece.

"Do realise how good it is," she implored. "Eat it imaginatively. Roll your eyes if you can and taste it on the breath. It's not a sandwich from the hatter's bag—it's the kind of cake that might have been mentioned in the Book of Genesis. . . . And God said: 'Let there be cake. And there was cake. And God saw that it was good.'"

"You needn't entreat me," said he. "Really you needn't. It's a queer thing but I always do notice what I eat here and never anywhere else. I suppose it comes of living alone so long and always reading while I feed . . . my habit of looking upon food as just food . . . something that's there, at certain times . . . to be devoured . . . to be . . . not there." He laughed. "That shocks you. Doesn't it?"

"To the bone," said she.

"But—look here—" He pushed away his cup and began to speak very fast. "I simply haven't got any external life at all. I don't know the names of things a bit—trees and so on—and I never notice places or furniture or what people look like. One room is just like another to me—a place to sit and read or talk in—except," and here he paused, smiled in a strange naïve way, and said, "except this studio." He looked round him and then at her; he laughed in his astonishment and pleasure. He was like a man who wakes up in a train to find that he has arrived, already, at the journey's end.

"Here's another queer thing. If I shut my eyes I can see this place down to every detail—every detail. . . . Now I come to think of it—I've never realised this consciously before. Often when I am away from here I revisit it in spirit—wander about among your red chairs, stare at the bowl of fruit on the black table—and just touch, very lightly, that marvel of a sleeping boy's head."

He looked at it as he spoke. It stood on the corner of the mantelpiece; the head to one side down-drooping, the lips parted, as though in his sleep the little boy listened to some sweet sound. . . .

"I love that little boy," he murmured. And then they both were silent.

A new silence came between them. Nothing in the least like the satisfactory pause that had followed their greetings—the "Well, here we are together again, and there's no reason why we shouldn't go on from just where we left off last time." That silence could be contained in the circle of warm, delightful fire and lamplight. How many times hadn't they flung something into it just for the fun of watching the ripples break on the easy shores. But into this unfamiliar pool the head of the little boy sleeping his timeless sleep dropped—and the ripples flowed away, away—boundlessly far—into deep glittering darkness.

And then both of them broke it. She said: "I must make up the fire," and he said: "I have been trying a new . . ." Both of them escaped. She made up the fire and put the table back, the blue chair was wheeled forward, she curled up and he lay back among the cushions. Quickly! Quickly! They must stop it from happening again.

"Well, I read the book you left last time."

"Oh, what do you think of it?"

They were off and all was as usual. But was it? Weren't they just a little too quick, too prompt with their replies, too ready to take each other up? Was this really anything more than a wonderfully good imitation of other occasions? His heart beat, her cheek burned, and the stupid thing was she could not discover where exactly they were or what exactly was happening. She hadn't time to glance back. And just as she had got so far it happened again. They faltered, wavered, broke down, were silent. Again they were conscious of the boundless, questioning dark. Again, there they were—two hunters, bending over their fire, but hearing suddenly from the jungle beyond a shake of wind and a loud, questioning cry. . . .

She lifted her head. "It's raining," she murmured. And her voice was like his when he had said: "I love that little boy."

Well. Why didn't they just give way to it—yield—and see what will happen then? But no. Vague and troubled though they were, they knew enough to realise their precious friendship was in danger. She was the one who would be destroyed—not they—and they'd be no party to that.

He got up, knocked out his pipe, ran his hand through his hair and said: "I have been wondering very much lately whether the novel of the future will be a psychological novel or not. How sure are you that psychology *qua* psychology has got anything to do with literature at all?"

"Do you mean you feel there's quite a chance that the mysterious non-existent creatures—the young writers of to-day— are trying simply to jump the psycho-analyst's claim?"

"Yes, I do. And I think it's because this generation is just wise enough to know that it is sick and to realise that its only chance of recovery is by going into its symptoms—making an exhaustive study of them—tracking them down—trying to get at the root of the trouble."

"But oh," she wailed. "What a dreadfully dismal outlook."

"Not at all," said he. "Look here . . ." On the talk went. And now it seemed they really had succeeded. She turned in her chair to look at him while she answered. Her smile said: "We have won." And he smiled back, confident: "Absolutely."

But the smile undid them. It lasted too long; it became a grin. They saw themselves as two little grinning puppets jigging away in nothingness.

"What have we been talking about?" thought he. He was so utterly bored he almost groaned.

"What a spectacle we have made of ourselves," thought she. And she saw him laboriously—oh, laboriously—laying out the grounds and herself running after, putting here a tree and there a flowery shrub and here a handful of glittering fish in a pool. They were silent this time from sheer dismay.

The clock struck six merry little pings and the fire made a soft flutter. What fools they were—heavy, stodgy, elderly—with positively upholstered minds.

And now the silence put a spell upon them like solemn music. It was anguish—anguish for her to bear it and he would die— he'd die if it were broken. . . . And yet he longed to break it. Not by speech. At any rate not by their ordinary maddening chatter. There was another way for them to speak to each other, and in the new way he wanted to murmur: "Do you feel this too? Do you understand it at all?" . . .

Instead, to his horror, he heard himself say: "I must be off; I'm meeting Brand at six."

What devil made him say that instead of the other? She jumped—simply jumped out of her chair, and he heard her crying: "You must rush, then. He's so punctual. Why didn't you say so before?"

"You've hurt me; you've hurt me! We've failed!" said her secret self while she handed him his hat and stick, smiling gaily. She wouldn't give him a moment for another word, but ran along the passage and opened the big outer door.

Could they leave each other like this? How could they? He stood on the step and she just inside holding the door. It was not raining now.

"You've hurt me—hurt me," said her heart. "Why don't you go? No, don't go. Stay. No—go!" And she looked out upon the night.

She saw the beautiful fall of the steps, the dark garden ringed with glittering ivy, on the other side of the road the huge bare willows and above them the sky big and bright with stars. But of course he would see nothing of all this. He was superior to it all. He—with his wonderful "spiritual" vision!

She was right. He did see nothing at all. Misery! He'd missed it. It was too late to do anything now. Was it too late? Yes, it was. A cold snatch of hateful wind blew into the garden. Curse life! He heard her cry "au revoir" and the door slammed.

Running back into the studio she behaved so strangely. She ran up and down lifting her arms and crying: "Oh! Oh! How stupid! How imbecile! How stupid!" And then she flung herself down on the *sommier* thinking of nothing—just lying there in her rage. All was over. What was over? Oh—something was. And she'd never see him again—never. After a long long time (or perhaps ten minutes) had passed in that black gulf her bell rang a sharp quick jingle. It was he, of course. And equally, of course, she oughtn't to have paid the slightest attention to it but just let it go on ringing and ringing. She flew to answer.

On the doorstep there stood an elderly virgin, a pathetic creature who simply idolised her (heaven knows why) and had this habit of turning up and ringing the bell and then saying, when she opened the door: "My dear, send me away!" She never did. As a rule she asked her in and ler her admire everything and accepted the bunch of slightly soiled-looking flowers—more than graciously. But to-day . . .

"Oh, I am so sorry," she cried. "But I've got someone with me. We are working on some wood-cuts. I'm hopelessly busy all evening."

"It doesn't matter. It doesn't matter at all, darling," said the good friend. "I was just passing and I thought I'd leave you some violets." She fumbled down among the ribs of a large old umbrella. "I put them down here. Such a good place to keep flowers out of the wind. Here they are," she said, shaking out a little dead bunch.

For a moment she did not take the violets. But while she stood just inside, holding the door, a strange thing happened. . . . Again she saw the beautiful fall of the steps, the dark garden ringed with glittering ivy, the willows, the big bright sky. Again she felt the silence that was like a question. But this time she did not hesitate. She moved forward. Very softly and gently, as though fearful of making a ripple in that boundless pool of quiet, she put her arms round her friend.

"My dear," murmured her happy friend, quite overcome by this gratitude. "They are really nothing. Just the simplest little thrippenny bunch."

But as she spoke she was enfolded—more tenderly, more beautifully embraced, held by such a sweet pressure and for so long that the poor dear's mind positively reeled and she just had the strength to quaver: "Then you really don't mind me too much?"

"Good night, my friend," whispered the other. "Come again soon."

"Oh, I will. I will."

This time she walked back to the studio slowly, and standing in the middle of the room with half-shut eyes she felt so light, so rested, as if she had woken up out of a childish sleep. Even the act of breathing was a joy. . . .

The *sommier* was very untidy. All the cushions "like furious mountains" as she said; she put them in order before going over to the writing-table.

"I have been thinking over our talk about the psychological novel," she dashed off, "it really is intensely interesting. . . ." and so on and so on.

At the end she wrote: "Goodnight, my friend. Come again soon."

16 JANUARY 1923

VIRGINIA WOOLF

KATHERINE [Mansfield] has been dead a week, & how far am I obeying her "do not quite forget Katherine" which I read in one of her old letters? Am I already forgetting her? It is strange to trace the progress of one's feelings. Nelly said in her sensational way at breakfast on Friday "Mrs Murry's dead! It says so in the paper!" At that one feels—what? A shock of relief?—a rival the less? Then confusion at feeling so little—then, gradually, blankness & disappointment; then a depression which I could not rouse myself from all that day. When I began to write, it seemed to me there was no point in writing. Katherine wont read it. Katherine's my rival no longer. More generously I felt, But though I can do this better than she could, where is she, who could do what I can't! Then, as usual with me, visual impressions kept coming & coming before me—always of Katherine putting on a white wreath, & leaving us, called away; made dignified, chosen. And then one pitied her. And one felt her reluctant to wear that wreath, which was an ice cold one. And she was only 33. And I could see her before me so exactly, & the room at Portland Villas. I go up. She gets up, very slowly, from her writing table. A glass of milk & a medicine bottle stood there. There were also piles of novels. Everything was very tidy, bright, & somehow like a dolls house. At once, or almost, we got out of shyness. She (it was summer) half lay on the sofa by the window. She had her look of a Japanese doll, with the fringe combed quite straight across her forehead. Sometimes we looked very steadfastly at each other, as though we had reached some durable relationship, independent of the changes of the body, through the eyes. Hers were beautiful eyes—rather doglike, brown, very wide apart, with a steady slow rather faithful & sad expression. Her nose was sharp, & a little vulgar. Her lips thin & hard. She wore short skirts & liked "to have a line round her" she said. She looked very ill—very drawn, & moved languidly, drawing herself across the room, like some suffering animal. I suppose I have written down some of the things we said. Most days I think we reached that kind of certainty, in talk about books, or rather about our writings, which I thought had something durable about it. And then she was inscrutable. Did she care for me? Sometimes she would say so— would kiss me—would look at me as if (is this sentiment?) her eyes would like always to be faithful. She would promise never never to forget. That was what we said at the end of our last talk.

She said she would send me her diary to read, & would write always. For our friendship was a real thing we said, looking at each other quite straight. It would always go on whatever happened. What happened was, I suppose, faultfindings & perhaps gossip. She never answered my letter. Yet I still feel, somehow that friendship persists. Still there are things about writing I think of & want to tell Katherine. If I had been in Paris & gone to her, she would have got up & in three minutes, we should have been talking again. Only I could not take the step. The surroundings—Murry & so on—& the small lies &

treacheries, the perpetual playing & teasing, or whatever it was, cut away much of the substance of friendship. One was too uncertain. And so one let it all go. Yet I certainly expected that we should meet again next summer, & start fresh. And I was jealous of her writing—the only writing I have ever been jealous of. This made it harder to write to her; & I saw in it, perhaps from jealousy, all the qualities I disliked in her.

For two days I felt that I had grown middle aged, & lost some spur to write. That feeling is going. I no longer keep seeing her with her wreath. I don't pity her so much. Yet I have the feeling that I shall think of her at intervals all through life. Probably we had something in common which I shall never find in anyone else. (This I say in so many words in 1919 again & again.) Moreover I like speculating about her character. I think I never gave her credit for all her physical suffering & the effect it must have had in embittering her.

The Nation is probably sold over Massingham's head; L. has a violent cold. I have been in bed, 101, again. Fergusson threatens to cut my tonsils.

DIARY OF A SOMEBODY
CHRISTOPHER MATTHEW

Wednesday, February 1st

PENELOPE's birthday. It will be eight years this summer since we decided we were not really meant for each other, yet I often think about her still. On an impulse, I decided to ring her, but found that the last number I had for her was the Queensgate flat. After much telephoning, I finally traced her whereabouts through Harry Jeavons, of all people, who told me that she had finally married an out-of-work sociologist and become self-sufficient in a converted ploughman's cottage near Barnstaple. Got through after lunch. Surprised to discover my heart gave a little jump at the sound of her voice, just as it always used to. She seemed genuinely pleased to hear from me again after all this time, and suggested I might like to drive down for lunch on Saturday.

I said that I thought it was rather a long way to come for lunch, but she said, "In that case, why not stay the night? We've got plenty of room, as long as you don't expect the Savoy. I know Ben would really love to meet you."

Oddly enough, I have been thinking more and more recently about the possibility of escaping the rat-race for a simpler, more wholesome existence in the country, and I shall be most interested to see how they have got on.

Thursday, February 2nd

Still no sign of my wildlife book, but so looking forward to seeing Penelope again that scarcely anything else seems to matter. Refused coffee from the machine for the first time in four years. From now on I shall avoid touching food or drink that has not been made from natural products.

At lunchtime popped out to buy the Seymours' book on self-sufficiency. It makes fascinating reading. Am particularly interested in the section on the cow. They write: "The cow should be absolutely central to the economy of a smallholding." I could not agree more. Section on the pig less interesting.

Planted some mustard and cress in an old ice-cream container.

Friday, February 3rd

Called in at my local grocer's on the way home to buy half a dozen eggs. When the girl produced them, I asked her if they were fresh.

"Fresh in yesterday," she replied in an off-hand manner.

"I am not interested in the date you received them. It's the date they were laid that I need to know," I said.

"How should I know when they were laid?" she replied. "I'm a shop assistant, not a chicken farmer."

I told her that there was no necessity to take that tone with me, and although it may not be a shop assistant's job to watch eggs being laid, it *was* her job to be civil to customers. I then asked her if they were farm eggs. "Says so on the box," she said with a shrug. "Dairyfield Farm."

I said that sounded like a made-up name if ever I had heard one, and reminded her that it is an offence against the Trade Descriptions Act to describe eggs as farm eggs if such is not the case.

"Here," she said, "are you some sort of policeman, or what?"

I said, "Merely an ordinary member of the public who wants to know precisely what he is paying for."

"If you ask me," she said, "you're making a lot of fuss over nothing. You asked me for six large eggs, and I gave you six large eggs. For all I know they may be ostrich eggs that have been interfered with by the head-shrinkers of Papua, but that's no concern of mine. Now, do you want them or don't you?"

I said not unless she could guarantee to me that they were real fresh farm eggs, adding for good measure that there were no ostriches in Papua. She simply put the eggs back on the shelf and walked away without so much as a word.

I could have pursued the matter with the manager, given the time and patience, but a quiet word with the Trades Description people will certainly prove very much more effective. I shouldn't be surprised if there isn't quite a stink about this.

No sign yet of my mustard and cress—or of my wildlife book.

Saturday, February 4th

Made an early start for Barnstaple, but traffic terrible anyway. Is it any wonder people like Penelope and Ben opt out of modern society?

Finally drove in through the open gate and immediately ran over a chicken or, to be more precise, a cockerel. Apparently he

was the very first creature they bought when they arrived. By way of consolation I remarked that they must have become used by now to sudden set-backs. Ben said: "Yes, but not quite as sudden as that."

Had for some reason pictured Penelope in a long, flowing

patterned dress, looking very romantic and beautiful like Dorelia John, and was most disappointed when she appeared in the doorway in jeans and T-shirt looking rather fat and unwashed— just like every other girl one sees in London. Ben looked more the part, in his collarless shirt with sleeves rolled up to his biceps, his old army trousers tied up with string and his heavy brown boots. He might have stepped straight out of the pages of a novel by D. H. Lawrence. He also hadn't shaved, I noticed.

After a while they offered me a glass of their home-made wine which tasted exactly like mouldy vinegar.

Then the children came in to be introduced—Seth aged seven, Job five, and Amos three. Penelope said, "It's about time you started a family." I felt like saying, "Not if they turn out to look like these."

They all appeared to have the most extraordinary number of holes in their pullovers, and when I remarked on this fact, Ben said, "They're meant to be like that. It's called open weave. We finished them only the other day on the hand loom."

Penelope said, "We thought they were rather successful."

Ben added, "And they cost only a fraction of the sort of thing you find in the shops."

And look it, I thought.

Lunch took an extraordinarily long time to prepare so that it was difficult for me to refuse a second glass of their vinegary wine. It was unfortunate that they had chosen to make every single stick of furniture with their bare hands since there was not a single chair or bench that was remotely comfortable.

Needless to say, there was no gas or electricity; such heating as there was came from open wood fires, and lighting was all by oil lamps. I noticed there were only two bedrooms, but did not like to ask where I would be sleeping—in the stable no doubt with the three sheep, two goats, cow, donkey, pregnant white New Zealand doe rabbit, eight Khaki Campbells and as many Buff Orpingtons as had escaped the wheels of visitors' cars. Lunch appeared finally at 2.15 in a large, steaming casserole.

"How delicious," I said. "Chicken."

"Yes," said Penelope. "To be precise, the one you ran over this morning. Nothing goes to waste here."

Ben then produced a small jug of their home-made ale which tasted to me exactly the same as their wine. I hoped they might close the window while we ate, since there was a cold wind out and it was blowing straight down my neck. But when I drew

Ben's attention to this, he said: "You city people don't know what fresh air is. You'll soon get used to it." I daresay I might have done had it not been for the appalling stench of manure that came in with it. It was so strong that at one point I really wondered if I was going to be able to finish what was on my plate.

When I mentioned Tim and Vanessa, whom Penelope had known, she said, "We're different now, and there's no point in pretending we're not."

After lunch Ben slaughtered one of the goats and Penelope sprayed the fruit trees with tar wash, some of which splashed on to my suede shoes, leaving a nasty mark. Later we had a cup of dried pea tea which seemed to me to taste no different from the wine and the beer. They seemed genuinely disappointed when I announced that I had suddenly remembered I had a lot of work to do in the morning and would therefore be unable to stay the night after all. However, I promised to return again in the summer and try some of the goat's-hoof jelly. As I drove out through the gate, I felt a strange bump under my rear wheel but decided not to stop.

Sunday, February 5th

Got up late. Still tired after long drive yesterday. Weather cold and wet. Thank goodness I decided not to stay. Went into the kitchen and found someone had moved my mustard and cress. Hunted high and low all morning, but without success. Mentioned the matter to Beddoes when he finally appeared at tea time. He said, "Oh, Birgit and I decided to have a tidy up yesterday and we threw it out with the rest of the rubbish. We wondered what it was." When I asked him who Birgit was that she should take it upon herself to interfere with other people's property, he told me airily that she was "a piece of Scandinavian tail" that he'd picked up on Aldgate East Underground station on Friday afternoon. I did not conceal my distaste at the crudeness of his language, and commented coldly that, as I understood it, he was going out with Victoria.

He said, "Well, I'm not now, so there."

While I am relieved to hear that Victoria has seen sense at last, the fact that some foreign girl whom I have never met, and never want to meet, should decide to throw away my mustard and cress is something which I can neither forgive nor forget. Thought about penning a note to the Trade Descriptions people re the eggs, but really I have better things to do with my time.

Suddenly the winter seems very long indeed.

From
Diary of a Somebody

———— ❧ ————

MR POOTER

GEORGE AND WEEDON GROSSMITH

*A conversation with Mr Merton on Society. Mr
and Mrs James, of Sutton, come up. A miserable
evening at the Tank Theatre. Experiments with
enamel paint. I make another good joke; but
Gowing and Cummings are unnecessarily offended.
I paint the bath red, with unexpected result.*

April 19

Cummings called, bringing with him his friend Merton, who is
in the wine trade. Gowing also called. Mr Merton made himself at
home at once, and Carrie and I were both struck with him
immediately, and thoroughly approved of his sentiments.

He leaned back in his chair and said: "You must take me as I
am"; and I replied: "Yes—and you must take us as we are.
We're homely people, we are not swells."

He answered: "No, I can see that", and Gowing roared with
laughter; but Merton in a most gentlemanly manner said to
Gowing: "I don't think you quite understand me. I intended to
convey that our charming host and hostess were superior to the
follies of fashion, and preferred leading a simple and wholesome
life to gadding about to twopenny-halfpenny tea-drinking afternoons, and living above their incomes."

I was immensely pleased with these sensible remarks of
Merton's, and concluded that subject by saying: "No, candidly,
Mr Merton, we don't go into Society, because we do not care
for it; and what with the expense of cabs here and cabs there,
and white gloves and white ties, etc., it doesn't seem worth the
money."

Merton said in reference to *friends*: "My motto is 'Few and
True'; and, by the way, I also apply that to wine, 'Little and

Good'." Gowing said: "Yes, and sometimes 'cheap and tasty', eh, old man?" Merton, still continuing, said he should treat me as a friend, and put me down for a dozen of his "Lockanbar" whisky, and as I was an old friend of Gowing, I should have it for *36s.*, which was considerably under what he paid for it.

He booked his own order, and further said that at any time I wanted any passes for the theatre I was to let him know, as his name stood good for any theatre in London.

April 20

Carrie reminded me that as her old school friend, Annie Fullers (now Mrs James), and her husband had come up from Sutton for a few days, it would look kind to take them to the theatre, and would I drop a line to Mr Merton asking him for passes for four, either for the Italian Opera, Haymarket, Savoy, or Lyceum. I wrote Merton to that effect.

April 21

Got a reply from Merton, saying he was very busy, and just at present couldn't manage passes for the Italian Opera, Haymarket, Savoy, or Lyceum, but the best thing going on in London was the *Brown Bushes*, at the Tank Theatre, Islington, and enclosed seats for four; also bill for whisky.

April 23

Mr and Mrs James (Miss Fullers that was) came to meat-tea, and we left directly after for the Tank Theatre. We got a bus that took us to King's Cross, and then changed into one that took us to the "Angel". Mr James each time insisted on paying for all, saying that I had paid for the tickets and that was quite enough.

We arrived at theatre, where, curiously enough, all our busload except an old woman with a basket seemed to be going in. I walked ahead and presented the tickets. The man looked at them, and called out: "Mr Willowly! do you know anything about these?" holding up my tickets. The gentleman called to came up and examined my tickets, and said: "Who gave you these?" I said, rather indignantly: "Mr Merton, of course." He said: "Merton? Who's he?" I answered, rather sharply: "You ought to know, his name's good at any theatre in London." He replied: "Oh! is it? Well, it ain't no good here. These tickets, which are *not* dated, were issued under Mr Swinstead's management, which has since changed hands." While I was having some very unpleasant words with the man, James, who had gone upstairs with the ladies, called out: "Come on!" I went up after them, and a very civil attendant said: "This way, please, box H." I said to James: "Why, how on earth did you manage it?" and to my horror he replied: "Why, paid for it, of course."

This was humiliating enough, and I could scarcely follow the play, but I was doomed to still further humiliation. I was leaning out of the box, when my tie—a little black bow which fastened on to the stud by means of a new patent—fell into the pit below. A clumsy man, not noticing it, had his foot on it for ever so long before he discovered it. He then picked it up and eventually flung it under the next seat in disgust. What with the box incident and the tie, I felt quite miserable. Mr James, of Sutton, was very good. He said: "Don't worry—no one will notice it with your beard. That is the only advantage of growing one that I can see." There was no occasion for that remark, for Carrie is very proud of my beard.

To hide the absence of the tie I had to keep my chin down the rest of the evening, which caused a pain at the back of my neck.

April 24

Could scarcely sleep a wink through thinking of having brought up Mr and Mrs James from the country to go to the theatre last night, and his having paid for a private box because our order was not honoured; and such a poor play, too. I wrote a very satirical letter to Merton, the wine merchant, who gave us the pass, and said, "Considering we had to *pay* for our seats, we did our *best* to appreciate the performance." I thought this line rather cutting, and I asked Carrie how many p's there were in appreciate, and she said "One". After I sent off the letter I looked at the dictionary and found there were two. Awfully vexed at this.

Decided not to worry myself any more about the Jameses; for, as Carrie wisely said, "We'll make it all right with them by asking them up from Sutton one evening next week to play at Bézique."

April 25

In consequence of Brickwell telling me his wife was working wonders with the new Pinkford's enamel paint, I determined to try it. I bought two tins of red on my way home. I hastened through tea, went into the garden and painted some flower-pots. I called out Carrie, who said: "You've always got some new-fangled craze"; but she was obliged to admit that the flower-pots looked remarkably well. Went upstairs into the servant's bedroom and painted her washstand, towel-horse, and chest of drawers. To my mind it was an extraordinary improvement, but as an example of the ignorance of the lower classes in the matter of taste, our servant, Sarah, on seeing them, evinced no sign of pleasure, but merely said "she thought they looked very well as they was before".

April 26

Got some more red enamel paint (red, to my mind, being the best colour), and painted the coalscuttle, and the backs of our *Shakespeare*, the binding of which had almost worn out.

April 27

Painted the bath red, and was delighted with the result. Sorry to say Carrie was not; in fact, we had a few words about it. She said I ought to have consulted her, and she had never heard of such a thing as a bath being painted red. I replied: "It's merely a matter of taste."

Fortunately, further argument on the subject was stopped by a voice saying, "May I come in?" It was only Cummings, who said, "Your maid opened the door, and asked me to excuse her showing me in, as she was wringing out some socks." I was delighted to see him, and suggested we should have a game of whist with a dummy, and by way of merriment said: "*You* can be the dummy." Cummings (I thought rather ill-naturedly) replied: "Funny as usual." He said he couldn't stop; he only called to leave me the *Bicycle News*, as he had done with it.

Another ring at the bell; it was Gowing, who said he "must apologize for coming so often, and that one of these days *we* must come round to *him*". I said: "A very extraordinary thing has struck me." "Something funny, as usual," said Cummings. "Yes," I replied; "I think even *you* will say so this time. It's concerning you both; for doesn't it seem odd that Gowing's always *coming* and Cummings' always *going*?" Carrie, who had evidently quite forgotten about the bath, went into fits of laughter, and as for myself, I fairly doubled up in my chair, till it cracked beneath me. I think this was one of the best jokes I have ever made.

Then imagine my astonishment on perceiving both Cummings and Gowing perfectly silent, and without a smile on their faces. After rather an unpleasant pause, Cummings, who had opened a cigar-case, closed it up again and said: "Yes—I think, after that, I *shall* be going, and I am sorry I fail to see the fun of your jokes." Gowing said he didn't mind a joke when it wasn't rude, but a pun on a name, to his thinking, was certainly a little wanting in good taste. Cummings followed up by saying, if it had been said by anyone else but myself, he shouldn't have entered the house again. This rather unpleasantly terminated what might have been a cheerful evening. However, it was as well they went, for the charwoman had finished up the remains of the cold pork.

April 28

At the office, the new and very young clerk Pitt, who was very impudent to me a week or so ago, was late again. I told him it would be my duty to inform Mr Perkupp, the principal. To my surprise, Pitt apologized most humbly and in a most gentlemanly fashion. I was unfeignedly pleased to notice this improvement in his manner towards me, and told him I would look over his unpunctuality. Passing down the room an hour later, I received a smart smack in the face from a rolled-up ball of hard foolscap. I turned round sharply, but all the clerks were apparently riveted to their work. I am not a rich man, but I would give half a sovereign to know whether that was thrown by accident or design. Went home early and bought some more enamel paint—black this time—and spent the evening touching up the fender, picture-frames, and an old pair of boots, making them look as good as new. Also painted Gowing's walking-stick, which he left behind, and made it look like ebony.

April 29, Sunday

Woke up with a fearful headache and strong symptoms of a cold. Carrie, with a perversity which is just like her, said it was "painter's colic", and was the result of my having spent the last few days with my nose over a paint-pot. I told her firmly that I knew a great deal better what was the matter with me than she did. I had got a chill, and decided to have a bath as hot as I could bear it. Bath ready—could scarcely bear it so hot. I persevered, and got in; very hot, but very acceptable. I lay still for some time.

On moving my hand above the surface of the water, I experienced the greatest fright I ever received in the whole course of my life; for imagine my horror on discovering my hand, as I thought, full of blood. My first thought was that I had ruptured an artery, and was bleeding to death, and should be discovered, later on, looking like a second Marat, as I remember seeing him in Madame Tussaud's. My second thought was to ring the bell, but remembered there was no bell to ring. My third was, that there was nothing but the enamel paint, which had dissolved with boiling water. I stepped out of the bath, perfectly red all over, resembling the Red Indians I have seen depicted at an East-End theatre. I determined not to say a word to Carrie, but to tell Farmerson to come on Monday and paint the bath white.

From *The Diary of a Nobody*

THOUGHTS ON
"THE DIARY OF A NOBODY"

JOHN BETJEMAN

The Pooters walked to Watney Lodge
  One Sunday morning hot and still
Where public footpaths used to dodge
  Round elms and oaks to Muswell Hill.

That burning buttercuppy day
  The local dogs were curled in sleep,
The writhing trunks of flowery May
  Were polished by the sides of sheep.

And only footsteps in a lane
  And birdsong broke the silence round
And chuffs of the Great Northern train
  For Alexandra Palace bound.

The Watney Lodge I seem to see
  Is gabled gothic hard and red,
With here a monkey puzzle tree
  And there a round geranium bed.

Each mansion, each new-planted pine,
  Each short and ostentatious drive
Meant Morning Prayer and beef and wine
  And Queen Victoria alive.

Dear Charles and Carrie, I am sure,
  Despite that awkward Sunday dinner,
Your lives were good and more secure
  Than ours at cocktail time in Pinner.

THE DOOR IN THE WALL

H. G. WELLS

I

ONE confidential evening, not three months ago, Lionel Wallace told me this story of the Door in the Wall. And at the time I thought that so far as he was concerned it was a true story.

He told it me with such a direct simplicity of conviction that I could not do otherwise than believe in him. But in the morning, in my own flat, I woke to a different atmosphere; and as I lay in bed and recalled the things he had told me, stripped of the glamour of his earnest slow voice, denuded of the focused, shaded table light, the shadowy atmosphere that wrapped about him and me, and the pleasant bright things, the dessert and glasses and napery of the dinner we had shared, making them for the time a bright little world quite cut off from everyday realities, I saw it all as frankly incredible. "He was mystifying!" I said, and then: "How well he did it! . . . It isn't quite the thing I should have expected him, of all people, to do well."

Afterwards as I sat up in bed and sipped my morning tea, I found myself trying to account for the flavour of reality that perplexed me in his impossible reminiscences, by supposing they did in some way suggest, present, convey—I hardly know which word to use—experiences it was otherwise impossible to tell.

Well, I don't resort to that explanation now. I have got over my intervening doubts. I believe now, as I believed at the moment of telling, that Wallace did to the very best of his ability strip the truth of his secret for me. But whether he himself saw, or only thought he saw, whether he himself was the possessor of an inestimable privilege or the victim of a fantastic dream, I cannot pretend to guess. Even the facts of his death, which ended my doubts for ever, throw no light on that.

That much the reader must judge for himself.

I forget now what chance comment or criticism of mine moved so reticent a man to confide in me. He was, I think, defending himself against an imputation of slackness and unreliability I had made in relation to a great public movement, in which he had disappointed me. But he plunged suddenly. "I have," he said, "a preoccupation——

"I know," he went on, after a pause, "I have been negligent. The fact is—it isn't a case of ghosts or apparitions—but—it's an odd thing to tell of, Redmond—I am haunted. I am haunted by something—that rather takes the light out of things, that fills me with longings . . ."

He paused, checked by that English shyness that so often overcomes us when we would speak of moving or grave or beautiful things. "You were at Saint Althelstan's all through," he said, and for a moment that seemed to me quite irrelevant. "Well" —and he paused. Then very haltingly at first, but afterwards more easily, he began to tell of the thing that was hidden in his life, the haunting memory of a beauty and a happiness that filled his heart with insatiable longings, that made all the interests and spectacle of worldly life seem dull and tedious and vain to him.

Now that I have the clue to it, the thing seems written visibly in his face. I have a photograph in which that look of detachment has been caught and intensified. It reminds me of what a woman once said of him—a woman who had loved him greatly. "Suddenly," she said, "the interest goes out of him. He forgets you. He doesn't care a rap for you—under his very nose . . ."

Yet the interest was not always out of him, and when he was holding his attention to a thing Wallace could contrive to be an extremely successful man. His career, indeed, is set with successes. He left me behind him long ago; he soared up over my head, and cut a figure in the world that I couldn't cut—anyhow. He was still a year short of forty, and they say now that he would have been in office and very probably in the new Cabinet if he had lived. At school he always beat me without effort—as it were by nature. We were at school together at Saint Althelstan's College in West Kensington for almost all our school-time. He came into the school as my co-equal, but he left far above me, in a blaze of scholarships and brilliant performance. Yet I think I made a fair average running. And it was at school I heard first of the "Door in the Wall"—that I was to hear of a second time only a month before his death.

To him at least the Door in the Wall was a real door, leading through a real wall to immortal realities. Of that I am now quite assured.

And it came into his life quite early, when he was a little fellow between five and six. I remember how, as he sat making his confession to me with a slow gravity, he reasoned and reckoned the date of it. "There was," he said, "a crimson Virginia creeper in it—all one bright uniform crimson, in a clear amber sunshine against a white wall. That came into the impression somehow, though I don't clearly remember how, and there were horse-chestnut leaves upon the clean pavement outside the green door. They were blotched yellow and green, you know, not brown nor dirty, so that they must have been new fallen. I take it that means October. I look out for horse-chestnut leaves every year and I ought to know.

"If I'm right in that, I was about five years and four months old."

He was, he said, rather a precocious little boy—he learned to talk at an abnormally early age, and he was so sane and "old-fashioned", as people say, that he was permitted an amount of initiative that most children scarely attain by seven or eight. His mother died when he was two, and he was under the less vigilant and authoritative care of a nursery governess. His father was a stern, preoccupied lawyer, who gave him little attention and expected great things of him. For all his brightness he found life grey and dull, I think. And one day he wandered.

He could not recall the particular neglect that enabled him to get away, nor the course he took among the West Kensington roads. All that had faded among the incurable blurs of memory. But the white wall and the green door stood out quite distinctly.

As his memory of that childish experience ran, he did at the very first sight of that door experience a peculiar emotion, an attraction, a desire to get to the door and open it and walk in. And at the same time he had the clearest conviction that either it was unwise or it was wrong of him—he could not tell which—to yield to this attraction. He insisted upon it as a curious thing that he knew from the very beginning—unless memory has played him the queerest trick—that the door was unfastened, and that he could go in as he chose.

I seem to see the figure of that little boy, drawn and repelled. And it was very clear in his mind, too, though why it should be so was never explained, that his father would be very angry if he went in through that door.

Wallace described all these moments of hesitation to me with the utmost particularity. He went right past the door, and then, with his hands in his pockets and making an infantile attempt to whistle, strolled right along beyond the end of the wall. There he recalls a number of mean dirty shops, and particularly that of a plumber and decorator with a dusty disorder of earthenware pipes, sheet lead, ball taps, pattern books of wall paper, and tins of enamel. He stood pretending to examine these things, and *coveting*, passionately desiring, the green door.

Then, he said, he had a gust of emotion. He made a run for it, lest hesitation should grip him again; he went plump with outstretched hand through the green door and let it slam behind him. And so, in a trice, he came into the garden that has haunted all his life.

It was very difficult for Wallace to give me his full sense of that garden into which he came.

There was something in the very air of it that exhilarated, that gave one a sense of lightness and good happening and well-being; there was something in the sight of it that made all its colour clean and perfect and subtly luminous. In the instant of coming into it one was exquisitely glad—as only in rare moments, and when one is young and joyful one can be glad in this world. And everything was beautiful there. . . .

Wallace mused before he went on telling me. "You see," he said, with the doubtful inflection of a man who pauses at incredible things, "there were two great panthers there. . . . Yes, spotted panthers. And I was not afraid. There was a long wide path with marble-edged flower borders on either side, and these two huge velvety beasts were playing there with a ball. One looked up and came towards me, a little curious as it seemed. It came right up to me, rubbed its soft round ear very gently against the small hand I held out, and purred. It was, I tell you, an enchanted garden. I know. And the size? Oh! it stretched far and wide, this way and that. I believe there were hills far away. Heaven knows where West Kensington had suddenly got to. And somehow it was just like coming home.

"You know, in the very moment the door swung to behind me, I forgot the road with its fallen chestnut leaves, its cabs and tradesmen's carts, I forgot the sort of gravitational pull back to the discipline and obedience of home, I forgot all hesitations and fear, forgot discretion, forgot all the intimate realities of this life. I became in a moment a very glad and wonder-happy little boy—in another world. It was a world with a different quality, a warmer, more penetrating and mellower light, with a faint clear gladness in its air, and wisps of sun-touched cloud in the blueness of its sky. And before me ran this long wide path, invitingly, with weedless beds on either side, rich with untended flowers, and these two great panthers. I put my little hands fearlessly on their soft fur, and caressed their round ears and the sensitive corners under their ears, and played with them, and it was as though they welcomed me home. There was a keen sense of homecoming in my mind, and when presently a tall, fair girl appeared in the pathway and came to meet me, smiling, and said 'Well?' to me, and lifted me and kissed me, and put me down and led me by the hand, there was no amazement, but only an impression of delightful rightness, of being reminded of happy things that had in some strange way been overlooked. There were broad red steps, I remember, that came into view between spikes of delphinium, and up these we went to a great avenue between very old and shady dark trees. All down this avenue, you know, between the red chapped stems, were marble seats of honour and statuary, and very tame and friendly white doves. . . .

"Along this cool avenue my girl-friend led me, looking down— I recall the pleasant lines, the finely-modelled chin of her sweet kind face—asking me questions in a soft, agreeable voice, and telling me things, pleasant things I know, though what they were I was never able to recall. . . . Presently a Capuchin monkey, very clean, with a fur of ruddy brown and kindly hazel eyes, came down a tree to us and ran beside me, looking up at me and grinning, and presently leaped to my shoulder. So we two went on our way in great happiness."

He paused.

"Go on," I said.

"I remember little things. We passed an old man musing among laurels, I remember, and a place gay with paroquets, and came through a broad shaded colonnade to a spacious cool palace, full of pleasant fountains, full of beautiful things, full of the quality and promise of heart's desire. And there were many things and many people, some that still seem to stand out clearly and some that are vaguer; but all these people were beautiful and kind. In some way—I don't know how—it was conveyed to me that they all were kind to me, glad to have me there, and filling me with gladness by their gestures, by the touch of their hands, by the welcome and love in their eyes. Yes——"

He mused for a while. "Playmates I found there. That was very much to me, because I was a lonely little boy. They played delightful games in a grass-covered court where there was a sun-dial set about with flowers. And as one played one loved. . . .

"But—it's odd—there's a gap in my memory. I don't remember the games we played. I never remembered. Afterwards, as a child, I spent long hours trying, even with tears, to recall the form of that happiness. I wanted to play it all over again—in my nursery— by myself. No! All I remember is the happiness and two dear playfellows who were most with me. . . . Then presently came a sombre dark woman, with a grave, pale face and dreamy eyes, a sombre woman, wearing a soft long robe of pale purple, who carried a book, and beckoned and took me aside with her into a gallery above a hall—though my playmates were loth to have me go, and ceased their game and stood watching as I was carried away. 'Come back to us!' they cried. 'Come back to us soon!' I looked up at her face, but she heeded them not at all. Her face was very gentle and grave. She took me to a seat in the gallery, and I stood beside her, ready to look at her book as she opened it upon her knee. The pages fell open. She pointed, and I looked, marvelling, for in the living pages of that book I saw myself; it was a story about myself, and in it were all the things that had happened to me since ever I was born. . . .

"It was wonderful to me, because the pages of that book were not pictures, you understand, but realities."

Wallace paused gravely—looked at me doubtfully.

"Go on," I said. "I understand."

"They were realities—yes, they must have been; people moved and things came and went in them; my dear mother, whom I had near forgotten; then my father, stern and upright, the servants, the nursery, all the familiar things of home. Then the front door and the busy streets, with traffic to and fro. I looked and marvelled, and looked half doubtfully again into the woman's face and turned the pages over, skipping this and that, to see more of this book and more, and so at last I came to myself hovering and hesitating outside the green door in the long white wall, and felt again the conflict and the fear.

"'And next?' I cried, and would have turned on, but the cool hand of the grave woman delayed me.

"'Next?' I insisted, and struggled gently with her hand, pulling up her fingers with all my childish strength, and as she yielded and the page came over she bent down upon me like a shadow and kissed my brow.

"But the page did not show the enchanted garden, nor the panthers, nor the girl who had led me by the hand, nor the playfellows who had been so loth to let me go. It showed a long grey street in West Kensington, in that chill hour of afternoon before the lamps are lit; and I was there, a wretched little figure, weeping aloud, for all that I could do to restrain myself, and I was weeping because I could not return to my dear playfellows who had called after me, 'Come back to us! Come back to us soon!' I was there. This was no page in a book, but harsh reality; that enchanted place and the restraining hand of the grave mother at whose knee I stood had gone—whither had they gone?"

He halted again, and remained for a time staring into the fire. "Oh! the woefulness of that return!" he murmured.

"Well?" I said, after a minute or so.

"Poor little wretch I was!—brought back to this grey world again! As I realised the fulness of what had happened to me, I gave way to quite ungovernable grief. And the shame and humiliation of that public weeping and my disgraceful home-coming remain with me still. I see again the benevolent-looking old gentleman in gold spectacles who stopped and spoke to me—prodding me first with his umbrella. 'Poor little chap,' said he; 'and are you lost then?'—and me a London boy of five and more! And he must needs bring in a kindly young policeman and make a crowd of me, and so march me home. Sobbing, conspicuous, and frightened, I came back from the enchanted garden to the steps of my father's house.

"That is as well as I can remember my vision of that garden—the garden that haunts me still. Of course, I can convey nothing of that indescribable quality of translucent unreality, that *difference* from the common things of experience that hung about it all; but that—that is what happened. If it was a dream, I am sure it was a day-time and altogether extraordinary dream. . . . H'm!—naturally there followed a terrible questioning, by my aunt, my father, the nurse, the governess—everyone. . . .

"I tried to tell them, and my father gave me my first thrashing for telling lies. When afterwards I tried to tell my aunt, she punished me again for my wicked persistence. Then, as I said, everyone was forbidden to listen to me, to hear a word about it. Even my fairy-tale books were taken away from me for a time—because I was too 'imaginative'. Eh? Yes, they did that! My father belonged to the old school. . . . And my story was driven back upon myself. I whispered it to my pillow—my pillow that was often damp and salt to my whispering lips with childish tears. And I added always to my official and less fervent prayers this one heartfelt request: 'Please God I may dream of the garden. Oh! take me back to my garden!' Take me back to my garden! I dreamt often of the garden. I may have added to it, I may have changed it; I do not know. . . . All this, you understand, is an attempt to reconstruct from fragmentary memories a very early experience. Between that and the other consecutive memories of my boyhood there is a gulf. A time came when it seemed impossible I should ever speak of that wonder glimpse again."

I asked an obvious question.

"No," he said. "I don't remember that I ever attempted to find my way back to the garden in those early years. This seems odd to me now, but I think that very probably a closer watch was kept on my movements after this misadventure to prevent my going astray. No, it wasn't till you knew me that I tried for the garden again. And I believe there was a period—incredible as it seems now—when I forgot the garden altogether—when I was about eight or nine it may have been. Do you remember me as a kid at at Saint Althelstan's?"

"Rather!"

"I didn't show any signs, did I, in those days of having a secret dream?"

2

He looked up with a sudden smile.

"Did you ever play North-West Passage with me? . . . No, of course you didn't come my way!"

"It was the sort of game," he went on, "that every imaginative child plays all day. The idea was the discovery of a North-West Passage to school. The way to school was plain enough; the game consisted in finding some way that wasn't plain, starting off ten minutes early in some almost hopeless direction, and working my way round through unaccustomed streets to my goal. And one day I got entangled among some rather low-class streets on the other side of Campden Hill, and I began to think that for once the game would be against me and that I should get to school late. I tried rather desperately a street that seemed a *cul-de-sac*, and found a passage at the end. I hurried through that with renewed hope. 'I shall do it yet,' I said, and passed a row of frowsy little shops that were inexplicably familiar to me, and behold! there was my long white wall and the green door that led to the enchanted garden!

"The thing whacked upon me suddenly. Then, after all, that the world of difference there is between the busy life of a school-boy and the infinite leisure of a child. Anyhow, this second time I didn't for a moment think of going in straight away. You see——. garden, that wonderful garden, wasn't a dream!"

He paused.

"I suppose my second experience with the green door marks For one thing, my mind was full of the idea of getting to school in time—set on not breaking my record for punctuality. I must surely have felt *some* little desire at least to try the door—yes. I must have felt that. . . . But I seem to remember the attraction of the door mainly as another obstacle to my overmastering determination to get to school. I was immensely interested by this discovery I had made, of course—I went on with my mind full of it—but I went on. It didn't check me. I ran past, tugging out my watch, found I had ten minutes still to spare, and then I was going downhill into familiar surroundings. I got to school, breathless, it is true, and wet with perspiration, but in time. I can remember hanging up my coat and hat. . . . Went right by it and left it behind me. Odd, eh?"

He looked at me thoughtfully. "Of course I didn't know then that it wouldn't always be there. Schoolboys have limited imaginations. I suppose I thought it was an awfully jolly thing to have it there, to know my way back to it; but there was the school tugging at me. I expect I was a good deal distraught and inattentive that morning, recalling what I could of the beautiful strange people I should presently see again. Oddly enough I had no doubt in my mind that they would be glad to see me. . . . Yes, I must have thought of the garden that morning just as a jolly sort of place to which one might resort in the interludes of a strenuous scholastic career.

"I didn't go that day at all. The next day was a half-holiday, and that may have weighed with me. Perhaps, too, my state of inattention brought down impositions upon me, and docked the margin of time necessary for the *détour*. I don't know. What I do know is that in the meantime the enchanted garden was so much upon my mind that I could not keep it to myself.

"I told—what was his name?—a ferrety-looking youngster we used to call Squiff."

"Young Hopkins," said I.

"Hopkins it was. I did not like telling him. I had a feeling that in some way it was against the rules to tell him, but I did. He was walking part of the way home with me; he was talkative, and if we had not talked about the enchanted garden we should have talked of something else, and it was intolerable to me to think about any other subject. So I blabbed.

"Well, he told my secret. The next day in the play interval I found myself surrounded by half a dozen bigger boys, half teasing, and wholly curious to hear more of the enchanted garden. There was that big Fawcett—you remember him?—and Carnaby and Morley Reynolds. You weren't there by any chance? No, I think

I should have remembered if you were. . . .

"A boy is a creature of odd feelings. I was, I really believe, in spite of my secret self-disgust, a little flattered to have the attention of these big fellows. I remember particularly a moment of pleasure caused by the praise of Crawshaw—you remember Crawshaw major, the son of Crawshaw the composer?—who said it was the best lie he had ever heard. But at the same time there was a really painful undertow of shame at telling what I felt was indeed a sacred secret. That beast Fawcett made a joke about the girl in green——"

Wallace's voice sank with the keen memory of that shame. "I pretended not to hear," he said. "Well, then Carnaby suddenly called me a young liar, and disputed with me when I said the thing was true. I said I knew where to find the green door, could lead them all there in ten minutes. Carnaby became outrageously virtuous, and said I'd have to—and bear out my words or suffer. Did you ever have Carnaby twist your arm? Then perhaps you'll understand how it went with me. I swore my story was true. There was nobody in the school then to save a chap from Carnaby, though Crawshaw put in a word or so. Carnaby had got his game. I grew excited and red-eared, and a little frightened. I behaved altogether like a silly little chap, and the outcome of it all was that instead of starting alone for my enchanted garden, I led the way presently—cheeks flushed, ears hot, eyes smarting, and my soul one burning misery and shame—for a party of six mocking, curious, and threatening schoolfellows.

"We never found the white wall and the green door. . . ."

"You mean——?"

"I mean I couldn't find it. I would have found it if I could.

"And afterwards when I could go alone I couldn't find it. I never found it. I seem now to have been always looking for it through my school-boy days, but I never came upon it—never."

"Did the fellows—make it disagreeable?"

"Beastly. . . . Carnaby held a council over me for wanton lying. I remember how I sneaked home and upstairs to hide the marks of my blubbering. But when I cried myself to sleep at last it wasn't for Carnaby, but for the garden, for the beautiful afternoon I had hoped for, for the sweet friendly women and the waiting play-fellows, and the game I had hoped to learn again, that beautiful forgotten game. . . .

"I believed firmly that if I had not told—— . . . I had bad times after that—crying at night and woolgathering by day. For two terms I slacked and had bad reports. Do you remember? Of course you would! It was *you*—your beating me in mathematics that brought me back to the grind again."

3

For a time my friend stared silently into the red heart of the fire. Then he said: "I never saw it again until I was seventeen.

"It leaped upon me for the third time—as I was driving to Paddington on my way to Oxford and a scholarship. I had just one momentary glimpse. I was leaning over the apron of my hansom smoking a cigarette, and no doubt thinking myself no end of a man of the world, and suddenly there was the door, the wall, the dear sense of unforgettable and still attainable things.

"We clattered by—I too taken by surprise to stop my cab until we were well past and round a corner. Then I had a queer moment, a double and divergent movement of my will: I tapped the little door in the roof of the cab, and brought my arm down to pull out my watch. 'Yes, sir!' said the cabman, smartly. 'Er—well—it's nothing,' I cried. '*My* mistake! We haven't much time! Go on!' And he went on. . . .

"I got my scholarship. And the night after I was told of that I sat over my fire in my little upper room, my study, in my father's house, with his praise—his rare praise—and his sound counsels ringing in my ears, and I smoked my favourite pipe—the formidable bulldog of adolescence—and thought of that door in the long white wall. 'If I had stopped,' I thought, 'I should have missed my scholarship, I should have missed Oxford—muddled all the fine career before me! I begin to see things better!' I fell musing deeply, but I did not doubt then this career of mine was a thing that merited sacrifice.

"Those dear friends and that clear atmosphere seemed very sweet to me, very fine but remote. My grip was fixing now upon the world. I saw another door opening—the door of my career."

He stared again into the fire. Its red light picked out a stubborn strength in his face for just one flickering moment, and then it vanished again.

"Well," he said and sighed, "I have served that career. I have done—much work, much hard work. But I have dreamt of the enchanted garden a thousand dreams, and seen its door, or at least glimpsed its door, four times since then. Yes—four times. For a while this world was so bright and interesting, seemed so full of meaning and opportunity, that the half-effaced charm of the garden was by comparison gentle and remote. Who wants to pat panthers on the way to dinner with pretty women and distinguished men? I came down to London from Oxford, a man of bold promise that I have done something to redeem. Something— and yet there have been disappointments. . . .

"Twice I have been in love—I will not dwell on that—but once, as I went to someone who, I knew, doubted whether I dared to come, I took a short cut at a venture through an unfrequented road near Earl's Court, and so happened on a white wall and a familiar green door. 'Odd!' said I to myself, 'but I thought this place was on Campden Hill. It's the place I never could find somehow—like counting Stonehenge—the place of that queer daydream of mine.' And I went by it intent upon my purpose. It had no appeal to me that afternoon.

"I had just a moment's impulse to try the door, three steps aside were needed at the most—though I was sure enough in my heart that it would open to me—and then I thought that doing so might delay me on the way to that appointment in which my honour was involved. Afterwards I was sorry for my punctuality —I might at least have peeped in and waved a hand to those panthers, but I knew enough by this time not to seek again belatedly that which is not found by seeking. Yes, that time made me very sorry. . . .

"Years of hard work after that, and never a sight of the door. It's only recently it has come back to me. With it there has come a sense as though some thin tarnish had spread itself over my world. I began to think of it as a sorrowful and bitter thing that I should never see that door again. Perhaps I was suffering a little from overwork—perhaps it was what I've heard spoken of as the feeling of forty. I don't know. But certainly the keen brightness that makes effort easy has gone out of things recently, and that just at a time—with all these new political developments—when I ought to be working. Odd, isn't it? But I do begin to find life toilsome, its rewards, as I come near them, cheap. I began a little while ago to want the garden quite badly. Yes—and I've seen it three times."

"The garden?"

"No—the door! And I haven't gone in!"

He leaned over the table to me, with an enormous sorrow in his voice as he spoke. "Thrice I have had my chance—*thrice*! If ever that door offers itself to me again, I swore, I will go in, out of this dust and heat, out of this dry glitter of vanity, out of these toilsome futilities. I will go and never return. This time I will stay. . . . I swore it, and when the time came—*I didn't go.*

"Three times in one year have I passed that door and failed to enter. Three times in the last year.

"The first time was on the night of the snatch division on the Tenants' Redemption Bill, on which the Government was saved by a majority of three. You remember? No one on our side—perhaps very few on the opposite side—expected the end that night. Then the debate collapsed like eggshells. I and Hotchkiss were dining with his cousin at Brentford; we were both unpaired, and we were called up by telephone, and set off at once in his cousin's motor. We got in barely in time, and on the way we passed my wall and door—livid in the moonlight, blotched with hot yellow as the glare of our lamps lit it, but unmistakable. 'My God!' cried I. 'What?' said Hotchkiss. 'Nothing!' I answered, and the moment passed.

"'I've made a great sacrifice,' I told the whip as I got in. 'They all have,' he said, and hurried by.

"I do not see how I could have done otherwise then. And the next occasion was as I rushed to my father's bedside to bid that stern old man farewell. Then, too, the claims of life were imperative. But the third time was different; it happened a week ago. It fills me with hot remorse to recall it. I was with Gurker and Ralphs—it's no secret now, you know, that I've had my talk with Gurker. We had been dining at Frobisher's, and the talk had become intimate between us. The question of my place in the reconstructed Ministry lay always just over the boundary of the discussion. Yes—yes. That's all settled. It needn't be talked about yet, but there's no reason to keep a secret from you. . . . Yes—thanks! thanks! But let me tell you my story.

"Then, on that night things were very much in the air. My position was a very delicate one. I was keenly anxious to get some definite word from Gurker, but was hampered by Ralphs' presence. I was using the best power of my brain to keep that light and careless talk not too obviously directed to the point that concerned me. I had to. Ralphs' behaviour since has more than justified my caution. . . . Ralphs, I knew, would leave us beyond the Kensington High Street, and then I could surprise Gurker by a sudden frankness. One has sometimes to resort to these little devices. . . . And then it was that in the margin of my field of vision I became aware once more of the white wall, the green door before us down the road.

"We passed it talking. I passed it. I can still see the shadow of Gurker's marked profile, his opera hat tilted forward over his prominent nose, the many folds of his neck wrap going before my shadow and Ralphs' as we sauntered past.

"I passed within twenty inches of the door. 'If I say good-night to them, and go in,' I asked myself, 'what will happen?' And I was all a-tingle for that word with Gurker.

"I could not answer that question in the tangle of my other problems. 'They will think me mad,' I thought. 'And suppose I vanish now!—Amazing disappearance of a prominent politician!' That weighed with me. A thousand inconceivably petty worldlinesses weighed with me in that crisis."

Then he turned on me with a sorrowful smile, and, speaking slowly, "Here I am!" he said.

"Here I am!" he repeated, "and my chance has gone from me. Three times in one year the door has been offered me—the door that goes into peace, into delight, into a beauty beyond dreaming, a kindness no man on earth can know. And I have rejected it, Redmond, and it has gone——"

"How do you know?"

"I know. I know. I am left now to work it out, to stick to the tasks that held me so strongly when my moments came. You say I have success—this vulgar, tawdry, irksome, envied thing. I have it." He had a walnut in his big hand. "If that was my success," he said, and crushed it, and held it out for me to see.

"Let me tell you something, Redmond. This loss is destroying me. For two months, for ten weeks nearly now, I have done no work at all, except the most necessary and urgent duties. My soul is full of inappeasable regrets. At nights—when it is less likely I shall be recognised—I go out. I wander. Yes. I wonder what people would think of that if they knew. A Cabinet Minister, the responsible head of that most vital of all departments, wandering alone—grieving—sometimes near audibly lamenting—for a door, for a garden!"

4

I can see now his rather pallid face, and the unfamiliar sombre fire that had come into his eyes. I see him very vividly to-night. I sit recalling his words, his tones, and last evening's *Westminster Gazette* still lies on my sofa, containing the notice of his death. At lunch to-day the club was busy with his death. We talked of nothing else.

They found his body very early yesterday morning in a deep excavation near East Kensington Station. It is one of two shafts that have been made in connection with an extension of the railway southward. It is protected from the intrusion of the public by a hoarding upon the high road, in which a small doorway has been cut for the convenience of some of the workmen who live in that direction. The doorway was left unfastened through a misunderstanding between two gangers, and through it he made his way.

My mind is darkened with questions and riddles.

It would seem he walked all the way from the House that night —he has frequently walked home during the past Session—and so it is I figure his dark form coming along the late and empty streets, wrapped up, intent. And then did the pale electric lights near the station cheat the rough planking into a semblance of white? Did the fatal unfastened door awaken some memory?

Was there, after all, ever any green door in the wall at all?

I do not know. I have told his story as he told it to me. There are times when I believe that Wallace was no more than the victim of the coincidence between a rare but not unprecedented type of hallucination and a careless trap, but that indeed is not my profoundest belief. You may think me superstitious, if you will, and foolish; but, indeed, I am more than half convinced that he had, in truth, an abnormal gift, and a sense, something—I know not what—that in the guise of wall and door offered him an outlet, a secret and peculiar passage of escape into another and altogether more beautiful world. At any rate, you will say, it betrayed him in the end. But did it betray him? There you touch the inmost mystery of these dreamers, these men of vision and the imagination. We see our world fair and common, the hoarding and the pit. By our daylight standard he walked out of security into darkness, danger, and death.

But did he see like that?

TRUE STRANGE STORY

J. B. PRIESTLEY

I make no claim to psychic power or anything of that kind. Yet the following story is true in every detail. A few years after the Second War I was staying with an old friend in New York. He was officially connected with the American Poetry Society and as he had to attend its annual prize-giving banquet, he took me along with him. He had to sit at a high top table with other officials of the Society and the poets who were to receive its awards. I was at one of the round tables below, sitting next to a pretty woman-friend of his. After half an hour or so, I said to her—and this was not a familiar ploy and I do not know why it came into my mind—"I propose to make one of those poets wink at me, and I'll try the fifth one from the left, that dark, heavy-set, sombre woman, obviously no winker." After concentrating on her for a minute or two, it seemed to me that she winked at me, and I cried triumphantly, "She did it. I'm sure she did." But my neighbour did not believe me and I really was not sure myself, the top table being twenty or thirty feet away and the light not too good. However, after the speeches and awards had been made and we broke away from our tables, the dark, sombre woman poet, who had been one of the prize-winners, came up to me. "You're Mr Priestley, aren't you? Well, I must apologize for winking at you. I've never done such a thing before and I can't imagine what made me do it then. Just a sudden silly impulse, I guess!" I told her quite truthfully that she had made me very proud and happy, and then somebody else claimed her. I have forgotten her name but I do remember that my New York friend told me, two or three years later, that she had just died, though only, I think in her early forties. I have never tried the experiment since, preferring to rest on this one triumph. Perhaps I ought to add here that I did not wink at her, just commanded her to wink at me. Also, I suspect that halfway through a boring public dinner, when everybody's mind is emptying, is probably the best time to attempt this feat.

From
Outcries and Asides

A NEW LOOK AT THE PARANORMAL

COLIN WILSON

IN 1977 I was asked to present on BBC television one of the most remarkable poltergeist cases in the history of psychical research. It took place in the office of a German lawyer, Herr Sigmund Adam, who lived in Rosenheim, south-west of Munich. In 1967 Adam's electric lights began to go wrong; strip lights kept failing, and even exploding. When the local electricity board investigated, they discovered that there were sudden violent surges of current, which burned out the lights. But there seemed to be nothing wrong with the power lines. Soon afterwards Herr Adam received his telephone bill, and was shocked by its size. He called in the telephone authority, and their examination revealed that someone had been dialling the automatic clock over and over again, dozens of times a day. But there was something odd about this too. It took seventeen seconds to get through to the automatic clock, and it was thus impossible to make more than three complete calls a minute, even if you hung up immediately. But the records showed that the calls were being made at a rate of four or five a minute—a total impossibility, unless some expert electrician was getting straight through to the relays.

Local newspapers ran stories about the "spook" in Herr

Adam's office. These were noticed by the distinguished "psychical investigator" Hans Bender, whose laboratory is in Freiburg. Bender went along to investigate, and it was his young assistant who made the observation that cracked the case. He was standing in the corridor, and a young girl walked past him. As she walked under the lights, they began swinging, as if an invisible hand had pushed them.

Her name was Anne-Marie Schaberl, and she seemed a perfectly ordinary teenager; she had been working in Adam's office for two years. When told that she could be causing the strange happenings she was frankly incredulous, but nevertheless she reluctantly agreed to spend some time in Bender's laboratory. At first the results were disappointing; tests in Extra Sensory Perception—ESP—showed no abnormality. Then Bender began asking her questions about her childhood and home life. She started to talk about her difficult family background and a long and painful illness, and had obvious trouble controlling her emotions. Bender seized the opportunity to test her again. This time the results were astonishing; she clearly possessed considerable telepathic ability, and looking at the results Anne-Marie had reluctantly to admit that she could—indeed, that she *must*—be the cause of the strange disturbances. According to Bender, she seemed rather pleased that she possessed these curious powers.

The knowledge that she was "psychic" seems to have increased her powers. When she got back to the office, pictures began turning on walls, drawers shot out of filing cabinets as if pushed from inside, and a heavy cabinet was moved several feet. Finally, Herr Adam felt he had had enough; he sacked her.

Anne-Marie took more office jobs, and the same weird disturbances made life impossible every time; she was always dismissed. She took a job in a factory, but when someone had a bad accident, her workmates suspected that the poltergeist was at work again, and she had to leave. Her boyfriend jilted her because the electronic equipment at the Catholic youth club began to go wild as soon as Anne-Marie walked into the building; various games—like bowling (with its mechanised pin-setting and scoring equipment)—became impossible. Eventually Anne-Marie married somebody else and had a baby, and the phenomena suddenly ceased.

The poltergeist has been observed for many centuries. There are thousands of accounts of "spooks" that cause objects to fly through the air and doors to open and close when no one is near them. Poltergeist means "rattling ghost". But it was not until the late nineteenth century, after the foundation of the Society for Psychical Research, that investigators noticed that there is nearly always a child or teenager in the house where the disturbances occur. And when Freud popularised the notion of the unconscious mind, these researchers finally identified the real culprit. Put very simply, it seems that when teenagers begin to experience the sexual changes of adolescence, they generate some extraordinary energies which can, in certain circumstances, cause events that seem to be the work of a mischievous "ghost". It is not clear whether the energies are always sexual in nature; sometimes the child concerned may be well under the age of adolescence, but in most such cases the child is going through some intense emotional disturbance.

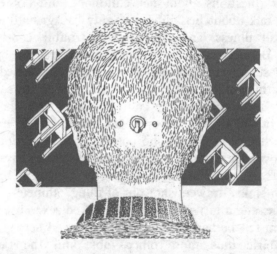

I begin this survey with the poltergeist because it seems to be one of the really well-authenticated examples of a "psychical phenomenon". A few sceptical scientists still persist in believing that all poltergeists are really naughty children throwing stones in order to attract attention. The Rosenheim case is so important because there is no way in which Anne-Marie could have faked the phenomena; there is no known way of causing violent surges of electric current, or of dialling an automatic clock five times a minute.

So here, at least, we have one concrete fact that contradicts all our normal sensible assumptions about the physical world. A disturbed teenager can, *without knowing it*, cause events that run counter to the laws of nature. One particular ability of the poltergeist is more baffling than all the others; it seems to be able to break the law of nature that says that two objects cannot be in the same place at the same time. Hans Bender has described a case in which he left a house with all the doors and windows locked; as he walked down the garden path a heavy object that he had left on the table whizzed past his head. In another case, the poltergeist caused water to flow through a tightly sealed pipe without breaking it. In a poltergeist case in Croydon, a picture fell out of its frame on to the floor without breaking the seal at the back of the frame. The poltergeist appears to know the secret of "interpenetration of matter".

From the commonsense point of view, the paradoxical thing about poltergeists is that the person causing the phenomenon is usually altogether ignorant that he or she is responsible. It raises an interesting legal problem. If someone were actually killed through a piece of poltergeist activity—they cause fires, for example, and make heavy objects fall off shelves—could the "focus" of the disturbances be charged with manslaughter?* The answer is probably no; because the person responsible is, in fact, completely and genuinely unaware of being the cause. And this somehow affronts our sense of logic. Of course, Freud taught us that the unconscious mind often behaves like a separate individual; but that is only in a manner of speaking. If I leave my umbrella behind in a house I want to revisit, no one doubts that it is "I" who am absent-minded. But in poltergeist activity, it seems that "another you" is responsible.

A scientific discovery made in recent years, however, *does* throw an interesting light on the problem. In the late 1930s, surgeons discovered that they could cure epileptic patients by cutting through a part of the brain called the *corpus callosum*, which is a thick bridge of nerve fibres that joins the right and left hemispheres of the upper brain *(cerebrum)*. Since this operation appeared to cause the patient no harmful side-effects, the interesting question was raised: what on earth is the corpus callosum for? In the 1950s R. W. Sperry of Cal Tech had another look at the problem, studying patients whose brain had been divided to cure epilepsy. He stumbled on the solution: the two halves of the brain seem to have completely different purposes. The left side of the brain is for speaking, for reasoning, for dealing with everyday problems. The right side is concerned with recognition,

* As far as I know, there is no known case of anyone being killed, or even badly hurt, by a poltergeist.

with intuition. In short, you could say that the left side is a scientist while the right is an artist.

But the most interesting discovery was still to come. It was this: that *there are two people living inside our heads*. And it is the one in the left hemisphere who calls himself "I". The person who lives in the right half has no language. If a split-brain patient looks at an open book down its centre margin, the left-hand page is a blank. If he wants to read it, he has to move his head so that the right eye can see it. (For some strange reason, the left side of our body is connected to the right brain, and vice versa.) If you show a split-brain patient an orange with the right eye, and an apple with the left, and you *ask* him what he has seen, he will reply "orange". But if you ask him to *write* what he has seen with his left hand, he will write "apple". If you ask him what he has just written, he will reply "orange".

Stranger still, if a split-brain patient is shown a "naughty" picture with the right half of the brain, he will blush or giggle. If asked why he is blushing, he will truthfully reply "I don't know". The person he *calls* "I" lives in the left half of the brain, the logical half. And a few inches away there is another person who feels that he has just as much right to be called "I". Carl Sagan has an amusing story of a man who, when smoking marihuana, had a sensation that there was someone watching him from the right half of his head. He asked "Who are you?", and the answer came back "Who wants to know?".

It is also significant that the "person" who lives in the right brain can be made to blush with embarrassment. The right half of the brain is involved with our *feelings*. And poltergeist activity seems to be due to repressed feelings.

It seems, then, that science has confirmed that there *are* two people living inside our heads, and that, although they are kept in close touch by the great bridge of nerve fibre joining the two halves, they are nevertheless separate individuals. And it also gives a glimpse of how poltergeists "work". Anne-Marie was a good Catholic who had been brought up in a rigidly Catholic home; her father was a dominant character of whom she was afraid. As a child, she must have learned to repress her feelings— as we all do if we are rigidly disciplined. When she went to work in Herr Adam's office, at the age of fifteen, she hated working in a town—she much preferred the country. But she forced herself to stick at it, repressing her feelings of frustration and resentment, and one day that "I" in the other half of the brain, whose feelings were always being ignored and suppressed, lost its temper and began interfering with the electric current in Herr Adam's office.

At the time I was working with Hans Bender on the television programme about the Rosenheim case, I was also involved in a private investigation of my own. The subject was the well-known "psychic" Uri Geller. I had—like most people—seen Geller bending spoons on television by gently stroking them with his finger, and I had read denunciations of Geller by many stage magicians, who claimed that it was all trickery and sleight of hand. The first time I met Geller, we went to a Mayfair restaurant for lunch, during the course of which he bent several spoons simply by rubbing them gently with his finger. I could not detect any trickery, but had to admit that any good conjuror could probably duplicate the "trick". But Geller performed one feat that left me baffled and convinced me of his genuineness. He turned his back on me, and asked me to make a drawing on the back of the menu card. I did a kind of comic monster that I draw for my children. He made me cover it with my hand before he turned round. It would have been impossible for him to see what I had drawn—another person was sitting beside me, watching him closely—as I was myself. He then asked me to concentrate hard and try to "transmit" the drawing to him telepathically. After two false starts, he duplicated my drawing with amazing exactitude.

Subsequently I saw a great deal of Geller, and watched him repeat the same kind of feat many times. He himself obviously has no idea of "how he does it". What interested me most was that many of the things that tend to happen when you are with Geller are completely unexpected, and apparently surprise him as much as they surprise you. Light bulbs fall out of their sockets; objects ping across the room. This experience convinced me that Geller is simply producing a special kind of poltergeist effect, although he *can*, to a certain extent, control it. He was, for example, trying hard to read my mind. He obviously makes an effort of concentration when he bends spoons. He is never certain whether it will work, and very often it doesn't. Nevertheless it seems that, to some extent, the left-brain "I" *can* persuade its partner in the other half to perform certain tricks. The Anne-Marie case demonstrates the same point; when she became upset, talking about her illness, she began making high scores in ESP tests. It seems probable that she could, if she tried hard, learn to create the mental conditions that would "trigger" her "psi powers".

How far does this get us towards saying with confidence that psychic powers really exist? To answer that question, it is necessary to glance back over the history of psychical research in the past hundred years.

In the early 1850s, a novelist named Catherine Crowe wrote a book called *The Night Side of Nature, or Ghosts and Ghost Seers*. It became an instant bestseller, and continued to go into edition after edition right up to the end of the century. By modern standards, it is little more than a collection of old wives' tales. We are told of a German youth, an apprentice, who dreamed that he had been murdered on a road near Bergsdorff. He made the mistake of telling his master who, to demonstrate his disbelief in premonitions, sent him to Bergsdorff with some money for his brother-in-law. Near Bergsdorff the apprentice saw a steward he knew, told him the story, and asked if a workman could accompany him for the remainder of the journey. The next day the youth's body was found, with its throat cut. The workman was arrested, and admitted that he had killed the apprentice, saying that the story of the dream had given him the idea. . . . All this sounds just a little too neat and well-constructed to be true; people certainly experience premonitory dreams, but I can think of no case in which the premonition has *caused* its own fulfilment. It sounds like a story invented to illustrate the moral that no man can escape his fate. This applies to many of the stories in the book. They seem designed to illustrate some moral— that crime doesn't pay, that murder will out . . .

In 1882, a group of Cambridge dons decided to form the Society for Psychical Research, whose purpose was to collect reports of hauntings, premonitions, "spectres of the living" and similar phenomena, and to encourage their scientific study. What very soon emerged was that most psychic experiences have no moral of any kind. Ghosts do not usually come back to haunt their murderers, or walk around moaning and clanking chains. Most apparitions look like ordinary solid human beings, and there seems to be no logic in their appearance or disappearance. Most psychic occurrences seem to be oddly pointless. Here is a typical example, cited in Tyrrell's famous *Apparitions*. Canon Bourne was out hunting with his two daughters; the daughters decided to return home with the coachman, while Bourne went on. Suddenly, the girls saw their father signalling frantically to them from the other side of the valley; the coachman saw him too. His horse looked dirty, as if it had had an accident.

Now if this story had been told by Catherine Crowe, we would expect to learn that Canon Bourne *had* just been thrown from his horse, or murdered by ruffians, who were caught because the ghost signalled to his daughters. In fact, the girls searched the hillside and found no sign of their father. Later, he arrived home perfectly well and unharmed, and said that he had not been anywhere near the field where they had seen him waving.

It is tempting to believe that the girls simply mistook a passing traveller for their father; but Tyrrell adds that "a similar appearance of Canon Bourne was seen on another occasion". In fact, this is an example of a fairly well-known class of phenomenon known as "phantasms of the living", of which there are thousands of recorded examples. The modern view is that certain people can unconsciously project mental images of themselves to other places. Canon Bourne was probably a highly imaginative man, who, when his daughters had left him alone, began to daydream about having a serious accident. It is even possible that the whole incident was simply an example of telepathy between himself and his daughters—except that the coachman saw it too.

The founders of the Society for Psychical Research had tremendous hopes. The nineteenth century was the age of invention; science had solved all kinds of difficult problems. Now that the subject of the paranormal was being investigated scientifically, there seemed every reason to believe that it would soon yield up its secrets. Nothing of the sort happened. Serious investigators accumulated a vast body of evidence to prove the existence of ghosts, phantasms of the living, precognition and telepathy; but they came no nearer to explaining them. Science feels thoroughly uncomfortable with unexplained phenomena. It prefers to believe that they are non-existent. So although the pioneers of psychical research devised hundreds of impressive experiments to prove the existence of "psi" powers, paranormal research continued to be regarded with suspicion by most scientists. Some of the experiments were very impressive indeed. In the 1920s, Dr Eugene Osty designed an apparently foolproof test to prove that some people could foresee the future. A psychic was taken into a room containing dozens of empty chairs, and asked to predict who would be sitting in various chairs at some date in the near future. His descriptions were carefully written down by researchers. Later, an audience was invited to come to the room to witness the result. As they entered, each person drew a number out of a bag, and sat in the chair of the same number. When they were all seated, the psychic's predictions were read aloud: "Chair number 28; a middle aged man wearing a grey suit, with a blue bow tie . . ." Osty's "empty chair test" demonstrated beyond all doubt that certain psychics could accurately predict who would be sitting in a certain chair. Yet it still failed to explain how. As a result, this remarkable experiment went out of fashion, until it was revived—with equally successful results—in recent years.

That was the real problem: the total absence of explanation. In the history of crime, unsolved cases hold a special place, and people speculate endlessly about the identity of Jack the Ripper, or whether Lizzie Borden really murdered her parents with an axe. But scientific man loathes unsolved mysteries, and if they remain unsolved for too long he is inclined to dismiss them as frauds and delusions. In the 1930s, for example, the novelist Upton Sinclair became interested in telepathy, and wrote a book about it called *Mental Radio*. It achieved wide popularity. But a Russian scientist, Professor L. L. Vasiliev, conducted a series of experiments in which he showed that telepathy still worked perfectly well even if the "sender" was shut up in a lead chamber. So telepathy could not depend on some form of "radio wave". In 1949, the biologist Sir Alister Hardy addressed the British Association, and spoke about telepathy. "There has appeared on the horizon something which many of us do not like to look at. If it is pointed out to us, we say: 'No, it can't be there, our doctrines say it is impossible.' . . . [Yet] I believe that no one who examines the evidence with an unbiased mind can reject it." So, are scientists in 1979 any more inclined to accept telepathy than in 1949? Unfortunately, no. It remains unexplainable; therefore it is best to ignore it.

Modern psychical research thus finds itself in an embarrassing position. It has a vast body of impressive evidence—no longer the old wives' tales of *The Night Side of Nature*, but hundreds of laboratory experiments demonstrating the reality of telepathy, precognition and clairvoyance. In the early 1930s, Dr J. B. Rhine of Duke University gave an immense new impetus to the subject when he began testing gamblers to see if they could really influence the fall of the dice. Gamblers were asked to try to throw double-sixes, and their success rate proved to be well above average. Other subjects were asked to guess what cards an assistant was looking at in the next room; again, the success rate was above average. Subjects were even asked to guess what would be the *next* card the assistant would turn up from the pack; again, the results were above average. So Rhine had proved, beyond all shadow of doubt, the reality of telepathy, precognition and psychokinesis (moving material objects with the mind). A few scientists agreed that his results were impressive; the majority flatly declined to believe that it proved anything at all.

The same thing applies to a discovery that has aroused widespread interest in recent years: Kirlian photography. In 1939, Professor Semyon Kirlian was watching a patient who was receiving treatment with a high frequency generator. When glass electrodes were brought near the patient's skin, there was a tiny spark, like the flash of electricity when you switch on a neon light. In a neon tube, this is due to the presence of the gas. What was causing it here? A layer of moisture round the patient's body? To find out, Kirlian tried photographing his own hand, placing it between two metal plates charged by a high frequency current. When the photograph was developed, it showed Kirlian's hand surrounded by a glowing corona. When he placed a leaf between the plates, the photograph showed tiny flares of energy exploding around its edges. What was even stranger was that when Kirlian tried photographing a leaf from which a fragment had been torn, the photograph still showed the whole leaf.

The explanation that suggested itself to Kirlian was that his camera was photographing the "life field" of the object, some kind of emanation caused by life.

In fact, such a life field had already been discovered in the early 1930s by two American scientists, Harold Burr and F. S. C. Northrop. They tried attaching very delicate voltmeters to trees, and discovered that the tree has a faint electrical field that varies with storms, sunspots and the time of the year. In fact, the field seems to vary with the tree's "life energy". When attached to animals, the voltmeter was able to register when they ovulated. It was soon discovered that it would also indicate when a human female would ovulate—making it easy for her to determine when she could conceive. It could also show the presence of latent diseases, revealing cancers long before they were detectable by more conventional means.

So it looked as if Kirlian had discovered a method of photographing the field of life—what occultists like to call "the living aura"—the envelope of life that surrounds all living creatures. Many scientists began to test Kirlian photography. Some of them, like Dr Thelma Moss, soon became convinced that it worked. Others, like Professor John Taylor, were unable to obtain satisfactory results, and finally decided that Kirlian photography was some purely electrical phenomenon. Forty years after it was discovered, Kirlian photography is still as far from general acceptance as ever.

I am not suggesting that scientists should be more credulous. But the widespread refusal to take "the paranormal" seriously is not due to lack of evidence. It is due to lack of a convincing theory. There is far less evidence for the existence of "black holes" in space—whirlpools of collapsed matter, so dense that not even light can escape from them—or of "tachyons", particles that are supposed to travel faster than light. But scientists can explain tachyons and black holes with a convincing theory; so no one regards them as delusions. No one dismisses them scornfully as the products of superstition or wishful thinking.

The odd thing is that there always *have* been convincing theories of the paranormal around, some of them surprisingly perceptive. For example, in the 1890s an American Patents Examiner named Thomas Jay Hudson wrote an exciting book called *The Law of Psychic Phenomena*. Hudson was deeply interested in such matters as hypnotism, telepathy and second-sight. He came up with the interesting theory that man possesses two "minds", which he called objective and subjective. The objective mind is our commonsense personality, the consciousness that deals with everyday living, the outside world. The subjective mind is a kind of intuition. "It is the seat of the emotions and the storehouse of memory. It performs its highest functions when the objective senses are in abeyance."

Hudson was fascinated by hypnosis. He had been present when an intelligent young student was hypnotised, and asked if he believed in spirits. He said no. The hypnotist said: "That's a pity, because we've brought the spirit of Socrates to speak to you." The young man looked at the corner of the room indicated by the hypnotist, and began to blush and stammer. The hypnotist assured him that he could ask Socrates any questions he liked, and asked him to translate the answers into English. Thereupon ensued an incredible "dialogue", in which "Socrates" answered all the questions at length. What amazed everyone present, says Hudson, was "the remarkable system of spiritual philosophy involved", so clear, so plausible, and so original. Later, the hypnotist offered to call up more recently dead philosophers; the subject's manner changed completely; but the "system" of philosophy he continued to translate was amazingly consistent.

Hudson did not believe that the student was talking to spirits; what amazed him was the tremendous skill and originality displayed by his "subjective mind". Its skills extend far beyond inventing "spiritual philosophies". In the 1820s, a Frenchman named Didier, who had been hypnotised many times, used to fall into spontaneous trances as he sat reading the newspaper. His two sons, Alexis and Adolphe, would sometimes sneak the paper out of his hands; but Didier would continue to read aloud, just as if he still held it. Later, Alexis became famous as a "hypnotic clairvoyant". He was extensively tested by doctors and scientists, who would place him in a trance, then ask him to describe things that were happening elsewhere. Asked to visit the home of one of the experimenters (whom he had only just met) Didier was able to describe it in detail. With his eyes bandaged, and a barrier in the middle of the table, he was still able to play an impeccable game of cards with one of the investigators. These, and hundreds of similar experiments, were described in a massive four-volume work on *Abnormal Hypnotic Phenomena* by E. J. Dingwall. But then, science in the 1840s regarded hypnotism as another fraud and delusion. It was not until Charcot and Freud made it respectable that doctors ceased to deride it and to persecute its practitioners. But by then, it had become an accepted dogma that hypnosis cannot in any way increase the subject's paranormal powers. So the early experiments were forgotten.

We can now see that the most astonishing thing about Hudson's theory of man's two minds is that it is remarkably accurate. His subjective mind is the right cerebral hemisphere; the objective mind is the left. Their different functions are precisely as Hudson described them. The moral is clear. If some scientist had taken Hudson seriously in the 1890s, and attempted to find a physiological basis for the "two minds", Sperry's discovery of the functions of the two cerebral hemispheres might have been made half a century earlier. The basic difference between the two hemispheres was known, even a century ago; in 1864, the neurologist Hughlings Jackson remarked: "Expression on the left, recognition on the right." If Hudson had known about brain physiology, he might have made the connection himself. But no scientist was interested in Hudson, for a simple *a priori* reason: it was easier to believe that all psychic phenomena were delusions, and that Hudson was a fool to waste his time with them. So his brilliantly perceptive theory was ignored.

At this point, it is necessary to admit that many students of the paranormal are inclined to take a more optimistic view of the present state of affairs. Dr. John Randall, in his classic *Parapsychology and the Nature of Life*, performs a brilliant analysis of the determinist views of nineteenth-century science, and shows the way in which they have been successfully challenged by researchers like Rhine, Soal and Thouless. Randall feels that the great breakthrough occurred in the 1950s, when researchers into the paranormal began to make use of various types of machine to test subjects for extra-sensory perception. Many die-hard sceptics had insisted that even Rhine's experiments with dice and Zena cards could have been faked. That suspicion arises because all such experiments involve at least two people: one doing the "guessing", the other turning up the cards—or whatever—in the next room. (For example, Alexis Didier's feats under hypnosis could be explained as telepathy rather than clairvoyance; i.e. he didn't actually "travel" to the home of the investigator, but merely read his mind.) If this second person could be replaced by a machine, which would make completely random choices, then the experiment should be watertight. Soon, various machines had been designed to flash lights or turn up numbers in an absolutely random sequence. The psychic's job was to guess what would turn up next. Again, the results were remarkable. (I recommend the curious to look them up in Randall's book.) The machines were even used to test mice, to see if they could use extra-sensory perception to avoid electric shocks generated in a random manner; the positive results excited parapsychologists all over the world.

But these experiments were performed more than ten years ago. If an experiment had been performed to demonstrate that atomic nuclei can be made to loop the loop in a magnetic field, every scientist in the world would now accept it as fact. Then why, in view of these recent experiments, do most scientists continue to ignore paranormal research? Not because they believe the experimenters to be frauds, or because they doubt their scientific abilities. It comes back again to the lack of a theory. What good does it do to know that mice can somehow read the future, if it simply contradicts all your premises about the nature of time?

I suspect that scientists themselves are only dimly aware that this is what is bothering them. They like to insist that they remain unconvinced by paranormal research because the evidence is inadequate or contradictory. They can always think up various objections to any experiment you describe to them—even if it has to come down, finally, to a suggestion of deliberate fraud. So conscientious researchers go on trying to devise more and more foolproof experiments, and then wonder why their colleagues still remain uninterested. It never occurs to them to ask why, for example, Freud converted the whole scientific world with his "sexual theory" without the aid of a single "foolproof experiment". None of Freud's case studies were repeatable in the laboratory; yet the scientific world accepted them as proof of his theories for years. The simple truth is that it was Freud's *theory* that struck his fellow scientists as plausible.

So let us, for the moment, stop worrying about the laboratory side of "psi" research, and recognise that a single plausible theory—like Hudson's two minds—is worth a hundred experiments with mice in electrified cages. It may, of course, prove to be untrue. But at least it stimulates the right approach—an attempt to understand what is going on, instead of merely picking holes in individual bits of evidence.

Let us look more deeply at the results of the split-brain experiments. At first, we find it very hard to grasp that the "I" lives in the left side of the head. But then it begins to seem less bizarre. After all, I may sometimes fall into a mood of abstraction, in which I stare blankly out of a window, merely watching the falling rain. My "I" has vanished altogether in such experiences. Sperry observed that when his split-brain patients walked around the room, they did not notice if they bumped into things with their left side (connected to the right brain). They only noticed if they bumped into things with the right side. The "I" noticed. And this is just what we would expect. Hudson said that the "objective mind" looks outward "to man's physical necessities". It is the look-out, standing on guard to warn us of the approach of problems. This clearly implies that the "other self" in the right brain is looking elsewhere—probably "inwards".

The majority of us are, fortunately, not split brain patients. We can, to some extent, contemplate the activities of that mysterious "intuitive self" with the rational ego. (It is important to remember that you *identify* with the rational ego.) For example, if you happen to be a music lover it is not difficult to observe yourself when you are enjoying music. (It is the right brain that appreciates music.) How do we appreciate music? We do it, as anyone can verify, by looking inward. We take the music inside ourselves, and allow it to expand. And when we recognise this, we can observe another important feature of right brain activity. When we are interested in something, it has the effect of causing a tiny spring of pure vitality to rise inside us. You can be completely exhausted; but as soon as you become deeply interested in anything you heave a sigh of relief, and energy begins to trickle gently into your reserve tanks, like a cistern refilling after a bath. The right brain seems to control our energy supplies. The left uses up energy; the right replaces it.

Recent experimenters have made an interesting observation. If an electro-encephalograph—a machine for measuring brainwaves—is connected to the right hemisphere when the subject is working out mathematical calculations, the right seems to go to sleep; it shows the "idling" rhythms known as alpha waves. Bored with this rational activity, it puts its hands in its pockets and stares out of the window. This explains a great deal about our modern psychological ailments. Because we spend an enormous amount of time in various kinds of calculations and verbalisations, the right hemisphere spends much of its time sitting around idly. It gets into a habit of idleness. But since the right is our energy supplier, this means that we spend much of our time in an under-energised state. We actually come to long for emergencies, for "something to happen", to galvanise the right into getting up off its behind, and making us feel "alive".

Suddenly it becomes possible to see a dim outline of what happens in poltergeist activity. Anne-Marie is a country girl; she responds to hedgerows, trees and birds, not to boring offices. Two years in Herr Adam's office leave her feeling utterly stifled and bored, and her "intuitive self", her energy supplier, is almost permanently asleep. Most normal people would "break out"—go and get drunk, or provoke a violent quarrel, or buy an expensive hat. Anne-Marie has been too well-disciplined for that. She is also of an age when her sexual energies are awakening; but good Catholics in Bavaria keep their desires suppressed. Finally, that person in the other side of her brain loses its temper; it is sick of being ignored and suppressed.

And then, of course, it does something that leaves us baffled. We cannot conceive "action at a distance"—a beam of pure energy making lights explode and drawers shoot in and out. All that part of its activity is still a mystery. But at least, our knowledge of the functions of the "two selves" begins to give us an idea of how the process is triggered. In fact, I think I can go one step further than that. A few years ago I discovered, to my amazement, that I could "dowse". If I approached ancient standing stones holding a divining rod in my hands, the rod would twist violently upwards. "I" (i.e. my "left" self) felt nothing. I can only suppose that my "other self" is picking up certain energies from the stones, or the earth itself, and causing my muscles to contract automatically—a pure reflex, like tapping your knee. This seems to suggest that, in some odd way, my right-brain can "tune in" to the energies of the earth. Could it not, perhaps, make use of these energies in poltergeist activity? This might also explain another phenomenon that still baffles scientists: spontaneous combustion. There are dozens of well-authenticated cases of people bursting spontaneously into flame and being charred to a cinder. There is also the puzzling phenomenon of "human electric eels", usually teenagers, who suddenly build up voltages large enough to knock a grown man unconscious; no one knows why, but it seems related to poltergeist activity. A Missouri teenager, Frank McKinistry, used to develop a powerful electric charge at night, which he would lose as the day wore on; but while he was highly charged, his feet stuck to the ground so that he had difficulty in walking. This again suggests that the energy came from the earth itself.

A French investigator of poltergeists, Adolphe D'Assier, put forward an interesting theory, which I throw in for good measure: that inanimate objects possess a kind of "double", a phantasmal image—similar in principle, perhaps, to the "double" projected by Canon Bourne. One of the most remarkable of modern investigators, the late T. C. Lethbridge, reached the same conclusion from his own experiments with a dowsing rod and pendulum.

All this is, of course, pure speculation; but it is, I would argue, speculation moving in the right direction, speculation based upon new scientific insights. Obviously the real problem with modern "parascience" is that it simply contradicts the insights of common sense. But then, science needs to recognise that it is still looking at the world through Newtonian spectacles—that is, with the basic assumption that the universe is a kind of huge clock, and that "mind" (or life) plays no real part in the mechanism; it is merely a bystander. Einstein changed all this more than half a century ago, with the theory that light is somewhere half between a particle and a wave, and that space itself can be "curved". Yet science has never adjusted to this insight. It has not even adjusted to the insight of Immanuel Kant, to the effect that perhaps space and time are illusions, "added" to the outside world by our minds.

This comes altogether closer, however, to the insights provided by split-brain research. We have to grasp that the "I" of the scientist is also that "left brain" self, which works in terms of logic and language. The left brain also has a strong sense of time; the right has none at all. (This is why, when you are deeply absorbed in something, "time flies by".) Kant compared his "categories" to a pair of spectacles that we have to wear on our noses all the time. But in order to grasp what the left brain does to your perceptions, you need to imagine something more like a thick sheet of glass, interposed like a window between you and the world out there. Moreover, this sheet of glass is covered all over with fine squares, like graph paper—our logical categories. Yet we have become so accustomed to its presence that we do not even notice it—until it suddenly lifts, like the drop curtain in a theatre, and the fresh air blows in, making us aware that we spend most of our time in a kind of prison cell. And we realise that the reality we saw through the glass was a lifeless image; it lacked a whole dimension of being.

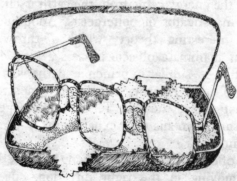

If we could substitute this image of reality for the one we hold at the moment (i.e. reality is merely the material world out there), we might be in a position to grasp some of those strange possibilities presented to us by the world of the paranormal. I agree that this is incredibly difficult, since we have all acquired a lifelong habit of seeing the world through the spectacles of the left brain. I can say, rationally, that perhaps the right can see into the future because time is an invention of the left cerebral hemisphere; but it doesn't really mean much to me. The only way I can begin to grasp it is by thinking in terms of music, or of those sudden moments of rapt intensity when time becomes unreal. By thinking in this way, I can begin to grasp that scientific thinking is *not* realistic; reality is somehow thicker, deeper, more real. If we want to move forward to that next step, we must somehow learn a completely new way of thinking.

I have to admit that, as I write these words, the idea scares me—which just goes to show how much of the old fashioned scientist is still left in me. Let us hope our children will be more open-minded.

To a Poet
a Thousand Years Hence
John Heath-Stubbs

I who am dead a thousand years
And wrote this crabbed post-classic screed
Transmit it to you—though with doubts
That you possess the skill to read,

Who, with your pink, mutated eyes,
Crouched in the radioactive swamp,
Beneath a leaking shelter, scan
These lines beside a flickering lamp;

Or in some plastic paradise
Of pointless gadgets, if you dwell,
And finding all your wants supplied
Do not suspect it may be Hell.

But does our art of words survive—
Do bards within that swamp rehearse
Tales of the twentieth century,
Nostalgic, in rude epic verse?

Or do computers churn it out—
In lieu of songs of War and Love,
Neat slogans by the State endorsed
And prayers to *Them*, who sit above?

How shall we conquer?—all our pride
Fades like a summer sunset's glow:
Who will read me when I am gone—
For who reads Elroy Flecker now?

Unless, dear poet, you were born,
Like me, a deal behind your time,
There is no reason you should read,
And much less understand, this rhyme.

INVENTING THE FUTURE
LYALL WATSON

PETER Laurie points out that scientific truth today, "which is supposed to be completely independent of time, place or person, is actually based entirely on political or social evidence" and not on observation or fact.

For example, I believe in the electron as a basic building block of matter. But on what evidence do I base this belief? I haven't got, and even if I did have wouldn't know how to work, the apparatus necessary to demonstrate its existence. Instead I take the word of the Wykeham Professor of Physics in the University of Oxford, and I ignore the opinion of the Professor of Cosmic Knowledge in the University of Light who insists that electrons are actually tiny transformations of the souls of the departed. Experiments about electrons boil down in the end to experiments about professors.

And why do I choose to believe one rather than the other? Simply because the Oxford opinion is one verified by an elaborate system of rival researchers who duplicate, largely with the hope of discrediting, each other's work. A system of commenting and criticising, weighing, assessing and refereeing in which experts sit in judgement on the facts, ultimately reaching a consensus, selecting what is true and rejecting the remainder as false. But, in the final analysis, this is a political process not a scientific one.

Somewhere between the question and the answer there is room for opinion. The answers are only approximate and Knowledge, it seems, is very largely a matter of belief. The rigid experimental protocols, the strict scientific procedures which were thought to hold individuality in abeyance, have probably always been contaminated. Total objectivity may be nothing but a myth.

If this is so—and few of those involved in any way with quantum physics now deny that the observer, simply by being there, influences the outcome of the experiment—then we face a dilemma.

If faith is part of the scientific process, lying clearly in the path between question and answer, then might it not also intrude between Nature and the question? Is it possible that Man, by his interrogation, changes Nature itself?

I believe he can, and does.

Consider one dynamic paradigm—man's changing view of the solar system: Hipparchus, the greatest of Greek astronomers, developed in the second century BC the first comprehensive scheme in which all the observed motions of the planets were accounted for by a complex of epicycles based on the implicit assumption that earth was the unmoving centre of the universe. Why go to all this trouble with difficult mathematics when Aristarchus, a century earlier, had proposed a simpler solution in which it was assumed that the heavenly bodies revolved around the sun? For two reasons. Firstly, the scheme of Hipparchus worked. Using it, he was able to predict the positions of all known planets at any given time. This was important for astrology and the timing of rituals. And secondly it is very hard to think of the whole earth flying through space, unless you have been taught this description of reality as a child, and will believe anything.

Claudius Ptolemy, two centuries later, carried on the work of Hipparchus and elaborated it further into a geocentric system that came to be called Ptolemaic and which lasted, and functioned very well, for fourteen centuries. It was only displaced in 1543 on publication, by Copernicus, of a mathematical system that could cope with the calculation of planetary orbits on a heliocentric basis, and come to terms with the notion of an earth that moved.

Now, in 1977 we have a book by Robert Newton of Johns Hopkins University which suggests that Ptolemy was a fraud. Working backwards from modern astronomical tables, this twentieth-century Newton finds that Ptolemy's observations are so accurate that they could never have been made with the instruments and attitudes described in his great thirteen volume work *The Almagest*. Robert Newton concludes that Ptolemy's work did "more damage to astronomy than any other work ever written, and astronomy would be better off if it had never existed". Ptolemy, he suggests, is "not the greatest astronomer of history, but something still more unusual; he is the most successful fraud in the history of science".

There is cause to quibble with Robert Newton about the deleterious effects of Ptolemy's geocentric theory. One of the basic tools of new physics is the correspondence principle which suggests that every new theory, if it is to prove useful and secure knowledge without undue loss of past achievement, must offer a limiting transition to the old theory which it replaces. Or else, in terms of a modern metaphor, you end up tossing the baby out with the bath water.

But a more fundamental criticism of Robert Newton's strangely shrill attack on someone who died two millennia ago, is that it could be based on a fallacious assumption. Namely that if he is right, Ptolemy must be wrong, and therefore dishonest. It does seem strange that the Greek astronomer, holding hypotheses which we see as invalid, and working with instruments which we consider inadequate, should nevertheless have arrived at what we believe to be the right answers. At least it appears odd unless we change our basic assumption and suggest instead that Robert Newton and Claudius Ptolemy both reached the same answers using different tools, because they used them on different models of reality. And that neither of these models is necessarily the "right" one, but that both bear some sort of intrinsic relationship to the true nature of things.

In other words, all facts are laden with theory, and Nature has a way of turning out to be partly what is, and partly what we want it to be.

But that's heresy, so let's return for a moment to our shifting paradigm: One hundred and fifty years after the death of Copernicus, his finds, and those of Galileo after him, were codified into the famous three laws of motion by the true Newton, Isaac, who, in *Principia Mathematica* made an intuitive leap to the notion that the same laws applied to earthly and to heavenly bodies. With the aid of his law of universal gravitation, Newton developed an overall scheme of things, which was so precise, so elegant in its construction that, almost unaided, it ushered in the Age of Reason.

If anyone slowed the growth of astronomy it was Isaac Newton himself, who cast such a long shadow that many of his heirs thought he had left them nothing new to discover. Another century and a half passed before William Herschel in 1781 brought a breath of fresh air to the science by discovering a new planet, Uranus. In the following sixty years it became apparent that the new planet was not behaving precisely as Newton's laws

demanded and in 1856 John Adams in England and Urbain Leverrier in France, working without knowledge of each other and reasoning only with pen and paper, decided that the irregularities in the orbit must be due to the presence of another planet beyond Uranus. Both calculated where it should be visible and on the very first evening that a large enough telescope was turned to the prescribed spot, there it was, right on cue. And we now know it as Neptune.

This discovery is usually seen as a triumphant endorsement of Newton's laws, as further proof that all problems can be solved by careful observation and the skilful use of mathematics. But it seems to have been overlooked that both Adams and Leverrier were calculating partly on the basis of Bode's Law (a now disproved notion that the planets orbit at distances from the sun which can be predicted by a scale of proportions which rise by a constant increment in this way—4:7:10:16:28:52:100:196:388:etc.) If it is assumed that the asteroid belt is the remains of a planet that once lay between Mars and Jupiter at position 28, then all the inner seven planets fit the scale exactly. So it was generally assumed that, if there was an eighth planet, it would be found at position 388. But it is nowhere near there. Neptune is much further away and yet, on 23rd September 1846, when Johann Galle aligned the great Berlin reflector according to instructions, the planet was right in place, on demand.

Adams and Leverrier, using the wrong tools, making the wrong assumptions, came up quite independently with the right answer. Should we now begin looking for an international conspiracy to defraud? I doubt it. But I am very intrigued to know that, since the discovery of Neptune, it has been found that even those famous calculations didn't take all the discrepancies in the motion of Uranus into account.

Uranus still tends to wander off its predicted orbit by a fraction, so in the last years of the nineteenth century Percival Lowell turned the resources of his private observatory in Arizona over to a search for yet another member of the solar system. He called it Planet X. Precise calculations predicted where it ought to be found and a careful search was made, but the ninth planet didn't materialise until fourteen years after Lowell's death.

On 13th March 1930, Clyde Tombaugh—then a young un-qualified assistant in the Lowell observatory, finished a year of painstaking picking through comparative photographs of the critical part of the sky. And there, moving almost imperceptibly across a field of four hundred thousand equally faint stars, was Pluto, god of the nether darkness. It is no accident that the first two letters of the new planet's name should be the initials of the man who decided where to look. And it seems fitting too that, following Tombaugh's discovery, it was revealed that Milton Humason of the Harvard Observatory had a few years previously taken a photograph of the precise location where Pluto should have been, but seen nothing there. This mysterious failure is officially attributed to the fact that Humason must have succeeded in obtaining the image of Pluto—after all, anyone can do it now—but that it fell right on a tiny flaw in his photographic plate.

I am well aware of the pattern of synchronicity in scientific discovery; of how different workers in widely separated laboratories, completely without collusion, simultaneously produce answers to questions that seemed insoluble for years. And how, once the barrier is broken, the solutions often seem so painfully simple it is difficult to understand why they weren't obvious to everyone right from the start.

I am not necessarily suggesting, by presenting a brief history of our discovery of the solar system in this way, that the outer planets didn't exist until we began to look for them. But neither am I prepared to dismiss this possibility out of hand.

From
Lifetide

COSMIC EVOLUTION

ARTHUR KOESTLER

IN all previous generations man had to come to terms with the prospect of his death as an individual; the present generation is the first to face the prospect of the death of our species. *Homo sapiens* arrived on the scene about a hundred thousand years ago, which is but the blinking of an eye on the evolutionary time-scale. If he were to vanish now, his rise and fall would have been a brief episode, unsung and unlamented by other inhabitants of our galaxy. We know by now that other planets in the vastness of space are humming with life; that brief episode would probably never have come to their notice.

Only a few decades ago it was generally thought that the emergence of life out of inanimate chemical compounds must have been an extremely improbable, and therefore extremely rare event, which may have occurred only once, on this privileged planet of ours, and nowhere else. It was further thought that the formation of solar systems, such as ours, was also a rare event, and that planets capable of supporting life must be even rarer. But these assumptions, flavoured by "earth-chauvinism", have been refuted by the rapid advances of astrophysics. It is now generally accepted by astronomers that the formation of planetary systems, including inhabitable planets, is "a common event"; and that organic compounds, potentially capable of giving rise to life, are present both in our immediate neighbourhood, on Mars, and in the interstellar dust-clouds of distant nebulae. Moreover, a certain class of meteorites was found to contain organic materials whose spectra are the same as those of pollen-like spores in pre-Cambrian sediments. Sir Fred Hoyle and his Indian colleague, Professor Chandra Wickranashinghe, proposed (in 1977) a theory, which regards "pre-stellar molecular clouds such as are present in the Orion nebula, as the most natural 'cradles' of life. Processes occurring in such clouds lead to the commencement and dispersal of biological activity in the Galaxy . . . It would now seem most likely that the transformation of inorganic matter into primitive biological systems is occurring more or less continually in the space between the stars."

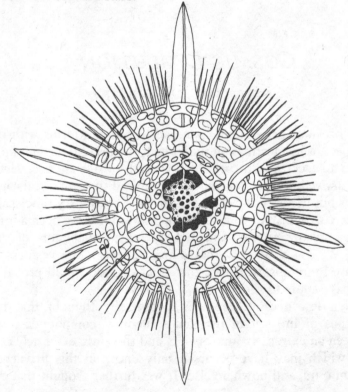

As for the pollen-like structures in meteorites, the authors hold it to be possible that they "represent primitive, interstellar 'proto-cells' in a state of suspended animation". At present "some hundred tons of meteoritic material enter the earth's atmosphere every day; but in earlier geological epochs the accumulation rate may have been much higher". Part of this material may have originated in the "cradles of life"—the dust-clouds pre-dating the formation of stars.

Thus the doctrines of "terran chauvinism" have become untenable, like so many other cherished beliefs of nineteenth-century science. We are not alone in the universe—not the only spectators in the theatre, surrounded by empty seats. On the contrary, the universe around us is teeming with life, from primitive "proto-cells", floating in interstellar space, to millions of advanced civilizations far ahead of us—where "far" might mean the distance we have travelled from our reptilian or amoebic ancestry. I find this perspective comforting and exhilarating. In the first place, it is nice to know that we are not alone, that we have company out there among the stars—so that if we vanish, it does not matter too much, and the cosmic drama will not be played out before an empty house. The thought that we are the only conscious beings in this immensity, and that if we vanish, consciousness would vanish from it, is unbearable. Vice versa, the knowledge that there are billions of beings in our galaxy, and in other galaxies, infinitely more enlightened than our poor sick selves, may lead to that humility and self-transcendence which is the source of all religious experience.

This brings me to a perhaps naive, but I think plausible consideration regarding the nature of extraterrestrial intelligences and civilizations. Terrestrial civilization (from the start of agriculture, written language, etc.) is, at a generous estimate, around 10,000 years old. To make guesses about the nature of extraterrestrial civilizations a few *million* years older than ours is of course totally unrealistic. On the other hand, it is entirely reasonable to assume that sooner or later—within, say, its first 10,000 years—each of these civilizations would have discovered thermonuclear reactions—i.e., met the anno zero of its own calendar. From this point onward natural selection—or rather, the "selective weed-killer" as I have called it—takes over on a cosmic scale. The sick civilizations engendered by biological misfits will sooner or later act as their own executioners and vanish from their polluted planet. Those civilizations which survive this and other tests of sanity will grow, or have already grown, into a cosmic élite of demi-gods. More soberly speaking, it is a comforting thought that owing to the action of the cosmic weed-killer, only the "goodies" among these civilizations will survive, whereas the "baddies" will annihilate themselves. It is nice to know that the universe is a place reserved for goodies and that we are surrounded by them. The established religions take a less charitable view of the cosmic administration.

From
Janus

THE COMPULSIVE COMMUNICATORS

DAVID ATTENBOROUGH

Homo sapiens has suddenly become the most numerous of all large animals. Ten thousand years ago, there were about ten million individuals in the world. They were ingenious, communicative and resourceful, but they seemed, as a species, to be subject to the same laws and restrictions which govern the numbers of other animals. Then, about four thousand years ago, their number began to increase rapidly. Two thousand years ago it had risen to three hundred millions; and a thousand years ago, the species began to overrun the earth. Today, there are over four thousand million. By the turn of the century, on present trends, there will be over six thousand million. These extra-ordinary creatures have spread to all corners of the earth in an unprecedented way. They live on the ice of the Poles and in the tropical jungles on the equator. They have climbed the highest mountains where oxygen is cripplingly scarce and dived down in special suits to walk on the bed of the sea. Some have even left the planet altogether and visited the moon.

Why did this happen? What power did man suddenly acquire that turned him into the most successful of all species? The story starts five million years ago on the plains of Africa. The grass and scrub-covered landscape was then much as it is today. Some of the creatures that lived there were giant versions of modern species— a pig as big as a cow with tusks a metre long, an immense buffalo, and an elephant standing a third as tall again as the one that is found there now—but others were very like contemporary species —zebra, rhinoceros and giraffe. There were also ape-like creatures about the size of chimpanzees. They were descendants of a forest-living ape that had been widespread through not only Africa but Europe and Asia about ten million years ago. The first fossils of the plains-living ape were discovered in southern Africa and it was accordingly named Australopithecus, Southern Ape, but now several more kinds have been discovered in Africa and a great deal of work is going on in an attempt to disentangle their genealogies. Every time a fresh piece of fossil evidence is unearthed, the debates are renewed with great intensity, for all researchers are agreed that among these creatures are the ancestors of modern man. As a group, they can be conveniently called ape-men.

They were not abundant and their fossilised bones are rare, but enough have been found to give a fairly clear idea of what they were like in life. Their hands and feet resembled those of their tree-climbing ancestors and were very good at grasping things with nails on the digits, not claws. The limbs were not particularly well-suited to running and were certainly not nearly as effective for that purpose as those of either the antelopes or the carnivores. Their skulls also show clear signs of their forest-dwelling past. The eyes, as can be judged from the sockets, were well developed. Clearly sight was of great importance for these animals as it is for all monkeys and apes. By contrast their sense of smell must have been relatively poor, for the skulls have short nasal clefts. The teeth are small and rounded and not well suited to grinding grass or pulping fibrous twigs. Neither do they have shearing blades, like those of a carnivore. On what, therefore, did these creatures feed out on the plain? They may have grubbed up roots and gathered berries, nuts and fruit, but they also, in spite of the inadequacies of their anatomy, became hunters.

The structure of their hip bones shows that, right at the beginning of their colonisation of the plains, they began to stand upright. The tendency towards a vertical torso was already present among the tree-living primates that used their hands for plucking fruit and leaves. Many of these had also been able to stand up on their hind legs for short periods when they descended to the ground. For a life on the plains, however, a permanent upright posture must have been very useful. The ape-men were small, defenceless and slow, compared with the predators of the plains, so advance warning of the approach of enemies must have been of the greatest importance and the ability to stand upright and look around might make the difference between life and death. It would also have been of great value in hunting. All the predators on the plain—lions, hunting dogs, hyenas—gather a great deal of information from smell. They keep their noses to the ground. But for the ape-men, sight was the most important sense as it had been in the trees. There was more to be gained from getting the head high and looking into the distance than there was from sniffing a patch of dusty grass. The patas monkey, that spends almost all of its time in open grassland, adopts just such tactics, standing up on its hind legs whenever it is alarmed.

The upright stance is certainly not a way of achieving speed. If anything, it must have slowed down the ape-men. A highly-trained human athlete, probably the best two-legged runner there has ever been among primates, can barely maintain a speed of 25 kilometres an hour for any distance, whereas monkeys, galloping on all fours, can go twice as fast. But bipedalism did bring one further advantage. The ape-men had hands with a precise and powerful grip, developed by their ancestors in response to the demands of a tree-climbing life. If they stood upright, these hands could be ready at all times to compensate for the lack of teeth and claws. If the animals were threatened by enemies they could defend themselves by hurling stones and wielding sticks. Faced with a carcass, they might not be able to open it with their teeth as a lion could do, but they could cut it open using the sharp edge of a stone, held in the hand. They could even take one stone, strike it against another and so shape it. Stones deliberately struck in such a way have facets on them that are quite different from those on stones that have been chipped by rolling in streams or split by frost. They can thus be identified and many such have been found associated with the skeletons of ape-men. The animals had become tool-makers. So ape-men claimed a permanent place for themselves in the community of animals on the plains.

This state of affairs lasted for a very long time, probably as much as three million years. Slowly, generation after generation, the bodies of one line of ape-men became better adapted to the plains-living life. The feet became more suited to running, lost their ability to grasp and acquired a slight arch. The hips changed, the joint moved towards the centre of the pelvis to balance the upright torso, and the pelvis itself became more bowl-shaped and broader to provide a base for the strong muscles running between pelvis and spine that were needed to hold the belly in its new upright position. The spine developed a slight curve so that the weight of the upper part of the body was better centred. Most importantly, the skull changed. The jaw became smaller and the forehead more domed. The brain of the first ape-men had been about the same size as that of a gorilla, around 500 cubic centimetres. Now it was double the size. And the animal grew to a height of over a metre and a half. Science has given this creature a name that reflects its new stance and height—Homo erectus, Upright Man.

He was a much more skilled tool-maker than his predecessors. Some of the stones he chipped were carefully shaped with a tapering point at one end and a sharp edge on either side, and were of a size that fitted neatly into the hand. Evidence of one of his successful hunts has been unearthed at Olorgesailie in southwest Kenya. In one small area lie the broken and dismembered skeletons of giant baboons of a species that is now extinct. At least fifty adult animals and a dozen young appear to have been slaughtered here. Among their remains are hundreds of chipped stones and several thousand rough cobbles. All are of rock that does not occur naturally within 30 kilometres of the site. The implications are several. The way the stones have been chipped and shaped establishes that the hunters were Upright Men. The fact that the stones come from a distant site suggests that the hunts were premeditated and that the hunters had armed themselves long before they found their prey. Baboons, even the smaller living species, are very formidable creatures with powerful fanged jaws. Few men today, without firearms, would be prepared to tackle them. The numbers killed at Olorgesailie suggest that such hunts were regular team operations demanding considerable skill. Upright Man was clearly, by now, a very formidable hunter indeed.

Did he use what we would recognise as a language to discuss his plans and carry out such attacks? Attempts have been made to deduce from his skull and neckbones the structure of the soft parts of his throat and the current view is that although he was capable of making noise considerably more complex than the grunts and screams of modern apes, his speech, if indeed we can call it that, was probably slow and clumsy.

However, he had another medium of communication at his disposal—gestures—and we can make some confident guesses as to what they were and what they meant. Human beings have more separate muscles in their face than any other animal. They make it possible to move the various elements—lips, cheeks, forehead, eyebrows—in a great variety of ways that no other creature can match. There is little doubt, therefore, that the face was the centre of Upright Man's gestural communication.

One of the most important pieces of information it transmits is identity. We take it for granted that all our faces are very different from one another, yet this is a very unusual characteristic among animals. If individuals are to co-operate in an organised team in which each has his own responsibilities, then it is crucial for those taking part to be able to distinguish one from another immediately. Many social animals, such as hyenas and wolves, do this by smell. Men's sense of smell, however, was much less informative than their sight, so their identities were proclaimed not by fragrant glandular secretions but by the shape of the face.

DESPERATION. PACIFICATION. EXPECTATION. ACCLAMATION. REALIZATION
"IT'S FRY'S"

Since the features of the face are extremely mobile, they can also convey a great deal of information about changing moods and intentions. We still have little difficulty in understanding expressions of enthusiasm and delight, disgust, anger and amusement. But quite apart from such revelations of emotion, we also send precise messages with our faces—of agreement and dissent, of welcome and summons. Are the gestures we use today arbitrary ones that we have learned from our parents and share with the rest of the community simply because we have the same social background? Or are they deeply embedded in us and an inheritance from our prehistoric past? Some gestures, such as methods of counting or insulting, vary from society to society and are clearly learned. But others appear to be more universal and deep-seated. Did Upright Man, for example, nod agreement and shake his head in disapproval as we do? Clues to the answers can come from the gestures used by people from another society who have had no contact whatever with our own.

New Guinea is one of the last places in the world where such people might be found. Even there, very few can be considered to have escaped all influences of Western European man, for almost every part of the island has been explored, but ten years ago, one small patch of country remained unentered by outsiders in the forested mountains at the headwaters of the Sepik River. A pilot, flying over the area, had noticed in what everyone had assumed to be uninhabited territory, a few huts in clearings. The Australian administration, who at that time controlled the island, decided to discover who these unknown people were. A patrol was organised, led by a District Commissioner, and I was able to join it. A hundred men from the villages along the river were recruited to carry stores and tents. At the last known village on one of the tributaries, the people, themselves little visited, told us that they knew that somebody lived in the mountains ahead, but no one there had ever met them, knew what language they spoke or even what they called themselves. The river people referred to them as the Biami.

After we had been marching through the mountains for two weeks, drenched by daily rains, living entirely on the food we carried with us, we found foot-prints. Two people were ahead of us and travelling fast. We followed them. When we broke camp in the mornings, we found their tracks in the forest nearby and knew that they had been sitting watching us the previous evening. That night we left gifts in the forest, but they were not touched. We called greetings in the language of the river people, but we did not know whether or not the Biami could understand it. In any case, there was no reply. This continued, night after night, until eventually we lost the trail. After three weeks, we had almost given up hope of making contact. Then one morning, we awoke to find seven men standing in the bush within a few yards of our tent. They were very small, and naked but for cane wrapped round their waist with sprigs of green leaves thrust through it in the front and at the back. Some had ear-rings and necklaces of animal bones. One carried a woven bag full of roots and fruit.

As we scrambled out of our tents, they stood their ground. It was an act of great trust and we tried to demonstrate as quickly and convincingly as possible that our intentions were friendly. The river men spoke to them, but the Biami understood nothing. We had to rely entirely on such gestures as we had in common, and it turned out that there were many of them.

We smiled—and the Biami smiled back. The gesture may seem an odd one as an indication of friendliness, for it draws attention to the teeth, the only natural weapon that man has. But its essential element is not the teeth but the movement of the lips. In other primates, this is a gesture of appeasement, an indication by a young male chimpanzee, for example, to his dominant senior that he is not challenging authority. In the human species the gesture has become slightly modified by upturning the ends of the mouth and is used to convey welcome and pleasure. We can be sure that this expression has not been entirely learned from our parents and is part of our built-in repertoire of gesture because babies, born deaf and blind, will nonetheless smile when they are picked up to be fed.

We were anxious to extend our relationship with the Biami. We had brought goods for them—beads, salt, knives, cloth—but it seemed condescending and patronising simply to hand them out as gifts. We pointed to the net bag and raised our eyebrows questioningly. The Biami understood immediately and pulled out taro roots and some green bananas. We began to trade. Pointing at an object, touching fingers to indicate numbers, nodding our head in agreement, all these gestures were unambiguous. We all used our eyebrows a great deal. They are the most mobile features of the face. It is possible that they may serve to keep sweat from running into the eyes but that does not explain their great mobility. Their main function must surely be as signalling devices. The Biami drew their eyebrows together to express disapproval. When they accompanied this by shaking the head, they made it unequivocally clear that they did not want the beads that we offered. By raising their eyebrows when they examined our knives, they expressed wonder. When I caught the glance of a man standing hesitantly at one side of the group and raised my eyebrows momentarily at the same time giving a slight backward jerk of my head, the Biami man did the same, a gesture that seemed to be a recognition and a happy acceptance of one another's presence.

This eyebrow flash is used all over the world. It works as well in a Fijian market as in a Japanese store, with Indians in the Brazilian jungle as in an English pub. Its precise meaning may vary from place to place but that such signals are so widespread and used by such disparate groups suggests very strongly that they are the common inheritance of humanity. They may well have been used by Upright Man as he planned his hunts, greeted friends, collaborated in the killing of prey and brought back the carcasses to the delight of his mate and children.

With this improved talent for communication and skill in making tools, Upright Man became more and more successful. His numbers increased and he began to spread. From southeastern Africa he moved into the Nile valley and northwards to the eastern shores of the Mediterranean. His remains have been found farther east in Java, and in China. Whether he migrated into Asia from Africa or whether these people were the descendants of an Asiatic ape-man is still a question which we do not have enough evidence to answer with confidence. Some of the African groups reached Europe. A few crossed over a land bridge that once connected Tunisia, Sicily and Italy. Others travelled eastwards round the Mediterranean and up north through the Balkans.

Upright Man was in Europe in some numbers about a million years ago. But about 600,000 years ago the climate changed. It started to get very cold. The shift was gradual and by no means steady and continuous. There were long periods when the weather ameliorated and the ice sheets advancing down from the north paused and temporarily retreated. But the overall trend was a great cooling. So much water locked up in the ice caps caused a lowering of the sea-level and the emergence of more land bridges, so that eventually men were able to spread into the Americas across the Bering Strait and down the island chains of Indonesia towards New Guinea and Australia.

In Europe, Upright Man must have felt the increasing cold very keenly. He had evolved in the warmth of the African plain and did not have the protection of thick fur, like the mammals that had lived in these cooler regions for a long period. Doubtless, many creatures, in such circumstances, would have retreated to warmer parts or simply died out. Man, being dexterous of hand and inventive of mind, did neither. He hunted the furred animals, stripped the skins from their dead bodies and used them himself. And he found shelter in caves.

His living sites have been discovered in great numbers in southern France and Spain. Along the great limestone valleys of central France such as the Dordogne and in the foothills of the Pyrenees, the cliffs are riddled with caves and almost every one shows some sign of ancient habitation. From the objects that have been found in them, we know a great deal about these people. They used bone needles and sinew to sew clothes of skin and fur.

They fished with carefully carved multi-barbed bone harpoons and hunted in the woods with spears tipped with stone blades. Blackened stones show that they had control of fire and they must have treasured it, for it gave them desperately needed warmth in the winter and enabled them to cook meat that their small teeth could not otherwise have chewed.

Their teeth, indeed, had become even smaller than those of their ancestors, but their cranium had expanded and was now as big as our own. Judging from casts taken from the inside of their skulls, that part of the brain that controls speech was fully developed, so it is reasonable to assume that these men now spoke a language that was fluent and complex. In short, as far as the skeletons alone are concerned, there is no significant difference between a man who lived in the caves of France 35,000 years ago and ourselves. Anthropologists, accordingly, have given these people the same name as they use, somewhat immodestly, for all modern humans—Homo sapiens, Wise Man.

The difference between the life of a skin-clad hunter leaving a cave with a spear over his shoulder to hunt mammoth, and a smartly-dressed executive driving along a motorway in New York, London or Tokyo, to consult his computer print-out, is not due to any further physical development of body or brain during the long period that separates them, but to a completely new evolutionary factor.

Man has credited himself with several talents to distinguish him from all other animals. Once we thought that we were the only creatures to make and use tools. We now know that this is not so: chimpanzees do so and so do finches in the Galapagos that cut and trim long thorns to use as pins for extracting grubs from holes in wood. Even our complex spoken language seems less special the more we learn about the communications used by chimpanzees and dolphins. But we are the only creatures to have painted representational pictures and it is this talent which led to the developments which ultimately transformed the life of mankind.

Its first flowering can be seen in those ancient European caves. The men who lived there ventured deep into the black holes that lead from the back of many of them, finding their way by the feeble flickering light of stone lamps filled with animal fat. There, in some of the most remote parts of the caverns, sometimes in passages and chambers that could only have been reached after hours of crawling, they painted designs on the walls. For pigments they used the red, brown and yellow ochres of iron, and black from charcoal and manganese ore. For brushes, they used sticks burred at the end, their fingers, and sometimes blew paint on to the rock, probably from the mouth. Sometimes the designs are engraved with a flint tool and there are a few examples of carving in the round, and modelling in clay. Their subjects were almost always the animals they hunted—mammoth, deer, horse, wild cattle, bison and rhinoceros. Often they are superimposed, one on top of the other. There are no landscapes and only very rarely human figures. In one or two caves, the people left a particularly evocative symbol of their visit, the image of their hands made by blowing paint over them so that the outline is left stencilled on the rock. Scattered among the animals, there are abstract designs— parallel lines, squares, grids and rows of dots, curves that some say represent the female genitalia, chevrons that might be arrows. These are the least spectacular of the designs but the most significant for what was to come.

Even now, we do not know why these people painted. Perhaps the designs were part of a religious ritual—if the chevrons surrounding a great bull represented arrows, then maybe they

were drawn to bring success in hunting; if the cattle shown with swollen sides are intended to appear pregnant, then maybe they were made during increase rituals to ensure the fertility of the herds. Maybe their function was less complicated and the people painted simply because they enjoyed doing so, taking pleasure in art for art's sake. Perhaps it is a mistake to seek a single universal explanation. The most ancient of the paintings is thought to be about 30,000 years old, the youngest maybe 10,000. The interval between these two dates is about six times the length of the entire history of western civilisation, so there is no more reason to suppose that the same motives lay behind all these paintings than there is to believe that background music saturating a modern hotel serves the same function as a Gregorian chant. But whether they were directed at the gods, at young initiates or appreciative members of the community, they were certainly communications. And they still retain their power to communicate today. Even if we are baffled by their precise meaning, we cannot fail to respond to the perceptiveness and aesthetic sensitivity with which these artists captured the significant outlines of a mammoth, the cocked heads of a herd of antlered deer or the looming bulk of a bison.

Elsewhere in the world it is still possible to discover just what purposes rock painting can have to a hunting people. In Australia, the Aborigines still draw designs on rock that are, in many ways, very similar to the prehistoric designs of Europe. They are painted on cliffs and rock shelters, often in parts that are extremely difficult to reach; they are executed in mineral ochres; they are superimposed one on top of another; they include abstract geometrical designs and stencilled handprints; and very often, they represent creatures on which the aborigines rely for food— barramundi fish, turtles, lizards and kangaroo.

Some of these designs are repainted time and time again, in the belief that by keeping the image of the animals fresh on the rock they will continue to flourish in the surrounding bush. Elsewhere, men paint as an act of worship. The Walbiri people of the central desert believe that the world was created by a great spirit snake, the rainbow serpent, whose many-coloured trail appears in the sky after storms. The old men say that it lives in a hole at the base of a long sandstone cliff in the heart of the tribal territory. No man has ever seen the snake itself, though it sometimes leaves the marks of its passing in the sand. Many generations ago, the people painted the snake-god's image on the rock, a huge undulating curve in white ochre, outlined with red. Horseshoe shapes beside it, not unlike some of the geometric designs of prehistory, represent human beings who are descended from the snake. Beside them on the cliff are more symbols, parallel lines and concentric circles, dots and chevrons, that represent the footprints of ancestral animals, carpet snakes and spears.

These designs have been repainted regularly by generations of men. The process of doing so is, in itself, an act of worship, a communion with the snake god creator. The old Walbiri men went there regularly to chant the ancient myths and to meditate on their meaning. Relics of the snake, rounded stones engraved with abstract symbols, were kept in clefts in the rocks. The old men took them out reverently, anointed them with red ochre and kangaroo fat, and chanted. Young men used to be taken there to be initiated under the image of the snake, to be instructed in the meaning of the symbols, and to witness the re-enactment of the legends in mime and song.

There is no reason to suppose that the aborigines are any more closely related to the prehistoric cave dwellers of France than we are, but their way of life is still very close to that of the men of the Stone Age. Homo sapiens led such an existence, hunting animals and gathering fruits, seeds and roots everywhere in the world for many thousands of years. Such a life is hazardous and rough. Men, women and children are exposed to the pitiless sifting of an impersonal environment. The slow and the careless are likely to be killed by predators; the weak may starve; the old may fail to survive the torment of a drought. Those whose bodies were, by the chance of genetic variation, better suited to the conditions, had an advantage. They survived and reproduced, handing on that advantage to their children.

So the bodies of men responded to the impress of the world they lived in and made the most recent major physical changes to be incorporated in their genes. Those that lived in the tropics, like the Australian aborigines and the Africans, had dark skins. Pigmentation may have been acquired several times, quite independently, so a black skin is not by itself an indication of a close relationship to another black skin. Its purpose is protection. The rays of the sun, in excess, can be very harmful. Beating on an unprotected fair skin, they can produce a cancer. Dark pigment, however, provides an effective shield. Many people living in such environments, in Africa, India and Australia, also share another characteristic—thin, attenuated bodies. This shape is also a response to their hot dry surroundings. It provides a large area of skin surface in proportion to body weight, a greater expanse over which winds and evaporating sweat can cool the body.

In cold regions, the situation is reversed. The sun's rays, in moderate quantities, are important for health. Without them, the body cannot manufacture vitamin D, so in the north, where the sun is so often hidden, people like the Lapps of Scandinavia have fair skins. The Eskimo, living within the Arctic Circle, also have light-coloured skin and, in addition, a physique that is the opposite of the gangling tropical desert-dweller. They are short and squat, the shape with a low surface-to-weight ratio which best retains heat. Their lack of facial hair may also be an adaptation to a cold climate, for a beard and moustache, in these conditions, may ice up and become a real impediment.

Since such characters as these became fixed in the genes by natural selection, they remain apparent in individuals, generation after generation, no matter where they live, unless the processes similar to those that brought them into existence cause over many thousands of years further changes.

Communities who live by hunting and gathering still exist. The aborigines and the African bushmen live in deserts. Other groups find all they need from the rain forests in Central Africa, and Malaysia. They all live in harmony with the natural world around them, altering it not at all and making do with what it immediately provides. Nowhere are they overwhelmingly numerous. Their expectation of life is short, their birthrate and the survival of their children are curbed by the scarcity of food and the hazards of their lives. Such was the condition of man for almost all his existence. It is very close to the way in which Upright Man lived about a million years ago. And for about nine hundred and ninety thousand years afterwards, it was the life that he and his descendant, Homo sapiens, was to follow. Throughout that time, as far as we can judge, man's numbers increased by only about one-tenth of one per cent each century.

Then, with dramatic swiftness, about eight thousand years ago, that began to change. In lands outside the forests and the deserts, the human population began to increase. The trigger may well have been a wild grass that grew then, as it still does, on the sandy hills and fertile river deltas of the Middle East. It bears numerous seeds, full of nourishment, that are easily plucked and winnowed from their husks. Doubtless man, as he hunted across the open lands, had gathered it and eaten it whenever he encountered it. But a change in his fortunes came when he realised that he need not rely on chance encounters with the wild plant. If he forbore to eat all the seeds that he gathered but planted them in a convenient place, he would no longer be forced to wander in search of the plant the following summer. He could settle down beside his plots and wait for the grain to sprout, stop being a gatherer and become a farmer, build himself permanent huts and live in villages. So he founded the first towns.

Uruk, in Syria, was built on what was then the marshy reed-covered delta of the Tigris and Euphrates Rivers. Now it is a desert. The town was a complex one. The people planted fields of grain around it and kept herds of goats and sheep. They made pottery, fragments of which still lie all over the site. And in the centre of the town, they constructed an artificial mountain out of baked mud-bricks, held together with plaited layers of reeds. The settled life led by the citizens of Uruk enabled them to make a further crucial advance in man's techniques of communication. People who travel perpetually have to keep their material possessions to a minimum. People who live in houses, however, can accumulate all kinds of objects. In the remains of one of the buildings at Uruk a small clay tablet, covered with incisions, was found. It is the earliest known piece of writing. No one yet knows exactly what it means. It appears to be a record of rations of food. The shapes seem to be based on the appearance of the objects they represent, but there is no attempt at naturalistic portrayals. The marks are simple diagrams but ones that must have been recognised by the people for whom they were intended.

When the tablet was baked, men turned the surge of evolution into a new course. Now an individual had a means of conveying information to others in a way that was independent of his presence or indeed of his continued existence. People elsewhere and generations unborn could now learn about his successes and his failures, his insights and his strokes of genius. If they had a mind to, they could sift through accumulations of humdrum facts and extract a seed of significance that could lead to wisdom.

Other communities elsewhere, in the valley of the Nile, the jungles of Central America and the plains of China, made similar innovations. The diagrammatic representations of objects became simplified and took on new meanings. By using them as puns, they could represent sounds. At the eastern end of the Mediterranean, people developed them into a comprehensive system with which they represented every sound they spoke by shapes cut in stone, scored on clay or drawn on paper.

The revolution caused by the sharing of experience and the spread of knowledge had begun. The Chinese, a thousand years ago, gave it further impetus by devising mechanical means of reproducing such marks in great numbers. In Europe, Gutenberg independently, though much later, developed the technique of printing from movable type. Today, our libraries, the descendants of those mud tablets, can be regarded as immense communal brains, memorising far more than any one human brain could hold. Life began three and a half thousand million years ago when a molecule appeared in the primordial seas which, by its shape, could convey instructions for the building of a further generation of molecules. As evolution proceeded, these molecules increased enormously in size and complexity and became chromosomes carrying all the information necessary for the development of an entire organism. Animals, as they became more advanced, supplemented the physical inheritance of their offspring by teaching, so adding nurture to nature, but when, a few thousand years ago, man began to use physical objects to convey experience to generations unborn, then a new and immensely important threshold had been crossed. His pictographs and his writings, his books, micro-film and computer tapes can be seen as extra-corporeal DNA, adjuncts to our genetical inheritance as important and influential in determining the way we behave as the chromosomes in our tissues are in determining the physical shape of our bodies. It was this accumulated wisdom that eventually enabled us to devise ways of escaping the dictates of the environment. Our knowledge of agricultural techniques and mechanical devices, of medicine and engineering, of mathematics and space travel, all depend on stored experience. Cut off from our libraries and all they represent and marooned on a desert island, any one of us would be quickly reduced to the life of a hunter gatherer.

Man's passion to communicate and to receive communications seems as central to his success as a species as the fin was to the fish or the feather to the birds. We do not limit ourselves to our own acquaintances or even our own generation. Archaeologists labour to decipher clay tablets rescued with painstaking care from Uruk and other ancient cities in the hope that the same citizen long ago may have recorded a message of more significance than a boastful genealogy of a chief or a laundry list. In our own cities, dignitaries arrange for messages to be sent to future generations by burying writings in steel cylinders strong enough to survive even a nuclear catastrophe. And scientists, convinced that man's most refined language of all is that of mathematics, select a universal truth that they believe will be recognised through all eternity—a formula for the wavelength of light—and beam it towards other galaxies in the Milky Way to proclaim that here on earth, after three thousand million years of evolution, a creature has emerged that has for the first time devised its own way of accumulating and transferring experience across generations.

This last chapter has been devoted to only one species, ourselves. This may have given the impression that somehow man is the ultimate triumph of evolution, that all these millions of years of development have had no purpose other than to put him on earth. There is no scientific evidence whatever to support such a view and no reason to suppose that our stay here will be any more permanent than that of the dinosaur. The processes of evolution are still going on among plants and birds, insects and mammals. So it is more than likely that if men were to disappear from the face of the earth, for whatever reason, there is a modest, unobtrusive creature somewhere that would develop into a new form and take our place.

But although denying that we have a special position in the natural world might seem becomingly modest in the eye of eternity, it might also be used as an excuse for evading our responsibilities. The fact is that no species has ever had such wholesale control over everything on earth, living or dead, as we now have. That lays upon us, whether we like it or not, an awesome responsibility. In our hands now lies not only our own future, but that of all other living creatures with whom we share the earth.

From
Life on Earth

BAD BACKS

BRIAN INGLIS

THE first reasonably detailed account of the treatment of back disorders dates from the 5th century BC, in the works of Hippocrates. As with Homer, there is no contemporary account of Hippocrates as an individual; the writings, collected a couple of centuries later, may have been taken from a number of sources. But they were to be extremely influential, offering as they did the first calm and clear account of the disorders from which man suffered, and what could be done to ameliorate them.

Nothing very much, Hippocrates admitted, *could* be done, to alter the course of most illnesses, except by giving every assistance possible to the healing force of nature, with rest and an appropriate diet. But he accepted that it might be possible to do something about a spine which had been bent forward, whether by accident, habit, pain, or advancing years; with the aid of traction or succussion—shaking—to force the vertebrae apart, so that they could be maneuvered back into their correct position, by hand or some other means.

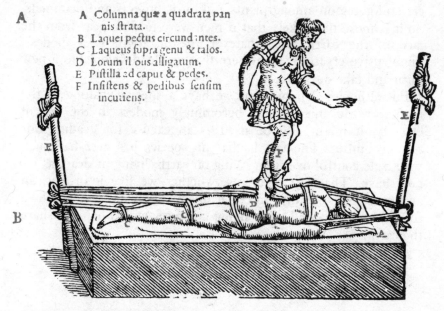

A   A Columna quæ a quadrata pannis ſtrata.
B Laquei pectus circundantes.
C Laqueus ſupra genu & talos.
D Lorum ilious alligatum.
E Piſtilla ad caput & pedes.
F Inſiſtens & pedibus ſenſim incutiens.

The method of traction he favoured involved placing the patient on a board, and tying thongs round his ankles, knees, loins and armpits. The physician "or some person who is strong, and not uninstructed, should apply the palm of one hand to the hump and then, having laid the other hand upon the former, he should make pressure, gauging whether this force should be applied directly downward, or toward the head, or toward the hips". The method, Hippocrates insisted, was safe. It was safe, too, for the doctor to put his foot on the bent spine, or even to bounce up and down on it, the better to straighten it out. And hazardous though the method now sounds, similar methods have been reported by anthropologists working with tribal communities, by historians, and by folk-lore enthusiasts collecting material, in many parts of the world; which has prompted the medical historian Dr Eiler Schiötz of Oslo to say that if such methods have been found effective in countries as far apart as Norway, Mexico and the Pacific islands, "over many, many centuries", the inference is that they must have some validity.

The alternative, succussion, involved strapping the patient to a ladder, which could be shaken up and down to loosen his vertebrae. Hippocrates was prepared to give credit to the individual who had thought of the idea, "or any other contrivance which is according to nature"; but so far as he knew, the method had never succeeded in straightening out anybody's bent spine. He was suspicious of it, too, because he had observed that it was "principally practised by those physicians who seek to astonish the mob —for to them, such things appear wonderful, when they see a man suspended and thrown down, or the like; they always extol such exhibitions and never concern themselves about whether the results of the experiment are good or bad". The doctors who used the method, in Hippocrates' experience, were not to be trusted. He was unwilling to reject the possibility that the spine might be helped by succussion, if it were properly understood and carried out; but for his part, he would not care to treat cases in this way, because such procedures were generally practised by charlatans.

From
The Book of the Back

SELF-HELP

JONATHAN MILLER

B Y the time anyone feels ill enough to call in a doctor, he has already been receiving free treatment from a private physician whose personal services have been available to him from the moment of his conception. By inheriting the premises in which we are condemned to spend the rest of our lives, we are born into a hospital whose twenty-four-hour services are, paradoxically, designed to overcome and counteract the risks of living in such a dangerous tenement. It is a hospital staffed by its only patient, and although we take no conscious part in our own therapeutic activities, the fact that we have ourselves on call around the clock means that we can overcome most common emergencies without having to summon outside help.

Prevention is, of course, better than cure, and ideally one would live in a world so free of risk that prevention and cure would be equally unnecessary. But it is hard to imagine what such an environment would be like. The womb is the nearest we ever come to it and, like the womb, such a world would be so monotonous and so unchallenging that any species which grew accustomed to it would soon lose the ability to survive anywhere else. The most versatile and ambitious species are those which have evolved mechanisms capable of recognising and facing threats before they have had a chance to inflict expensive and possibly irreparable damage.

Most of the protective mechanisms I am going to discuss are reactions or responses of one sort or another: they are called into existence when a threat makes its appearance. Once they have succeeded in forestalling the threat, they automatically subside—ready to issue forth again whenever the danger recurs. Creatures which have a large repertoire of such mechanisms are much more favourably placed than animals which rely on permanent protection. Shellfish, for example, depend for their safety, such as it is, on heavy mechanical armour, which is cumbersome and only occasionally useful. When an animal is as small as a water flea, the weight of its shell does not limit its mobility, but when it is as large as a turtle, most of its muscular energy is spent on moving its safety from one place to the next. Anyway, no armour is foolproof, and animals which rely on heavy shields are no match for ones which have invested in nimbleness, intelligence and ingenuity.

The same principle applies to unbreakable bones. Theoretically it would be possible to construct a skeleton which could resist all but the most extreme mechanical stresses. But the weight of such an apparatus would be quite prohibitive, and in the long run it is more profitable to have a nervous system which can anticipate dangerous falls, complemented by bones which can rapidly repair themselves in the event of unavoidable accident. As a general principle, living organisms distribute their insurance funds between a nervous system capable of forecasting threats, and tissues whose active and continuous growth enables them to repair unpreventable damage.

The way in which an animal reacts to a threat depends to a large extent on how far away the threat is when it first makes itself known. Remote dangers call forth a totally different type of behaviour from ones which first appear on or near the surface of the animal. The farther away the threat is, or the sooner it is recognised, the more opportunity there is to analyse the situation as a whole. When a predator announces its distant presence, the animal has time to rearrange its whole attitude and plan the most profitable course of action. If the opponent is larger, fiercer or faster, flight may be the best form of protection. If the opponents are more evenly matched, particularly if they are members of the same species, it may be more appropriate to put up a frightening show of aggressive behaviour—or a display of submission may be just as effective, since it often calls off the fight; but if battle is joined, the weaker contestant immediately arranges itself to minimise the expected injury: it folds up and offers the least vulnerable surface. These reactions are reinforced by physiological changes in the bloodstream. Alarm causes the automatic secretion of the hormone adrenalin, which, when released into the bloodstream, speeds the heart, raises the bristles, increases the blood sugar, and generally puts the animal in a favourable condition for either fight or flight.

As the threat approaches, the reactions become brisker, simpler and more localised: instead of involving the animal's whole attitude, they are limited to the threatened part itself: eyes blink and limbs flinch. The animal is, in other words, protected by concentric rings of vigilance. Vision, hearing and smell anticipate distant threats in time to plan strategic action. The behaviour connected with these sense organs is therefore judicious, hesitant and versatile. But anything which succeeds in sneaking past or breaking through the early-warning system poses a much more urgent problem. With the immediate threat of injury, there is no time to consider alternative actions, and the response must be simple, unhesitating and automatic.

The sequence repeats evolutionary history in reverse: urgency reduces behaviour to a simplicity which is comparable with that of our primitive ancestors. This principle also applies to the pursuit of satisfaction. The reactions which fulfil and consummate satisfaction are much less versatile and much more localised than the ones which are used to obtain it: swallowing food is a much more automatic affair than hunting for it; orgasm is much more stereotyped than courtship—which is probably why pornography is so much less interesting than literature.

There are some threats which, because they are too small to be seen or too quiet to be heard, always arrive at the surface unannounced and menace us before we have had time to prepare ourselves. Such dangers can usually be handled by short-range tactical mechanisms. The scratch reflex, for example, is so automatic and so primitive that animals can display it even when they have lost higher parts of the nervous system—a frog which has had its brain destroyed and is completely insensitive to visual or acoustic stimuli will nevertheless reach up and try to wipe away a cutaneous irritant. The eye has an even more efficient arrangement. Its surface is so delicate and the transparency of the window so important that it anticipates injury with a non-stop laundry of tears and blinks; when an irritant actually lands on it, the output of tears increases, and the eyelids go into protective spasm. These mechanisms are so automatic that it is easy to take

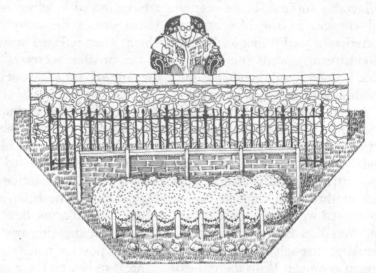

them for granted, but if illness dries up the tears and paralyses the blinking, the transparent surface soon ulcerates.

The lungs and intestines are also guarded by reflex mechanisms. Although these passages are folded away inside the torso, the membranes which line them are just as much part of the outside surface as the skin is. Fortunately, they have comparatively narrow entrances, and the disproportionate sensitivity of the nose, tongue and lips makes it easy to supervise their safety. Although the intake of food endangers the uptake of breath—to reach the stomach, food has to pass over the top of the windpipe—confusion is avoided by the subtle co-ordination of the two functions. The act of swallowing automatically postpones breathing and at the same time raises the larynx, so that the entrance to the lungs is brought under a little flap or lid just behind the tongue called the epiglottis—you can see this action quite clearly if you watch someone's Adam's apple when he swallows. If this co-ordination is paralysed, as it may be in cases of polio, for example, the patient is in danger of choking whenever he swallows.

This and other dangers call for a second line of defence. Any irritant which succeeds in entering the windpipe immediately excites the familiar cough reflex. The patient takes a breath, but as he starts to blow out, the larynx narrows, so that the act of expiration works for a moment against a strong resistance. When the air pressure inside the lung has been raised to a sufficiently high level, the larynx suddenly relaxes, and the explosive release of air blows the irritant out of the mouth or nose. This laryngeal action is extremely important: patients who have lost control over it may be able to puff and blow, but they can't raise the explosive power necessary to expel the foreign body.

A cough may be an irritating inconvenience, but it would be disastrous if the reflex failed. Doctors are sparing in their use of cough mixtures because, if it were extinguished, the unsuspecting lungs would lie open to the invasion of septic material. This is also why unconsciousness poses such a serious threat to the lungs. Loss of the cough reflex is now considered one of the most serious hazards of head injury: the victim of a road accident runs as much risk from drowning in his own secretions as he does from the immediate effects of the injury itself.

Recognition of this simple fact has led to a dramatic fall in the mortality of unconscious patients. It is amazing how easy it is to save life by turning the unconscious person on his front.

From
The Body in Question

SEASIDE SENSATION
D. J. ENRIGHT

The strains of an elastic band
Waft softly o'er the sandy strand.
The maestro stretches out his hands
To bless the bandiest of bands.

Their instruments are big and heavy—
A glockenspiel for spieling Glock,
A handsome bandsome cuckoo clock
For use in Strauss (Johann not Lévi),

Deep-throated timpani in rows
For symphonies by Berlioz,
And lutes and flutes and concertinas,
Serpents, shawms and ocarinas.

The sun is shining, there are miles
Of peeling skin and healing smiles.
Also water which is doing
What it ought to, fro- and to-ing.

But can the band the bandstand stand?
Or can the bandstand stand the band?
The sand, the sand, it cannot stand
The strain of bandstand and a band!

Now swallowed up are band and stand
And smiling faces black and tanned.
The sand was quick and they were slow.
You hear them playing on below.

1 *APRIL 1871*

FRANCIS KILVERT

I went to Whitney by the 2.6 train. Miss Hutchinson was at home at the Rectory. She is the niece of Mary Hutchinson, the wife of William Wordsworth the poet. And she was the god-daughter of Dorothy Wordsworth, William's sister. We had some interesting talk about the Wordsworth family. She showed me first a large brooch she was wearing containing on one side a beautiful coloured photograph of the poet, and on the other side

two locks of grey hair from the heads of the poet and his wife. This photograph is far the best and most pleasing likeness I have seen of the poet. It was taken from a picture painted by Haydon almost entirely from memory. The poet had written to the painter telling him with pride that he had ascended Helvellyn when he was 70 years old, and sending him a sonnet on the occasion. The painter was extremely pleased with the letter and the sonnet and immediately drew Wordsworth in a meditative mood composing the sonnet.

Miss Hutchinson said that once, when she was staying at the Wordsworths', the poet was much affected by reading in the newspaper the death of Hogg the Ettrick Shepherd. Half an hour afterwards he came into the room where the ladies were sitting and asked Miss Hutchinson to write down some lines which he had just composed. She did so, and these lines were the beautiful poem called the Graves of the Poets. He was very desultory and disinclined to write. His ladies were always urging him to do so however. And he would have written little if it had not been for his wife and sister. He could not bear the act of writing and he wrote so impatiently and impetuously that his writing was rarely legible. He was very absent and has been known to walk unconsciously through a flock of sheep without perceiving them. He had many books read to him in his later years when his eyesight grew weak. He did not care much for society and preferred the society of women to that of men. With men he was often reserved.

When William Howitt was at Rydal Mount looking about after Wordsworth's death he fell in with old James the gardener and asked him which was the poet's study. "This," said James pointing to the arbour and the grass mound from which Rydal Mount takes its name. William Wordsworth was a tall man. Dorothy was short and spare. She was a great walker in her youth and suffered physically and mentally as she grew old for having overtaxed her strength when she was young with excessively long walks. When she was middle aged and growing elderly she thought nothing of walking from Brinsop into Hereford, six miles and back, if she wanted a thimble. When she was staying at the Hutchinsons' farm in Radnorshire she would walk into Kington and back on the smallest excuse. During her imbecility she had frequent intervals when all her old brightness, liveliness and clearness of mind returned. Then she relapsed into her sad state. She and her brother used often to stay at Mrs. Monkhouse's at the Stow farm, Whitney. Dorothy had a lucid interval at her brother's death. She was deeply affected at his loss, left her room and came to his bedside when he was dying.

JANE AUSTEN'S SECRET
LORD DAVID CECIL

JANE AUSTEN's obsessive secrecy about her writing is the nearest thing to an eccentricity in her otherwise well-balanced character. She even tried to conceal her real name from her publisher; in her letter to Crosby she called herself Mrs Ashton Dennis. Meanwhile, at Chawton and elsewhere, her double life went on. Her neighbours knew her only as the daughter of a late

"So he said ___ ome sighs
"I'm the s ___ our eyes.
Oh! restore ___ please ___ "
By acc ___ ease.

J. A.

rector of Steventon and at home nobody was aware of her literary work except her closest relations and Martha Lloyd. She took elaborate pains to conceal it from anyone else: friends, visitors, servants. This is all the more significant because it was not easy. She had no private room to write in, except the small bedroom she shared with Cassandra. Leaving the sitting room to the other ladies, she chose to work in the combined front hall and dining room at a little table on which she had placed her mahogany desk. She wrote on small pieces of paper because this made it easier for her, if interrupted, to slip them into a drawer or under a blotter. The room led, by way of a swing door, to the kitchen and other offices. Though this door creaked disagreeably, Jane Austen asked that it should be allowed to go on doing so. Her unspoken reason was that the creak gave her warning that someone was coming, so that she had time to hide her manuscript before he or she entered. In later years, she seems to have relaxed her vigilance sufficiently to do some of her writing in the general sitting room, whether at home or staying with one of her brothers. Another of her nieces, Edward's daughter Marianne, remembers her sitting sewing by the fire of a winter's evening. Suddenly she would burst out laughing, jump up, run across to the writing table and scribble down a sentence there; then, without explanation, she would come back and resume her seat by the fire.

From
A Portrait of Jane Austen

RUDYARD KIPLING
LORD BIRKENHEAD

THERE have already been many criticisms and evaluations of Kipling's work, and it is certain that a host of others will follow, for the quarry is deep, tempting, and inexhaustible. Some have sought, with deep psychological insight, to fathom his real springs of thought and action, and to penetrate the fiercely guarded innermost bastion of this thought. Others, like the Swedish philosopher Leeb Lunberg, have made erudite inquiries into the philology of Kipling's work and the sources from which it was derived; others again, like the Danish writer C. A. Bodelsen, have analysed with remarkable acuteness the "obscure" stories which sorely puzzled some of Kipling's honest, if simpler, admirers in his later creative phase.

A biographer, attempting to describe his life, cannot be lured too far down these byways, and can only note the general trend of his writings and make some reference to the most significant. And here one is immediately struck by the violent fluctuations in his popularity and the esteem in which he was held. For Kipling, as for others, the idolatry was often greater abroad than in his own land. But in England, too, his triumph was at first almost complete —he had burst upon the country with the force of an electric shock, but had lived to see his reputation sadly eroded, and during the years of disillusionment he seemed, particularly to the young, an elderly blimp who symbolized the odious themes of duty, patriotism and military preparedness.

Yet there can be little doubt of Kipling's survival in the long term; as Maurice Baring observed, he is "safe in the Temple of Fame, which once you have entered you cannot leave. For this Temple is like a wheel. It goes round and round, and sometimes some of its inmates are in the glare of the sun, and sometimes they are in the shade, but they are there; and they never fall out."

We have already noted the variations in Kipling's early work. They continued in the books published in his interim period. So far his greatest success had been achieved as a writer of short stories and of verse, and it is clear that he was anxious to show that he was not confined to these forms, but could also master the full-length novel. That he was wrong in this belief is clearly

suggested by the appearance of *The Light that Failed* (1891), and *The Naulahka* (1892), which he wrote in collaboration with Wolcott Balestier. The first is a bad book, hardly to be classified indeed as a novel, and the second perhaps the worst that Kipling ever had a hand in. *The Light that Failed* was coldly received, and it was soon accurately described by hostile critics as "The Book that Failed".

Nor is it difficult to put one's finger on the weakness which prevented Kipling to the end from becoming a novelist. It was not that he was incapable of planning a full-length novel, but rather that his impatience, and weakness in the creation of character, made it difficult for him to sustain the reader's interest beyond the bounds of the short story, which was a perfect vehicle for his art. *Kim*, by far the most successful of his longer works, is not by any normal standards a novel at all, but a series of linked episodes in the progress of the Lama and Kim, most of which could be prised from their neighbours without disturbing the symmetry of the whole.

In the words of a contemporary critic: "Kipling cannot escape from his own subjectivity. His *dramatis personae* melt away rapidly out of the memory, leaving us nothing but an admirably piquant and clever delineation," while to another contemporary, Richard Le Gallienne, "the characters are little more than pegs on which to hang an anecdote". This shortcoming was not necessarily an impediment to the short story as practised by Kipling, but it was fatal in the novel.

"Kipling was rarely capable of creating a character," wrote another critic. "He could combine a collection of observed traits into a composite which would pass in ordinary daylight for a likeness; but there are few if any of his stories in which any single character gathers flesh upon his bones, inspires that flesh with nerves and a brain, and carries his progenitor away."

We may test this undoubted truth by comparing Kipling's characterization with that of W. Somerset Maugham. They were the two most widely-read writers of the short story of their day, but unlike Kipling, Maugham was also, at his best, a most capable novelist. And the reason for this difference lies in the fact that Maugham was profoundly interested in the quirks of human nature and fascinated by the good and evil at war in every human breast. He fashioned his characters out of close observation, allowing them time to stretch and grow and become authentic, so that the reader could believe that he actually knew them, and could form for them a positive love or detestation. He did not hero-worship "Great Men". He was not interested in political issues or technical miracles. But the study of human frailty absorbed him, and that, no doubt, although he was a far less naturally gifted writer than Kipling, is why his characters remain printed on the mind—the odious Townsend in *The Painted Veil*, the contemptible Alroy Kear in *Cakes and Ale*, the cynical Dr Saunders in *The Narrow Corner*—while Kipling's Stricklands, Helders and Pycrofts dissolve without leaving a trace.

This weakness of Kipling's, however, did not impede him in the short story, which he continued to fashion with gem-cutting perfection, and we should remember Maugham's own tribute to him:

> Rudyard Kipling alone among the English writers of the Short Story, can bear comparison with the masters of France and Russia. Though he captured the favour of the great public when first he began to write, and has retained a hold on it ever since, cultivated opinion has always been somewhat scornful of him. He has identified with an Imperialism which was obnoxious to many sensitive persons, and certain characteristics of his style have always been irksome to readers of fastidious taste. But he was a wonderful, varied, and original teller of tales. He had a fertile invention, a merit in any writer, and to a supreme degree the gift of narrating

incident in a surprising and dramatic fashion. His influence for a while was great on his fellow-writers, but perhaps greater on his fellow-men who led, in one way or another, the sort of life he dealt with. When one travelled in the East it was astonishing how often one came across men who had modelled themselves on the creatures of his invention.

From
Rudyard Kipling

A PICTURE OF FAULKNER

PAUL THEROUX

The protagonist in Paul Theroux's Picture Palace
*is Maude Coffin Pratt, a 71-year-old photographer,
who is led to review her life in a series of flashbacks
when she permits a retrospective exhibition of her
work. Towards the end of World War II, while
dining in a Hollywood restaurant with Aldous
Huxley, she caught sight of Raymond Chandler and
his elderly wife at another table. Camera in hand,
she approached them unnoticed and yelled
"Applesauce!". Chandler cursed and his wife
"inched over into a swoon". Maude instantly
regretted the pictures she had taken. A few days
later she atoned for her churlish behaviour by
treating William Faulkner in a much more kindly manner.*

THERE was only one more picture to do. I had been asked by *Life* to update their files. Their picture of William Faulkner was a studio shot that had obviously been retouched to make him look like a confederate colonel. "Get him looking human," the picture editor said. I remembered that Orlando had mentioned him and admired several of his books, one apparently dealing with Harvard, which he had started to read to me during my early blind period and then stopped, saying, "This wouldn't make any sense to you"—I suspected that he gave it to Phoebe to read, because for the next few days, engrossed in the book, she flicked pages and her body purred.

Faulkner, I learned, was staying at the Highland Hotel in Hollywood, a semirespectable residential hotel done up in a kind of ulcerated stucco. There was no one at the front desk the day I visited, so—seeing his name and room number on the key board—I went directly to his room. I knocked and waited, and getting no response I tried the door.

It was unlocked: I stole in. The curtain was half open and through the French windows I could see a bright balcony and an armchair. On a table near me were crumpled pages of typescript, an old newspaper, and two copies of *God Is My Co-Pilot*. In the air was a sweet rotten-walnut stink of bourbon whisky, but apart from the sound of traffic and the sizzle of California sunlight the room was quiet. I peeked into the next room—an empty unmade bed—and I was about to leave when I saw a half-filled glass next to the telephone and a bottle and ice bucket. It looked like an interrupted boozing session, as if he had just stepped out. The room had the lived-in appearance of a warm mangled nest, the disorder of anticipation, a certain nervous premonition.

I considered photographing the room—*Whose Room?*, another series: identify the inhabitant from the dents in the chairs and the dirty glasses and ashtrays and books. I had taken off my dust-cap to act on this impulse, and then I saw him.

He was lying face up on the floor, one hand across his chest, the other pillowing his head; and his legs were poised in a twinkle-toes angle, as if he had died in a dance-step. My first thought was that he was dead—he had busted a gut or had been robbed and killed. But there was no blood anywhere. I went closer and heard him breathe. A moment ago I hadn't heard it; now his snores filled the room with the ripsawing of his drunken doze. As he lay there on the cool floor I could see how small he was—tiny feet, tiny moustache, pretty hands, and in his shorts his hairy little legs. He had a typist's powerful shoulders and though he was flat on his back and unconscious he had a victim's innocent dignity.

This supine man in a bleak Hollywood hotel room would, I knew, be fixed in my mind as emblematic of art. I could not hear the world "literature" without thinking of Lawrence's halitosis or O'Neill's dandruff, or the word "photography" without remembering pictures I had never taken, such as our windmill in the rain. People pretended that art was complete, but it had another side that was hidden and human and wept and stank and snored and died; and I wondered whether it was not perhaps truer than creation.

If Faulkner had been dead I would have done him. But he was only drunk, poor man, and I guessed why. I went away and locked the door and never regretted not taking that picture. Indeed, I was glad it was I who found Faulkner that day, and not another photographer out to make a name for herself.

From
Picture Palace

THE FILMING OF "DEATH IN VENICE"
DIRK BOGARDE

FORWOOD was fingering through a small box of moustaches which Mauro had left behind in his grief. He handed me one at random. I stuck it on; it was bushy, greyish, Kipling. In another box of buttons, safety pins, hair grips, and some scattered glass beads he disentangled a pair of rather bent pince-nez with a thin gold chain dangling. I placed the hat back on my head, wrapped a long beige woollen scarf about my neck, took up a walking stick from a bundle of others which lay in a pile, and borrowing a walk from my paternal grandfather, heavily back on the heels, no knee caps, I started to walk slowly round and round the room emptying myself of myself, thinking pain and loneliness, bewilderment and age, fear and the terror of dying in solitude. Willing von Aschenbach himself to come towards me and slip into the vacuum which I was creating for his reception.

And he came, not all at once, but in little whispers . . . bringing with him the weight of his years, the irritability of his loneliness, the tiredness of his sick body, and stiffly he went out into the long, long corridor which led to the great staircase, walking heavily, thumping firmly with the stick for confidence, frighteningly aware of the rising sounds of voices and laughter from below, some idea of tears behind the glittering, pinching pince-nez. At the top of the staircase he stopped suddenly, one shaking hand holding the cool mahogany rail, trying to square the sagging shoulders which emphasised his agonising shyness; below, the hall seemed jammed with people he didn't know and had never seen before. Arrogance slid in like a vapour; carefully, firmly, no longer shaking now, he started to descend towards them, head held as high as it would go, legs as firm as they would allow, hand lightly touching the rail for moral support. There was a sudden hush in the crowded room. Faces swiftly turned upwards towards him, pink discs frozen. He continued slowly down, allowing himself the barest smile of German superiority. From a long way away he suddenly heard Visconti's voice break the almost unbearable stillness. "Bravo! Bravo!" it cried. "Look, look, all of you! Look! Here is my Thomas Mann!"

I led a curiously isolated and protected existence for the next five months. I seldom, if ever, joined in with the troupe, or the other players, or met Visconti, or anyone else for that matter, socially; my life was in a state of limbo. Daily I sat alone on the Lido beach in my little cabana aloof and distant, silent and yearning as Von Aschenbach himself. Indeed I had absolutely no doubt that I was him, and the exterior shell of my normal body was only the vessel which contained his spirit. My main objective at this time, which was understood and respected by everyone around me, was to remain in total, exhausting, concentration at all times and under all circumstances in order to contain this spirit which was so completely alien to myself. It was a fragile thing; I was constantly terrified that he would at one moment or another slip away from me. But he stayed. Eventually, even in the peace of Ca' Leone, alone in my garden massed now with nodding spikes of white hollyhocks, or walking through the silent piazzas of the city after I had changed into jeans and a tee-shirt, I still retained his walk and mannerisms which might have surprised anyone who didn't know that I walked as a man possessed without consciousness of the present world.

My relationship with Visconti was extraordinary. We were fused together in a world of total silence. We seldom spoke, and never ever about the film. We sat a little apart from each other, admitting each other's need for privacy, but never much more than a metre away. Incredibly we had no need of speech together. We worked as one person. I knew, instinctively, when he was ready, he knew when I was. We worked very much on sign language; a raising of eyebrows from him signified that all was set when I was. Should I shake my head, then he would sit again, and light another cigarette until such time as I felt myself in condition, and then I would touch his arm and walk towards the lights. We hardly ever shot two takes of anything—occasionally he would murmur, "Encora" and we would do it again—but that was all that was ever said and it happened very few times.

Our behaviour startled the occasional stranger to the set. An American female photographer, forced upon us by our American bosses, haunted us for a few days, and was dispirited and furious at the same time, at our total lack of co-operation, which must, I suppose, have seemed rude to her. One day, in a bitterly sarcastic whisper I heard her remark that she had just heard us say "good morning" to each other . . . right beside her.

"They've stopped feuding!" she said triumphantly.

Feuding! I told Visconti with a wry smile, and he patted my hand comfortably: "Non capisce matrimonio, hey?" And it was a marriage indeed. We had never, at any time, discussed how I should attempt to play von Aschenbach; there were no discussions at all about motivation or interpretation. He chose the three suits I should wear, the two hats, the three ties, all my luggage and the shabby overcoat and scarf—and he had chosen me. Apart from that not a word was spoken. Once, just before our departure from Rome, I requested him to give me just half an hour to discuss the role. He grudgingly agreed and, telling me to help myself to wine on the table beside him, asked me how many times I had read the book. When I told him at least thirty, he advised another thirty and that was that; nothing more was ever said.

I think that the only direct instruction he ever gave me was one morning when he requested that I should stand upright in my little motor-boat at the exact moment that I felt the mid-day sun strike my face as we slipped under the great arc of the Rialto bridge. I did not know why I had to make this specific movement at such a precise time until I saw the final film with him some months later, and it was only then, too, that I realised he had been choreographing the entire film, shot by shot, blending all my movements to the music of the man he had wanted to embody the soul of Gustav von Aschenbach. Gustav Mahler.

From
Snakes and Ladders

🌿 🌿 🌿 🌿

CINEMA

DILYS POWELL

IT seems only yesterday that the fearless voyagers of *Rocketship XM*, having through some miscalculation on the part of their feminine fuel officer missed their aim at the moon, made an unexpected planetary landing. "Well, Mars!" they cried. "Whaddya know!" As a matter of fact it was quite a while ago: roughly thirty years. 1950 might be taken as the starting-point for cinema space-exploration.

One laughed, of course, about *Rocketship XM*, and perhaps it wasn't meant to be taken absolutely seriously. Come to that one wasn't at the time taking the possibilities of actual space travel quite seriously; the fearful realities were yet to come. But in the cinema a brisk two-way traffic developed. Space-emissaries in flying saucers arrived bearing token gifts for the President of the United States; understandably taken for space-weapons the gifts were greeted with gunfire. A rescue party from earth found the survivor of an earlier mission reluctant to be rescued; his space-robot-valet could outdo Jeeves any day. Not until the end of the 1960s with *2001: A Space Odyssey* did space-fiction emerge from the sphere of comic fantasy. Stanley Kubrick's film was not only stylistically imaginative; there had been plenty of visual imaginativeness in the space-trips of the previous years. This time there was intellectual excitement.

The 1970s, then, find space-cinema triumphant. A year or two ago a friend working in the British industry assured me that the future of the screen was in science-fiction. I put his opinion down to the passion of the young for extravagant adventure and declined to believe him. But up to a point he was right. Consider the successes of the last years of the decade—successes more than commercial. *Star Wars* may be for the nursery, and one has to say that it contains some of the most idiotic character-drawing since *Son of the Sheik*. But visually it has brilliant passages. Its fantasy creatures linger in the memory. The final aerial battle is superbly done. As for Steve Spielberg's *Close Encounters of the Third Kind*, here is an honourable attempt at what I will call reconciliation. The arrival of the extra-terrestrial visitors is heralded by nothing more alarming than a heightening of the brilliance of lights in the heavens. True that the strangers have the golf-club heads of the invaders in the 1953 *The War of the Worlds*. But their expressions, so far as one can judge through the protective haze which envelopes them, are far nicer. In some strange way their leader is almost beautiful. And they come bearing the gift of friendship—of love, one could say. I admit that I find the long introduction to the meeting less stirring than I had hoped. But the last half-hour of the film—the great spaceship descending in a blaze of light, the hush as the earth-crowd waits, the steady advance of the planet-people—there is something

august about that climax. It is a treaty between earth and space.

There has been other evidence of a serious approach to the space-theme. The element of fantasy persists, and one can't expect the screen to give up its idea that the universe is populated by beings with heads like the operative end of a brassie. But the cinema is beginning to draw back and look with a touch of mischief at its space-reports. Once you can joke about yourself you are out of the nursery. In *Dark Star*, for instance, a notable new director, John Carpenter, presents a cruising space-ship with equipment which gets out of hand and attacks the personnel. *Capricorn One* goes further. This is the story of a space-mission which never was; the mission is faked and the public is gulled into watching scenes on Mars which have been photographed in Arizona. And nowadays distinguished players are ready to lend their prestige to science-fiction. Alec Guinness wields a laser-sword in *Star Wars*. Marlon Brando, got up in a space-toga, plays a pontificating elder in *Superman*. And there is more on the way. At the end of the 1970s the cinema is enjoying a sci-fi cycle.

A horror-cycle too. A few years ago the Locarno Festival showed, outside the official programme, Tobi Hooper's *The Texas Chainsaw Massacre*. The movie, based on a real-life case of maniac murder, was already notorious; duty as well as curiosity impelled one to watch the hideous bashings and slashings. And that winter *The Texas Chainsaw Massacre* was in the programme of the London Film Festival. Ever since the first great American *Frankenstein*, or come to that since Germany's silent classics *The Golem* and *Waxworks*, there has been a cult of horror. Britain's Hammer productions—variations on the Dracula theme, the Frankenstein theme, tales of zombies and resuscitated mummies and general bloodstainery—have had their devotees, even their literature. But there is a difference in the horror of the second half of the 1970s. *The Texas Chainsaw Massacre* is unlike, say, *Dracula has Risen from the Dead*, and *The Hills Have Eyes* (a prize-winner, by the way, at the Sitges International Festival) with its holiday family, driving to California, in the hands of a gang of deformed and ravenous mutants, is different in mood from Hammer's *Frankenstein Must be Destroyed*. Even at their most absurd the Hammer movies drew on legend or myth or some sort of literature. The new horror films, the cult movies of today, proceed by disgust. They are unredeemed. They live on squalor and screams.

I suppose that they represent the extremes of the taste for

violence which governs so much of contemporary cinema. It is probably a heritage from the war; the Gestapo gave the screen a model. And for the young spectators who make up the greater part of the cinema audience violence is less repellent than it is to an older generation with actual experience of war. After all violence can be born of idealism: false idealism sometimes, but powerful all the same. Looking at the screen in the late 1970s, one has to remember how sharply it is slanted towards the teenager and a generation still in its early twenties; hence the manner of not only the cinema of violence, not only the cinema of sex, but the cinema of light entertainment too. One of the commercial successes of 1978 was *Saturday Night Fever*: a new kind of dancing, a new young star. A public which venerated Fred Astaire, which idolised Gene Kelly, is not likely to swoon at the spectacle of John Travolta skidding through his routines. But the teenagers are hooked.

Difficult, reflecting on the current state of the screen, not to slip into gloom. One thinks of the great names now lost to us. Visconti is dead; his *Ludwig*, one of the monuments of London's screen in 1978, shows with its magnificent baroque imagery of the life and death of the poor mad Bavarian king how great is our loss. Pasolini is dead—and though Pasolini's work, as those who have seen *Salo* might agree, did indeed embrace horror the iniquities were not pointless. Jean Renoir is gone: no more of those beaming pictures of Provençal life, no more of his warm liberality over human love. And the New Wave whose members so much admired him—the novelty of their work has dimmed, their films lack the feeling of enthusiasm, of an excited response to life and the potentialities of the cinema which was so stirring when they appeared in the late 1950s.

Easy enough to go on lamenting: so rich the past achievements, so thick the dust of forgetfulness. But all the time the screen demands new names, new ideas. At that one regains one's sense of balance, for it was in talking of new areas of creation that I began this article. Visconti indeed has vanished, and Vittorio de Sica. But Fellini is active, and Bertolucci with *1900*—at any rate with the first half of this picture of an Italy succumbing to and then reviving from Fascism—brings huge command to the screen. In France Alain Resnais continues to explore the intricacies of memory, for his *Providence* is essentially a study in what at night the mind recalls of daylight human relationships; since the mind is a writer's, it translates the remembered images into the stuff of drama. Interesting, too, that Resnais should have used among his leading players two of this country's best actors: from the theatre John Gielgud, from the cinema Dirk Bogarde.

For though the British industry has rarely been a great encourager of imaginative and adventurous directors—Hitchcock was drawn away by the possibilities of Hollywood, John Schlesinger has been among those to follow him at any rate temporarily, and the Powell-Pressburger team, genuine bright stars, were allowed to fade—British players have often dominated the international screen. Anyway we shouldn't give all the laurels to the intellectual, the experimental, the "difficult" films which have reached us from the European continent. Looking back at the far past, it is of Lillian Gish in *Intolerance* tending her geranium one thinks, not of France's art-cinema and *The Assassination of the Duc de Guise*.

Critics have commented glumly on the fact that the British entry in the Delhi Festival of 1978–79 was a straightforward thriller, a second re-make of *The Thirty-Nine Steps*. Re-make: naturally one cherishes the reputation of the Hitchcock version of 1935—and one may prefer to forget Ralph Thomas's version of 1959. But Don Sharp's film with the Michael Robson script is fresh. The development of the chase has been transformed; the twists of narrative surprise. And the hero, the pale Gothic-featured Robert Powell, is coolly convincing. One should not, I think, overlook the value of the thriller in the annals of the screen or forget Britain's contribution to the genre. Pleasure, I know, has been degraded; a critic is not supposed to sit back and enjoy his work. I shall not apologise for saying that I found *The Thirty-Nine Steps* one of the most *enjoyable* films of its period.

But pleasure does not make for trends, though there is a certain pleasure in the rediscovery of an old theme. The year 1978 at any rate restored a favourite subject: bluntly, women. Equality of the sexes has done little for the actresses of the screen. One admires, one praises the beautiful and the gifted, but it can't be denied that for two decades and more women have been the second-class citizens of the cinema. No young Garbo appears, no heiress to Dietrich. The splendid Katharine Hepburn rations her rôles. Bette Davis was among the suspects in *Death on the Nile*, but one could have done with more of those consonantal emphases; Myrna Loy was reduced to playing Burt Reynolds' mother in the indifferent death-joke of *The End*. Such moments serve only to remind us of past delights—mainly romantic delights, for these, like Jean Arthur, like Claudette Colbert, were the stars of a romantic age in the cinema. The current cinema rejects romance.

Nevertheless there is a new mood. No good counting on a revival of romantic cinema. But within the last year or two the feminine principle has reasserted itself—in a new way. The women on the screen have become active rather than passive. They have become independent. And almost without warning the American screen has produced a group of films in which women have been dominant. One of the first portents was *Julia*, made by Fred Zinnemann, a director at once powerful and sensitive. Based on a story by Lillian Hellman which had autobiographical elements, it drew a portrait of two women, one an anti-Nazi fighter in Hitler's Germany, one a friend, a writer who goes to look for her. It gave shining opportunities to Vanessa Redgrave as the anti-Nazi as well as to Jane Fonda. But Miss Fonda as the girl searching for her own place in life, her own line as a writer, strengthened her position as one of America's stars— and without stressing the point restored the actress in the cinema to a leading position.

Or there was *Girlfriends*, again a study of two young women and a friendship, this time shaken when one of them marries, leaving the audience to concentrate on the career—struggling, doubting, but persistent—of the other, a beginner-photographer. This time the director is a woman, Claudia Weill; and that reminds me of another film about two girls who take different directions in the world, *One Sings, the Other Doesn't*, made by the Frenchwoman Agnès Varda: an argument for women's lib, but light-hearted, seductive.

And yet another portrait, another painting of two contrasting lives: *The Turning Point*, Herbert Ross's film about the girl who becomes a famous dancer and the girl who, having given up a career for marriage, secretly resents the triumph of her friend.

Always, you see, the two figures in contrast if not in opposition. Perhaps the cinema still doesn't think one actress enough to command the screen. But *An Unmarried Woman* takes the giant step; it shows a normal sexual woman who prefers to live her own life. Deserted by her husband, she looks round, experiments, chooses and rejects; endearingly played by Jill Clayburgh, she remains in fact unmarried. It is one of the best performances as well as one of the best films of 1978; and in a period when the anti-hero rather than the hero holds the screen the audience can for the first time for years watch a sterling domestic heroine.

Meanwhile there has been a lull in the cinema of disaster. No ships have turned turtle. No skyscrapers have caught fire. Planes may have crashed, but the survivors have refrained from eating one another. On the other hand good comedies have been scarce. Two of the best have come from France: *Pardon Mon Affaire* and its sequel, *Pardon Mon Affaire Too*, each with the grave Jean Rochefort in various degrees of domestic embarrassment (worth remembering that the best comedians are the gravest). From America, one moderate exercise in lunacy, *Foul Play*, but that at least had charming Goldie Hawn among those entangled in a preposterous plot to assassinate a benevolent travelling Pope. *Somebody Killed Her Husband* had to make do with Farrah Fawcett-Majors, a piece of casting which did nothing for the poor girl or indeed for anybody else; while even Woody Allen, with what I find the over-intense family relationships of *Interiors*, turned solemn. For the rest, extravaganzas: a series of parodies and jokes in an essay called *Kentucky Fried Movie*; and a picture of anti-authority carryings-on in an American college, *National Lampoon's Animal House*, a cult-film, I gather, in the United States but received in this country with a good many frozen faces.

And frozen faces for Robert Aldrich's *The Choirboys*: a tale of American cops at play. Aldrich, once capable of such quirky, Stygian death-comedy as *Whatever Happened to Baby Jane?*, here relapses into a vulgarity which retains the element of violence marked in his earlier work. Violence: still it governs every area of contemporary cinema, it permeates comedy, it invades even the inquiry into friendship and character. Why, in *The Turning Point* even the two women, the famous ballerina and the settled wife and mother, fly at one another in an ecstasy of jealousy, suspicion and remembered rivalry. And again one looks for a cause. The war? Its tentacles still creep across Europe, and Africa, across a world ever ready for fresh explosions, new fissures. But for the United States there is a special source of violence, a special experience. There is Vietnam.

The cinema takes time to reflect the cataclysms of war. Of course there are the immediate reactions: propaganda, outbreaks of patriotic fervour. But it was over a decade before Hollywood, after the First War, responded to the split between soldiers and civilians implicit in *All Quiet on the Western Front*. And it is only now that the American screen expresses the consequences of Vietnam. Something more than the experience of war itself is concerned. There is the experience of defeat. The returning soldier is scarred by the horror of battle and perhaps capture. But he feels defeated in himself. And the emotion of defeat is there in at any rate two of the recent films about Vietnam.

One is Hal Ashby's *Coming Home*, with Bruce Dern as the soldier who sets out in an atmosphere of celebration and returns to find his wife in love with a crippled veteran. But it is defeat, in a way the shame of war, not his personal circumstances, which leaves him unable to adjust to life.

The second film is *The Deer Hunter*—much argued over on political grounds since it credits the Viet Cong with inhuman treatment of prisoners. But the point of Michael Cimino's film is not in the exercise of war but in its aftermath. Like the husband in *Coming Home*, the soldiers here are fêted when they set off. But the homecoming is more than muted, it is almost despairing. The film is a fine piece of work; we shall be lucky if in 1980 we see many films as good. But in the present climate we must be prepared for violence, for savagery. Prepared, I suppose, for more science-fiction (to be going on with there is a good example in Philip Kaufman's new version of *Invasion of the Body Snatchers*).

Prepared, hopefully, for a new emphasis on the importance of the actress on the screen. And those of us devoted to the elegance of Fred Astaire or the vitality of Gene Kelly should steel ourselves to more John Travolta.

And something unpredictable. Emerging not long ago from obscurity, the Australian cinema has given us the graceful mystery of *Picnic at Hanging Rock* and the doom-laden prophecies of *The Last Wave*. The London Film Festival of 1978 opened with Australia's skilful dovetailing of fiction and documentary fact, *Newsfront*. Still more recently we have seen an evocation of a terrible incident in Australian racial history, *The Chant of Jimmy Blacksmith*. Always the fresh theme, style, an assured technique.

And once more, as so often with the cinema, at the prospect of a new creative drive one's spirits soar.

ART NOW

MARINA VAIZEY

THE *New Yorker* has never had a bedside book, but for some years that magazine ran an occasional column under the generic title "Onwards and Upwards with the Arts". When I now spend my own professional and non-professional working days looking at exhibitions—at frozen moments—I translate that blazing slogan of determined and optimistic progress, with its delicate tinge of irony, into my own question, also ironically shaded: whence and whither? The energies, tragedies and traumas of the art world and the art worlds of the 1960s, in which the impulses of the post-war period were both exaggerated and accelerated, were based on two premises: that reforms were passionately and wildly, widely desirable, and that change was not only inevitable, but inevitably for the better. Simultaneously, the new movements in art—abstract expressionism and pop art— were identified as American in origin. This has remained a widely held belief, although pop art was probably first discussed, and popular culture a force to be reckoned with in the "fine" arts, in the group centred at the Institute of Contemporary Art in London in the 1950s; and abstract expressionism too had European roots.

Overall in the entire post-war period there has been a massive capitalisation on the stylistic freedom that had characterised Europe from the 1870s on. Rather than a succession of styles, artistic activity could consciously encompass a variety of styles at the same time, just as Victorian architecture had once rifled the stock buildings and varied idioms of the European past to make something distinctive of its own, even in buildings which simultaneously displayed a variety of styles on one facade. The horizons were further stretched by the colonising of the inner mind, the insights of the psycho-analysts: the worth, even the deification of personal perception came to be added to the heady mixture of possibilities. For artists past, present and future were open.

The post-war world added another major ingredient to art. For in the past four decades patterns of cultural subsidy changed as dramatically as television has dramatically come to dominate the mass media.

The seeds for a new shift in attitude towards patronage—in state money supporting artists to produce work for the public— may perhaps be seen in President Roosevelt's New Deal of the 1930s. But now there are no murals on the quality of life and national aspirations. Patriotism is suspect, and in a mass society individuality is praised.

The Arts Council of Great Britain officially began after the last war, nurtured into being by the immense exhilarating war-time success of the Council for the Encouragement of Music and the Arts. In the United States, the tax system has favoured private philanthropy. It is the families of oil and steel, the Rockefellers and the Mellons for example, who have meta-phorically fuelled the institutions which preserve art for the gaze of the public. There has been public expenditure in America also: the National Endowment for the Arts—federal funding was founded in the 1960s. And with the new emphasis on the adjectives regional and ethnic in the funding of culture in Western societies, there has been an immensely wide proliferation of arts bodies and of labels for art activities. Tourism has played a significant part. In San Francisco, local hotel taxes support the opera. In Eastern Europe, the emphasis on the preservation of the distant past is complemented by the support of living artists, even though their possibilities of artistic expression may be severely restricted. In Western Germany there has been a double explosion in the visual arts: the rich industrialists have bought and bought and bought, donating and lending to public institutions. And the cities, once capital cities and now provincial capitals, are rivals. Dusseldorf for example has produced an illustrated book, a kind of Who's Who, simply called *Dusseldorf— City of Artists*, in which each artist—some avant-garde by almost any standards—is given a little spread, a page or two.

Artistic freedom, and an abundance of funding methods if not funds, have thus combined together to produce a curious phenomenon which has come more and more into prominence in the 1970s, perhaps especially in the visual arts: that is, to put it simply, patronage by institution, curator and committee. It has enormous variations from country to country. France has a Ministry of Culture, and has further centralised activity by the opening of the controversial (and hysterically popular with the visiting public) Centre Pompidou, known as the Beaubourg, in Paris in early 1977. American museum officials often feel, in contrast to Europeans, that their main role is that of fund-raiser from corporate and private donors. In Britain there is even talk— and some action—of educating art students in the methods and manners of the real world. In February 1979 there was a seminar called "Life After Art School", at the Institute of Contemporary Art (itself privately funded in the 1950s, now a massive public institution subsidised by the Arts Council) at the time of the New Contemporaries exhibition, a show drawn from student work all over Britain. The seminar, nick-named Is There Life After Art School? was addressed by dealers and by representatives of funding organisations. For artists now have to know how to approach commercial galleries, and how to write out grant applications.

The enormous and unprecedented growth of educational institutions is yet another source of support. There are artists in residence in colleges and universities. In Britain nearly fifty institutions offer undergraduates tuition in the fine arts. In so far as quantification is possible, there are more artists than ever before. And there are more artists doing their own thing.

The Gulbenkian Enquiry in the Visual Arts, begun in 1977, is billed as a "survey of artists, arts patronage, art publics, and art institutions in England, Scotland, and Wales". Among many problems, the committee discovered the difficulty of defining just what is an artist. In the course of their work in various parts of Britain they developed methods of evolving provisional lists of "likely professional artists". For this definition, public institutions are invaluable: commercial and subsidised art galleries, associations of artists, grant-giving bodies and associations, educational establishments, all help to define the artist.

What this means, almost universally, is that culture is increasingly assumed to fall within the province of official institutions. East and West Europe have long been accustomed to the State Theatre and State Opera House. Now state support is more and more important for the visual arts, whether by direct subvention, by tax concessions, or by the special status of educational institutions. The process has long been at work: but now in the 1970s we can see developing a particular kind of biography for the artist.

His credentials would be as follows: education in an art academy; probably some teaching experience; exposure in group and single exhibitions; a mixture of public and private support; fellowships and residencies; donation of his work by private supporters to some public institutions (especially in America and West Germany); and entry by purchase of his work into major public collections, and possibly official commissions. All this would be accompanied by a growing bibliography—mentions and articles in newspapers, art magazines—and eventually the most recognised accolade of all, the final imprimatur: the museum catalogue or the monograph.

These methods of support do two things at once, in my view. To a degree, they separate the artist from the general public by having such well developed methods of middle-man support— even the mediation of the critic, notably well developed in America, and the mediation of the art administrator or curator. Simultaneously, larger numbers of artists are existing and surviving—whether they flourish well or ill—than ever before. There is thus an artist-explosion: but at the same time each artist is paradoxically more on his own in finding ways to reach a public. In a world dominated by mass media and advertising, combined with the increasing role of subsidy, popularity is felt to be the measure of success. The elite, and elitism, are now words often used pejoratively. The appeal of "advanced" art to just a few was not called into question in quite the same way in the 1920s and 1930s as it is today. Even the revolutionary artists of Russia felt—before they were crushed by the State—that their role was to lead and persuade rather than acquiesce to the demands of the masses. Their task was to identify the real needs.

But in the 1970s, the most pessimistic of observers might

suggest that freedom has become a straitjacket, and that there is a search for the new for its own sake. And there is even more Art into Art. The extension of the possibilities for education and for travel, the expansion of museums, and the ubiquity of the mass media mean not only the growth of such concepts as Malraux's Museum without Walls, but a hitherto unimaginable expansion

of the global reference library of visual imagery. Picasso and Matisse may quote African sculpture and a myriad of European paintings. Younger generations quote not only the heroes of Modernism, the art of the past, but any source they choose to fancy. Francis Bacon quotes Velasquez and van Gogh, John Walker quotes Manet, R. B. Kitaj quotes Lorenzetti, and David Hockney quotes Hogarth; these are straight examples of art into art. But any source may be used: popular packaging design, photographs, the cinema.

This explosion in art institutions of all kinds, in education, and in the availability of visual imagery, has been paralleled by a perhaps now wholly unrelated development in art marketing. While thousands of living artists struggle to survive, a few are turned into stars: the brilliance of Andy Warhol at this activity— simply the value of publicity which becomes an art in its own right—is one example. And David Hockney's appearance in his last year at the Royal College of Art—with dyed golden hair and a gold lamé suit—certainly gave an added dimension to the warm desire of the art public to embrace some prodigious talent. We no longer have saints; but there is a hunger for stars, and a lack of heroes. Hence derives, perhaps, the almost fanatical devotion to such dead art-heroes, such rocks of individual dedication and disdain for the world, as Cézanne and van Gogh.

Meanwhile, the art of the past has its own records, promoted in the main by the publicity workers of the auction houses. There is hardly a major newspaper in the West where auctions don't make front page news and regular features. There is even a *Guinness Book of Art Facts and Feats*, which has recently joined the stable led by the *Guinness Book of Records*.

Now all these factors may be thought extrinsic to the work of living artists. But the market has shown that anything can be sold, and that the most extreme gesture can become a saleable commodity.

Some artists have become performers. Unlike earlier performances in the ferment of the arts at the beginnings of modernism, there is a branch of the visual arts so designated: performance art, with its concomitant categories, environments and happenings. No doubt the elaboration of the process by which art reaches its many publics, and the expansion of sheer information that is available about the art of past and present, have contributed to the more extreme positions in which many artists find themselves. Art may now be anything. Art may simply be what someone who calls himself an artist does. The British living sculptors, so-called, the duo Gilbert and George, who enjoyed a vogue at the beginning of the 1970s, do just that: poses and poise are their hallmarks, fragments of their real life their art. A sample: a videotape in which the artists, drinking, chant "Gordon's Makes Us Drunk, Gordon's Makes Us Very Drunk" and so on. The Italian artist Pier Manzoni (1933–63) has been described as a worker in the field of artistic research. The spread of his posthumous reputation accelerated in the 1970s. Among his gestures: the inscribing in public of his own signature on naked women, thereby turning the living flesh into an art work; and the making of a limited edition of tins containing his own excrement, a work known collectively as "Artist's Shit".

At the other end of the scale there is Land Art. In land art an artist creates his work by pushing bits of the real world about. The most seminal real gesture of this kind has perhaps been Robert Smithson's "Spiral Jetty", made in 1970, which is just that: a spiral jetty made of black basalt, limestone rocks and earth, winding 1,500 feet out into the Great Salt Lake, Utah, from a spot on the northeastern shore, some miles from Brigham City. The work is known to the thousands who make up the art world mostly through reproduction, for few have been able to afford the time and the money to journey to see it. Even in reproduction it is exceedingly impressive, the very inaccessibility adding to its interest. Smithson's Spiral Jetty seems in some respects the lineal descendant of the follies that decorated the gentleman's park in the 18th and 19th centuries, except that Spiral Jetty does not seem to have been invented with any thought of social utility (some memorials and follies were actually designed to alleviate unemployment). Smithson's work involved risks; the artist died young in an accident while surveying another area for a land art project. By 1978, Spiral Jetty was submerged by the waters of the Great Salt Lake.

The work of the Bulgarian, now American, sculptor Christo— his covered paths in Kansas City, his wrapped mile of Australian coastline, his Valley Curtain in Rifle Gap, Colorado, and perhaps above all his 24 mile, 18-foot high "Running Fence" in Marin County, California—comprises efforts which do not take place exclusively in wildernesses or in isolation. They are works which involve scores, even hundreds of workers and firms, large and small, who supply materials and technical advice. In several cases Christo even points with pride to firms kept in business because of his commissions. The projects are financed by the sales of Christo's drawings, which act as a kind of share or stock. So far his politically emotive project to wrap up the Reichstag in Berlin is still on the drawing board, but has entered political debate in that divided city. Another factor of course is that Christo's mammoth projects are not permanent. Each has a limited life, defined beforehand. Running Fence was years in the planning, weeks in the making, and had a fortnight's "life" in the early autumn of 1976. What remains—the marketable commodity if you like—are the artist's drawings, and a corpus of earlier portable wrapped works.

So on the one hand there is a very grand, ambitious involvement with "nature", even though that involvement may only leave traces and soon be overwhelmed by a cloak of invisibility. Parallel to this is a kind of eco-art, the artist who puts on a white coat to signify his involvement with nature. The theme of the 1978 Venice Biennale was Nature into Art, Art into Nature. While this portmanteau title included grand and eye-opening works, it was a little difficult to feel wholly convinced by a Dutchman sitting in a teepee and smoking fish in the name of art, a live bull seduced by a fake cow in the name of art, or the Israeli sculptor tending his live sheep in the Israeli pavilion, at least for the duration of the private and press views. The artist attempts to take on the trappings of the worker. He may indeed feel himself to be a manual worker. And he wishes to be part of the sophisticated back-to-nature movement in which the richer societies on this planet are now indulging.

At the same time, a kind of roughness is apparent in much art work, a deliberate rusticity. The Welsh sculptor David Nash is at present employed, not as a Town Artist, but as a Forest Artist; that is, an artist in residence with the British Forestry Commission. His own work is much involved with structures made of wood, and he has even used live trees to make living sculptures that the visitor might come across in a woodland clearing or rough field. Although there is a centuries-old tradition of landscape architecture—which is certainly a kind of living sculpture, a sculpture-in-time—the idea of a "fine" artist using organic and changing materials in this way is unusual, although there are certainly a number of other significant examples. In the 1960s sculptors often used brilliantly coloured plastics and industrial oddments. Now there seems more of a passion for scrap, debris, and "natural" materials, found materials, stone and wood.

Some artists have put on those white coats with a vengeance, and borrowed some of the trappings from the social and natural scientists, investigating societies with techniques borrowed and adapted from other disciplines.

Equally the "less is more" movement is gathering pace. Minimalism is hardly played out. Such painters as the British artist Bob Law and the American Robert Ryman continue in the late 1970s to explore an art which depends on the most subtle of retinal stimuli. Seemingly monochrome paintings turn out to be rich in hue and tone, as a slow and concentrated look reveals. In my view, the continued emphases on certain kinds of reductive art are a continuing and valid reaction to a world in which we are all saturated with visual information.

Where is it all at? In performance art, in video art, in the art of high technology and new techniques, or in the art of subject matter and new imagery? Amidst all the discussion and debate, the changing patterns of subsidy and patronage, and the hunger for culture, several characteristics of the "fine" arts of the Western, industrialised society of the 1970s emerge. Vitality of a sort infuses the mass arts, those that survive by audience approval. In visual terms the most telling and pervasive images are to be found in films, television, advertising and journalism. Photographs and film have been so all pervasive that their imagery has fed back into the fine arts: meanwhile advertising itself takes off from the fine arts.

In the areas of painting and sculpture and the off-shoots of these disciplines and media, we find artists who work traditionally. We live in a pluralist society, and juggle many values at once. Thus there is no officially accepted art or style, but a succession of styles which rapidly follow one another in intellectual or establishment favour, sometimes meeting themselves as they turn the corner.

Recently in the late 1970s, the intellectual interest has latched on to figurative, representational painting. Dazed with the new, people want certainty, not only form but recognisable content.

If we are to be cynical we can say that in the visual arts it is a time of apathy. If we want to be optimistic, we can say that it is a time for consolidation, in which the race for the new has for a moment paused. The traditional, even traditional modernism, revitalises itself. The hand-done painting is coming back, the hand-done painting based on observation of the real world: and that world is intimate, domestic, emotional and personal. It is a time of introspection, a time when artists—like others—are trying to shut out the din of the insistent, noisy, chaotic and uncertain reality in which we live.

MODERN MUSIC
HUGO COLE

T HE great majority of knowledgeable music-lovers have little will to come to terms with contemporary music, and can give plausible excuses for staying away from every sort of modern-music concert. Intellectual music is "too difficult" and "too abstruse" and makes them feel excluded from the game. The music is written ostensibly for their benefit; but they stay on the side-lines like children watching their fathers playing with the trains off the Christmas tree. Middle-of-the-road contemporary music is "too safe"; why listen to Robert Simpson when you might be listening to Sibelius or Nielsen, to Walton instead of Elgar, or Copland instead of Stravinsky? (These questions are, of course, only veiled excuses; there are plenty of good reasons for listening to all three.) Avant-garde music "plays for effect"; makes absurd noises and uses instruments in ways which affront their natures; is "pretentious" or "in doubtful taste". And so, the listener frees himself of his obligations to contemporary music.

It is tragic that contemporary music still wears such a fearful face for so many intelligent listeners; particularly when so much excellent music has been brought into the world in the last fifty years which would, given sympathetic performance and under-standing audiences, enrich many lives. We may have no great composers today; but we have numbers of resourceful and inventive craftsmen, many minor poets and some sound-engineers of formidable powers. It is an absurd position that, with so much talk of order and logic, unity and inevitability, in music, we cannot bring order and logic into our own musical interrelationships or promote the most important unity of all—that binding link between composer and listener, without which the act of composition becomes mere self-indulgence. But the gap grows no smaller. Audiences have not yet come to terms with Schoenberg's music, which is as simple compared to Elliott Carter's as Mozart's is compared to Schoenberg's. To suppose that *one day* audiences will come to appreciate Carter, Boulez or Babbitt as if by magic is as absurd as to suppose that a widening trade gap will suddenly vanish if we look the other way.

From
The Changing Face of Music

MANNERISMS TO IMPRESS

MICHAEL SCHAFFER

WHEN horses want to show off, they curve their neck in order to appear more powerful and bring their head down to their chest. The ears are pointed towards the object that has to be impressed, the nostrils are partly opened and the tail is carried well. Equidae impress or show off only at the trot and I believe that the trot was developed for this purpose. With the exception of the Trotter, which has been selectively bred for this particular gait, free-running horses usually move at the walk or canter. Of course, such free horses do break into a trot before setting off at the canter or gallop, but it is only a transitionary movement to help them obtain sufficient impetus and has nothing to do with showing off. The high showy trot, which even very young foals can do, although normally they can canter from a stand, extends from dancing on the line whilst being led in hand—the favourite gait of stallions in front of a mare—to the piaffe, a high-stepping trot on the spot, the cadence and the action depending upon the type of horse.

When horses are prevented from moving forward by some kind of obstacle, they are often obliged to do the piaffe in order to impress their contemporaries. The half pass, a traversale, is also a very impressive movement and horses will freely execute this movement at the trot without a rider. Mares show off to the same degree as stallions, but I think they are less inclined to do the piaffe. Perhaps their behaviour derives from the masculine repertoire, since autocratic high-ranking mares sometimes show off with the same effective behaviour mannerisms as stallions do.

If horses want to reach their objective quickly, they may forget to show off and the trot turns into a strong or "butcher boy" trot. This gait is not the high action of the passage, but is a long, stretched action of all four legs and feet, and, since the horse is not collected, he usually pokes his nose out and this "impressive" action seems to be common to most wild asses and members of the *equus hemionus* species.

Earlier in this text I wrote of making an exception of Trotters since they are selectively bred to trot, but that they too have inherited the natural tendency to show off at the trot can be seen by the following incident in my own stable. One of my Trotter colt foals had to manage without a playmate for the first year of his life, because of which he always walked or cantered, although his parents were extremely good Trotters and his mother rarely cantered in the paddock. We decided that he had been alone too long and turned out another colt of the same age, and it was then that my belief that the trot was originally a movement designed purely to impress was again absolutely confirmed. The home-bred yearling immediately tried to impress his rival by arching his neck and, fully collected, he broke into a high cadenced trot. It is interesting to note that he retained this gait from then on as an alternative to the walk and canter.

Snaking the head is another movement aimed to impress and indicates resentment or animosity. It is a different movement to the one used to shake off flies, when the nose is perpendicular. When "snaking", horses are in various stages of collection turning slowly in circles and figures of eight. Such action does not necessarily indicate that the horse will attack, but it does mean that he has surplus aggression and it is, therefore, generally noticed in vicious animals of either sex which are separated from their companions and want to reach them or which do not like the people in their vicinity.

From
The Language of the Horse

VET IN A SPIN

JAMES HERRIOT

THIS was a very different uniform. The wellingtons and breeches of my country vet days seemed far away as I climbed into the baggy flying suit and pulled on the sheepskin boots and the gloves—the silk ones first then the big clumsy pair on top. It was all new but I had a feeling of pride.

Leather helmet and goggles next, then I fastened on my parachute, passing the straps over my shoulders and between my legs and buckling them against my chest before shuffling out of the flight hut on to the long stretch of sunlit grass.

Flying Officer Woodham was waiting for me there. He was to be my instructor and he glanced at me apprehensively as though he didn't relish the prospect. With his dark boyish good looks he resembled all the pictures I had seen of Battle of Britain pilots and in fact, like all our instructors, he had been through this crisis in our history. They had been sent here as a kind of holiday after their tremendous experience but it was said that they regarded their operations against the enemy as a picnic compared with this. They had faced the might of the Luftwaffe without flinching but we terrified them.

As we walked over the grass I could see one of my friends coming in to land. The little biplane slewed and weaved crazily in the sky. It just missed a clump of trees, then about fifty feet from the ground it dropped like a stone, bounced high on its wheels, bounced twice again then zig-zagged to a halt. The helmeted head in the rear cockpit jerked and nodded as though it were making some pointed remarks to the head in front. Flying Officer Woodham's face was expressionless but I knew what he was thinking. It was his turn next.

The Tiger Moth looked very small and alone on the wide stretch of green. I climbed up and strapped myself into the cockpit while my instructor got in behind me. He went through the drill which I would soon know by heart like a piece of poetry. A fitter gave the propeller a few turns for priming. Then "Contact!", the fitter swung the prop, the engine roared, the chocks were pulled away from the wheels and we were away, bumping over the grass, then suddenly and miraculously lifting and soaring high over the straggle of huts into the summer sky with the patchwork of the soft countryside of southern England unfolding beneath us.

I felt a sudden elation, not just because I liked the sensation but because I had waited so long for this moment. The months of drilling and marching and studying navigation had been leading up to the time when I would take to the air and now it had arrived.

FO Woodham's voice came over the intercom. "Now you've got her. Take the stick and hold her steady. Watch the artificial horizon and keep it level. See that cloud ahead? Line yourself up with it and keep your nose on it."

I gripped the joystick in my gauntleted hand. This was lovely. And easy, too. They had told me flying would be a simple matter and they had been right. It was child's play. Cruising along I glanced down at the grandstand of Ascot racecourse far below.

I was just beginning to smile happily when a voice crashed in my ear, "Relax, for God's sake! What the hell are you playing at?"

I couldn't understand him. I felt perfectly relaxed and I thought I was doing fine, but in the mirror I could see my instructor's eyes glaring through his goggles.

"No, no, no! That's no bloody good! Relax, can't you hear me, relax!"

"Yes, sir," I quavered and immediately began to stiffen up. I couldn't imagine what was troubling the man but as I began to stare with increasing desperation, now at the artificial horizon, then at the nose of the aircraft against the cloud ahead, the noises over the intercom became increasingly apoplectic.

I didn't seem to have a single problem, yet all I could hear were curses and groans and on one occasion the voice rose to a scream. "Get your bloody finger out, will you!"

I stopped enjoying myself and a faint misery welled in me. And as always when that happened I began to think of Helen and the happier life I had left behind. In the open cockpit the wind thundered in my ears, lending vivid life to the picture forming in my mind.

The wind was thundering here, too, but it was against the window of our bedsitter. It was early November and a golden autumn had changed with brutal suddenness to arctic cold. For two weeks an icy rain had swept the grey towns and villages which huddled in the folds of the Yorkshire Dales, turning the fields into shallow lakes and the farmyards into squelching mud-holes.

Everyone had colds. Some said it was flu, but whatever it was it decimated the population. Half of Darrowby seemed to be in bed and the other half sneezing at each other.

I myself was on a knife edge, crouching over the fire, sucking an antiseptic lozenge and wincing every time I had to swallow. My throat felt raw and there was an ominous tickling at the back of my nose. I shivered as the rain hurled a drumming cascade of water against the glass. I was all alone in the practice. Siegfried had gone away for a few days and I just daren't catch cold.

It all depended on tonight. If only I could stay indoors and then have a good sleep I could throw this off, but as I glanced over at the phone on the bedside table it looked like a crouching beast ready to spring.

Helen was sitting on the other side of the fire, knitting. She didn't have a cold—she never did. And even in those early days of our marriage I couldn't help feeling it was a little unfair. Even now, thirty-five years later, things are just the same and, as I go around sniffling, I still feel tight-lipped at her obstinate refusal to join me.

I pulled my chair closer to the blaze. There was always a lot of night work in our kind of practice but maybe I would be lucky. It was eight o'clock with never a cheep, and perhaps fate had decreed that I would not be hauled out into that sodden darkness in my weakened state.

Helen came to the end of a row and held up her knitting. It was a sweater for me, about half done.

"How does it look, Jim?" she asked.

I smiled. There was something in her gesture that seemed to epitomize our life together. I opened my mouth to tell her it was simply smashing when the phone pealed with a suddenness which made me bite my tongue.

Tremblingly I lifted the receiver while horrid visions of calving heifers floated before me. An hour with my shirt off would just tip me nicely over the brink.

"This is Sowden of Long Pasture," a voice croaked.

"Yes, Mr Sowden?" I gripped the phone tightly. I would know my fate in a moment.

"I've a big calf 'ere. Looks very dowly and gruntin' bad. Will ye come?"

A long breath of relief escaped me. A calf with probable stomach trouble. It could have been a lot worse.

"Right, I'll see you in twenty minutes," I said.

As I turned back to the cosy warmth of the little room the injustice of life smote me.

"I've got to go out, Helen."

"Oh, no."

"Yes, and I have this cold coming on," I whimpered. "And just listen to that rain."

"Yes, you must wrap up well, Jim."

I scowled at her. "That place is ten miles away, and a cheerless dump if ever there was one. There's not a warm corner anywhere." I fingered my aching throat. "A trip out there's just what I need—I'm sure I've got a temperature." I don't know if all veterinary surgeons blame their wives when they get an unwanted call, but heaven help me, I've done it all my life.

Instead of giving me a swift kick in the pants Helen smiled up at me. "I'm really sorry, Jim, but maybe it won't take you long. And you can have a bowl of hot soup when you get back."

I nodded sulkily. Yes, that was something to look forward to. Helen had made some brisket broth that day, rich and meaty, crowded with celery, leeks and carrots and with a flavour to bring a man back from the dead. I kissed her and trailed off into the night.

Long Pasture Farm was in the little hamlet of Dowsett and I had travelled this narrow road many times. It snaked its way high into the wild country and on summer days the bare lonely hills had a serene beauty; treeless and austere, but with a clean wind sweeping over the grassy miles.

But tonight as I peered unhappily through the streaming windscreen the unseen surrounding black bulk pressed close and I could imagine the dripping stone walls climbing high to the summits where the rain drove across the moorland, drenching the heather and bracken, churning the dark mirrors of the bog water into liquid mud.

When I saw Mr Sowden I realized that I was really quite fit. He had obviously been suffering from the prevalent malady for some time, but like most farmers he just had to keep going at his hard ceaseless work. He looked at me from swimming eyes, gave a couple of racking coughs that almost tore him apart and led me into the buildings. He held an oil lamp high as we entered a lofty barn and in the feeble light I discerned various rusting farm implements, a heap of potatoes and another of turnips and in a corner a makeshift pen where my patient stood.

It wasn't the two-week-old baby calf I had half expected, but a little animal of six months, almost stirk age, but not well grown. It had all the signs of a "bad doer"—thin and pot-bellied with its light roan coat hanging in a thick overgrown fringe below its abdomen.

"Allus been a poor calf," Mr Sowden wheezed between coughs. "Never seemed to put on flesh. Rain stopped for a bit this afternoon, so ah let 'im out for a bit of fresh air and now look at 'im."

I climbed into the pen and as I slipped the thermometer into the rectum I studied the little creature. He offered no resistance as I gently pushed him to one side, his head hung down and he gazed apathetically at the floor from deep sunk eyes. Worst of all was the noise he was making. It was more than a grunt—rather a long, painful groan repeated every few seconds.

"It certainly looks like his stomach," I said. "Which field was he in this afternoon?"

"I nobbut let 'im have a walk round t'orchard for a couple of hours."

"I see." I looked at the thermometer. The temperature was sub-normal. "I suppose there's a bit of fruit lying around there."

Mr Sowden went into another paroxysm, then leaned on the boards of the pen to recover his breath. "Aye, there's apples and pears all over t'grass. Had a helluva crop this year."

I put the stethoscope over the rumen and instead of the

normal surge and bubble of the healthy stomach I heard only a deathly silence. I palpated the flank and felt the typical doughy fullness of impaction.

"Well, Mr Sowden, I think he's got a bellyful of fruit and it's brought his digestion to a complete halt. He's in a bad way."

The farmer shrugged. "Well, if 'e's just a bit bunged up, a good dose of linseed oil 'ud shift 'im."

"I'm afraid it's not as simple as that," I said. "This is a serious condition."

"Well, what are we goin' to do about it, then?" He wiped his nose and looked at me morosely.

I hesitated. It was bitterly cold in the old building and already I was feeling shivery and my throat ached. The thought of Helen and the bedsitter and the warm fire was unbearably attractive. But I had seen impactions like this before and tried treating them with purgatives and it didn't work. This animal's temperature was falling to the moribund level and he had a sunken eye—if I didn't do something drastic he would be dead by morning.

"There's only one thing will save him," I said. "And that's a rumenotomy."

"A what?"

"An operation. Open up his first stomach and clear out all the stuff that shouldn't be there."

"Are you sure? D'ye not think a good pint of oil would put 'im right. It 'ud be a lot easier."

It would indeed. For a moment the fireside and Helen glowed like a jewel in a cave, then I glanced at the calf. Scraggy and long-haired, he looked utterly unimportant, infinitely vulnerable and dependent. It would be the easiest thing in the world to leave him groaning in the dark till morning.

"I'm quite sure, Mr Sowden. He's so weak that I think I'll do it under a local anaesthetic, so we'll need some help."

The farmer nodded slowly. "Awright, ah'll go down t'village and get George Hindley." He coughed again, painfully. "But by gaw, ah could do without this tonight. Ah'm sure I've got brown chitis."

Brown chitis was a common malady among the farmers of those days and there was no doubt this poor man was suffering from it but my pang of sympathy faded as he left because he took the lamp with him and the darkness closed tightly on me.

There are all kinds of barns. Some of them are small, cosy and fragrant with hay, but this was a terrible place. I had been in here on sunny afternoons and even then the dank gloom of crumbling walls and rotting beams was like a clammy blanket and all warmth and softness seemed to disappear among the cobwebbed rafters high above. I used to feel that people with starry-eyed notions of farming ought to take a look inside that barn. It was evocative of the grim comfortless other side of the agricultural life.

I had it to myself now, and as I stood there listening to the wind rattling the door on its latch a variety of draughts whistled round me and a remorseless drip-drip from the broken pantiles on the roof sent icy droplets trickling over my head and neck. And as the minutes ticked away I began to hop from foot to foot in a vain effort to keep warm.

Dales farmers are never in a hurry and I hadn't expected a quick return, but after fifteen minutes in the impenetrable blackness bitter thoughts began to assail me. Where the hell was the man? Maybe he and George Hindley were brewing a pot of tea for themselves or perhaps settling down to a quick game of dominoes. My legs were trembling by the time the oil lamp reappeared in the entrance and Mr Sowden ushered his neighbour inside.

"Good evening, George," I said. "How are you?"

"Only moderate, Mr Herriot," the newcomer sniffled. "This bloody caud's just—ah—ah—whooosh—just getting' a haud o' me." He blew lustily into a red handkerchief and gazed at me blearily.

I looked around me. "Well let's get started. We'll need an operating table. Perhaps you could stack up a few straw bales?"

The two men trailed out and returned, carrying a couple of bales apiece. When they were built up they were about the right height but rather wobbly.

"We could do with a board on top." I blew on my freezing fingers and stamped my feet. "Any ideas?"

Mr Sowden rubbed his chin. "Aye, we'll get a door." He shuffled out into the yard with his lamp and I watched him struggling to lift one of the cow byre doors from its hinges. George went to give him a hand and as the two of them pulled and heaved I thought wearily that veterinary operations didn't trouble me all that much but getting ready for them was a killer.

Finally the men staggered back into the barn, laid the door on top of the bales and the theatre was ready.

"Let's get him up," I gasped.

We lifted the unresisting little creature on to the improvised table and stretched him on his right side. Mr Sowden held his head while George took charge of the tail and the rear end.

Quickly I laid out my instruments, removed coat and jacket and rolled up my shirt sleeves. "Damn! We've no hot water. Will you bring some, Mr Sowden?"

I held the head and again waited interminably while the farmer went to the house. This time it was worse without my warm clothing, and cold ate into me as I pictured the farm kitchen and the slow scooping of the water from the side boiler into a bucket, then the unhurried journey back to the buildings.

When Mr Sowden finally reappeared I added antiseptic to the bucket and scrubbed my arms feverishly. Then I clipped the hair on the left side and filled the syringe with local anaesthetic. But as I infiltrated the area I felt my hopes sinking.

"I can hardly see a damn thing." I looked helplessly at the oil lamp balanced on a nearby turnip chopper. "That light's in the wrong place."

Worldessly Mr Sowden left his place and began to tie a length of plough cord to a beam. He threw it over another beam and made it fast before suspending the lamp above the calf. It was a big improvement but it took a long time, and by the time he had finished I had abandoned all hope of ever throwing off my cold. I was frozen right through and a burning sensation had started in my chest. I would soon be in the same state as my helpers. Brown chitis was just round the corner.

Anyway, at least I could start now, and I incised skin, muscles, peritoneum and rumenal wall at record speed. I plunged an arm deep into the opened organ, through the fermenting mass of stomach contents, and in a flash all my troubles dissolved. Along the floor of the rumen apples and pears were spread in layers, some of them bitten but most of them whole and intact. Bovines take most of their food in big swallows and chew it over later at their leisure, but no animal could make cud out of this lot.

I looked up happily. "It's just as I thought. He's full of fruit."

"Hhrraaagh!" replied Mr Sowden. Coughs come in various forms but this one was tremendous and fundamental, starting at the soles of his hob-nailed boots and exploding right in my face. I hadn't realized how vulnerable I was with the farmer leaning over the calf's neck, his head a few inches from mine. "Hhrraaagh!" he repeated, and a second shower of virus-laden moisture struck me. Apparently Mr Sowden either didn't know or didn't care about droplet infection, but with my hands inside my patient there was nothing I could do about it.

Instinctively I turned my face a little in the other direction.

"Whoosh!" went George. It was a sneeze rather than a cough, but it sent a similar deadly spray against my other cheek. I realized there was no escape. I was hopelessly trapped between the two of them.

But as I say, my morale had received a boost. Eagerly I scooped out great handfuls of the offending fruit and within minutes the floor of the barn was littered with Bramley's seedlings and Conference pears.

"Enough here to start a shop," I laughed.

"Hhrraaagh!" responded Mr Sowden.

"Whooosh!" added George, not to be outdone.

When I had sent the last apple and pear rolling into the darkness I scrubbed up again and started to stitch. This is the longest and most wearisome part of a rumenotomy. The excitement of diagnosis and discovery is over and it is a good time for idle chat, funny stories, anything to pass the time.

But there in the circle of yellow light with the wind whirling round my feet from the surrounding gloom and occasional icy

trickles of rain running down my back I was singularly short of gossip, and my companions, sunk in their respective miseries, were in no mood for badinage.

I was halfway down the skin sutures when a tickle mounted at the back of my nose and I had to stop and stand upright.

"Ah—ah—ashooo!" I rubbed my forearm along my nose.

"He's startin'," murmured George with mournful satisfaction.

"Aye, 'e's off," agreed Mr Sowden, brightening visibly.

I was not greatly worried. I had long since come to the conclusion that my cause was lost. The long session of freezing in my shirt sleeves would have done it without the incessant germ bombardment from either side. I was resigned to my fate and besides, when I inserted the last stitch and helped the calf down from that table I felt a deep thrill of satisfaction. That horrible groan had vanished and the little animal was looking around him as though he had been away for a while. He wasn't cheerful yet, but I knew his pain had gone and that he would live.

"Bed him up well, Mr Sowden." I started to wash my instruments in the bucket. "And put a couple of sacks round him to keep him warm. I'll call in a fortnight to take out the stitches."

The fortnight seemed to last a long time. My cold, as I had confidently expected, developed into a raging holocaust which settled down into the inevitable brown chitis with an accompanying cough which rivalled Mr Sowden's.

Mr Sowden was never an ebullient man but I expected him to look a little happier when I removed the stitches. Because the calf was bright and lively I had to chase him around his pen to catch him.

Despite the fire in my chest I had that airy feeling of success.

"Well," I said expansively. "He's done very well. He'll make a good bullock some day."

The farmer shrugged gloomily. "Aye, reckon 'e will. But there was no need for all that carry on."

"No need . . .?"

"Naw. Ah've been talkin' to one or two folk about t'job and they all said it was daft to open 'im up like that. Ah should just 'ave given 'im a pint of oil like I said."

"Mr Sowden, I assure you . . ."

"And now ah'll have a big bill to pay." He dug his hands deep into his pockets.

"Believe me, it was worth it."

"Nay, nay, never." He started to walk away, then looked over his shoulder. "It would've been better if you 'adn't come."

I had done three circuits with FO Woodham and on this third one he had kept fairly quiet. Obviously I was doing all right now and I could start enjoying myself again. Flying was lovely.

The voice came over the intercom again. "I'm going to let you land her yourself this time. I've told you how to do it. Right, you've got her."

"I've got her," I replied. He had indeed told me how to do it —again and again—and I was sure I would have no trouble.

As we lost height the tops of the trees appeared, then the grass of the airfield came up to meet us. It was the moment of truth. Carefully I eased the stick back, then at what I thought was the right moment I slammed it back against my stomach. Maybe a bit soon because we bounced a couple of times and that made me forget to seesaw the rudder bar so that we careered from side to side over the turf before coming to a halt.

With the engine stilled I took a deep breath. That was my first landing and it hadn't been bad. In fact I had got better and better all the time and the conviction was growing in me that my instructor must have been impressed with my initial showing. We climbed out and after walking a few steps in silence FO Woodham halted and turned to me.

"What's your name?" he asked.

Ah yes, here was the proof. He knew I had done well. He was interested in me.

"Herriot, sir," I replied smartly.

For a few moments he gave me a level stare. "Well, Herriot," he murmured, "that was bloody awful."

He turned and left me. I gazed down at my feet in their big sheepskin boots. Yes, the uniform was different, but things hadn't changed all that much.

From
Vet in a Spin

The Black Cat's Conversation

Elizabeth Jennings

Do not suppose
Because I keep to the fire,
Am out half the night,
Sleep where I fall,
Eye you with stares
Like your finest marbles,
That I am not conscious
Of your slightest changes
In mood. I never
Miss your temper
Although you attempt
To disguise it. I know

How envious you are
Of my lithe body,
My lack of self-consciousness,
My glossy coat,
My imperious air.
All this is instinct,
Something you've lost
Except when you cower
From the rats I bring in,
Proud of my haul.
I am proud of my pride
And I always win.

ACE HIGH

PETER FLEMING

THIS story begins in Guatemala. To be exact, it begins on the aerodrome outside the capital of Guatemala, and it begins very early in the morning, because in those days—it was about ten years ago—the air mail for Mexico used to take off as soon as it got light.

The mail plane, which is run by an American company, carries passengers. On this particular morning there were eleven of us. We stood meekly in the Customs shed, next door to the hanger, watching our suitcases being weighed by two small, suspicious men in straw hats. There was a heavy Christmas mail going north, and no one was allowed to take more than the minimum weight of luggage.

There was one other Englishman among the passengers, and naturally I noticed him at once. As a matter of fact, he was a very noticeable person. He was tall, and bronzed, and handsome. He had blue eyes and broad shoulders, and he was smoking a pipe. One cheek was furrowed by an intriguing scar. His suitcase was plastered with a galaxy of labels, all very exotic. He was a striking figure.

But striking in a very conventional way. That was the curious thing about him. It may sound far-fetched, but he conformed so aggressively to type that he seemed really rather an oddity. The trouble was that he was so *exactly* like the hero of almost any story in a magazine; he was too good to be true. And on top of it all—

on top of his blue eyes, and his hatchet face, and his clean limbs—
it turned out that his name was Carruthers. That made it harder
than ever to believe that he was a real person, because the heroes
in the magazine stories that I'd read had practically all been
called Carruthers.

You know how difficult it sometimes is to decide whether a
man is genuine or whether he's acting a part—putting it all on?
Well, it was particularly difficult with Carruthers, because if he
was acting he was so awfully well cast that you couldn't see how
much was sham and how much wasn't. I asked him what he'd
been doing in Guatemala, and he said in an off-hand way, Oh,
he'd been up-country, living with the Indians and doing a bit
of exploring. "Amazing people, those Mayan Indians," he said,
and a sort of far-away look came into his eyes which gave you to
understand that he'd probed the innermost secrets of their
civilization.

And where was he going now? Carruthers wasn't sure. Mexico
City for a bit; then probably south again to Yucatan. "I don't
seem to be able to sleep under a roof for long," he said with an
apologetic laugh.

He didn't boast. He wasn't a bit flamboyant. He got all his
effects by understatement; it was the things he left unsaid that
were meant to impress you. I say "meant to" because I made up
my mind almost at once that Carruthers was a fraud. I couldn't
help feeling that perhaps I was being unfair to him—that it was
wrong to condemn a large, laconic man simply because he
approximated so nearly to the strong silent heroes of fiction.
Everybody, after all, is acting a part most of the time, and it
seemed a little hard that Carruthers should forfeit one's confidence simply because his part was rather more dramatic and
conspicuous than most.

Still, there it was. I put down Carruthers as a sham. In the
course of the next twenty-four hours I changed my mind about
him twice.

Flying as a passenger in a big plane usually seems to me rather
dull. The world is reduced to a large, accurate relief map and its
inhabitants to small and uninteresting specks. But the flight
from Guatemala up to Mexico is far from boring. Most of the
way you skirt a big range of mountains. A lot of them are
volcanoes, with dense jungle climbing up their shoulders and
clouds of smoke oozing out of the peaks. You go quite close to

them, and far away on your left you can see the blue Pacific. As we roared through the sunlit air I felt very cheerful and mellow and decided that Carruthers ought to be given the benefit of the doubt.

An hour after we had started we were circling down to the landing field on the Mexican border. "Field" was a courtesy title. There was nothing but a dun rectangle of baked earth cut out of the heart of the jungle.

It's always a queer feeling when you land, and the engines are stopped. The silence is as sudden and as startling in its effect as a blow in the face. But this time there was something besides the silence which made the atmosphere seem odd. You couldn't have defined it, except in the light of what happened afterwards; you couldn't have said that there was disaster in the air. But I knew, and everybody knew, that there was something wrong.

Nobody had come out to meet us. The Customs shed, where our luggage had to be examined, stood at the far end of the clearing. Above it the red, white and green flag of Mexico flapped listlessly. There were no signs of life at all.

Carruthers and I and the two pilots began to walk towards the shed; it seemed suddenly a long way away. It was very hot.

The shed was empty. But next door there was a hut where the four men in charge of the frontier post lived. They were two soldiers and two Customs officials. When we went into the hut we found out what had happened. Indians had poisoned the water-tank. One soldier was dead; the two officials were delirious. The other soldier explained the situation in the intervals of being sick.

It was of course a terrible thing, but at first I couldn't understand why the pilots seemed to be taking it so much to heart. There was an American doctor on board—a fat, cheerful little man from Louisiana—and while he and I and Carruthers did what we could for the sick men, the pilots conferred together in low voices. I remember wondering what they were so upset about.

Ten minutes later I knew. All the passengers were summoned into the Customs shed. We stood round a long wooden table, most of us looking flustered and faintly horrified. Everyone had an uneasy feeling that the Indians who had done the poisoning were watching us from the edge of the clearing. In a slow apologetic voice the senior pilot explained the situation.

The first thing he said was that one of us had got to stay behind.
It was like this. The plane was carrying full weight already—

"maybe a bit over", the pilot confessed, glancing rather guiltily at a young honeymoon couple from Guatemala City who had cajoled him into taking an extra suitcase. Now we had three sick men on our hands, in urgent need of attention. By dumping all the passengers' luggage—the mails of course were sacrosanct—we should just be able to squeeze two of them in. There was only one way to make room for the third, and that was to leave one of the passengers behind.

The pilot said it wouldn't be more than ten hours, or say eleven at the outside, before they could send back a relief plane from Vera Cruz; it was bound to arrive before dusk. And he pointed out in a reassuring way that there was really hardly any danger from the Indians. They were a lot of quitters, anyhow, and seeing that there was no loot here it was a hundred to one that whoever stayed behind would be perfectly safe.

But he didn't sound very convinced of this himself, and while he was talking most of us cast furtive glances through the door behind him at the jungle on the other side of the clearing. That non-committal wall of trees had somehow acquired a very sinister air. Inside the shed there was a feeling of embarrassment: everyone was expecting a call for volunteers. Only Carruthers seemed to be entirely unmoved. His hand, as he held a match to his pipe, was almost ostentatiously steady; but I noticed that the pipe was lit already.

Meanwhile the second pilot had been sent back to the plane. Now he reappeared. He had a pack of cards in his hand. He asked us if we minded cutting for who stayed, because it seemed the fairest way. No one objected.

"O.K.," said the pilot. "Ace high, high stays. And the ladies aren't in on this."

Then he began to deal.

I remember the next two minutes very vividly. The casual, familiar patter of the cards on the wooden table: the scrabbling of a rat or a lizard in the thatch above our heads: an irritating, peevish whimper which came incessantly from one of the sick men: the heat shimmering on the baked earth outside. . . .

We got one card each. Nobody spoke. The squinting coffee-planter from Costa Rica, on the dealer's right, looked at his and was visibly relieved. The dapper Jew from God knows where looked at his and let his face show nothing. The nice little doctor seemed dubious, but beamed reassuringly at his wife. The two sinister Mexicans were respectively inscrutable and overjoyed.

The bald politician from Guatemala couldn't bring himself to pick up his card; he crossed himself over and over again, staring at the card as though he had been hypnotised by the baleful but well-developed lady whose bust was depicted on its back.

It was my turn now. A card slid across the table towards me. I felt as if I was going to be sick; it was a nasty moment. But I picked it up and it was a very low one—the six of Clubs—and the world became all of a sudden a much pleasanter place.

After me there were only the honeymoon couple and Carruthers, who was next to the dealer.

The little husband had his arm round the girl. He picked up his card with his free hand and showed it to her. Carruthers could see it too. He bit his lip. The girl began to cry, more or less silently. The husband seemed to be praying.

A card went to Carruthers—the last card. He looked at it, I noticed, without the least curiosity. Then he squared his shoulders and, catching my eye, smiled in a rather lofty and abstracted way. I wondered what he was up to.

We threw down our cards in the order they had been dealt in. They were mostly low—a three—an eight—another eight—a four —the more obviously unattractive of the Mexicans had the Knave of Clubs; everyone looked pleased, and he went rather green in the face.

But his luck was in. Without a word the poor little man on my right put down the King of Hearts and began to mop up his wife's tears with the end of a cheap fur she had round her neck. The fur tickled her nose and she sneezed. It was very pathetic.

Then, suddenly, Carruthers' clear, pleasant voice broke in on that emotional scene. "Wait a bit," he said. "I've got the Ace of Spades. I'm for it."

But he did not throw the card down and, as he put it in his pocket, he favoured me with what I can only describe as an otherworldly wink.

The engines roared and a great catharine wheel of dust flew up. We said good-bye to Carruthers. It was really a very moving scene. Only the honeymoon couple believed that he had actually drawn the ace, and of the rest of us only the Jew showed more of scorn than of admiration. The doctor's wife tried to insist on a re-deal; Carruthers wasn't to think, she said, that we didn't all appreciate how quixotic and chivalrous he had been; but she felt sure that one of those dagoes would draw the high card on a re-deal. Her husband, however, interrupted her; perhaps he had less faith than she in the race prejudice with which she credited the Gods of Chance. But he said that he was certainly proud to have met a man of Mr. Carruthers' calibre.

I waited till the others had gone on board. I felt bad about the whole thing. It was unpardonable of me to have thought of Carruthers as I had done. He had, actually, done the Big Thing, with capital letters; and I had disparaged him for looking like the sort of man who would. I felt a worm.

Was there anything I could do, in case anything—er—happened to him? Any messages, or anything?

Carruthers said No. There wasn't anybody much, he said, who —well, who cared about him. He looked excessively wistful as he said this, and once more I had that horrible, that unworthy feeling that he was acting a part.

I said, in a lame sort of way, that I was awfully sorry about the whole show.

"No need to be sorry," said Carruthers in a very manly voice. "It's just my luck. I never had any, at cards."

Then I told him impulsively that he oughtn't to have said that he had an ace when he hadn't.

"Oughtn't I?" said Carruthers, very gently.

I felt more of a worm than ever.

At dusk on the same day I landed for the second time in that clearing. The relief plane was full of Mexican soldiers from Vera Cruz. I had got a seat in it by saying that I was Carruthers' brother-in-law; the ties of family command a lot of respect in Latin America.

For the second time nobody came out to meet us. The lieutenant in charge lent me a revolver and we closed in on the shed in extended formation.

The Indians had been and gone. Carruthers was dead with two bullets in his body. They had cut off his head and taken it away with them, and also, judging by the blood, some dead and wounded of their own.

We·slept in the shed that night, and buried Carruthers before sunrise, on account of the flies. The grave was short as well as shallow. Poor Carruthers! They fired a ragged volley over him, partly out of respect for the dead, and partly to scare away Indians.

As we walked back to the shed for coffee the lieutenant said,

"He was a very valiant man, your brother-in-law". I agreed. The lieutenant was a nice little man, with large unmartial eyes like a deer's. Rather shyly he handed me a packet. It contained what they had found in Carruthers' pockets. Did I think there was anything missing?

I thanked him, and opened the packet. There wasn't much in it. An empty pocket-book, with the lining torn out. A snapshot of Carruthers, very upright on a horse. . . . Some keys and a handkerchief. His pipe. Two bills—one from London, one from an hotel in Guatemala City. And last of all a playing card. . . .

The lieutenant was saying something, but I do not remember what it was. The card was the Ace of Spades.

THE LITTLE WILLOW

FRANCES TOWERS

THE first evening, Simon Byrne was brought to the house by a friend of Charlotte's, one of those with whom she would have to settle an account after the war—unless, of course, he didn't come back. The stranger stood on the threshold and took in the room, and a look of such extraordinary delight came over his face that the youngest Miss Avery's heart gave a little leap, almost as if, independently of her mind and will, it greeted of its own accord another of its kind.

It was, of course, a peculiarly gracious room, with its high ceiling and Adam chimney piece. The shiny white walls were painted with light and dim reflections of colours, and a thick black hearthrug smudged with curly pink roses—an incongruous Balkan peasant rug in that chaste room—somehow struck a note of innocence and gaiety, like the scherzo in a symphony. That rug, and the photographs on the lid of the grand piano; the untidy stack of books on a table; and a smoky pseudo old master over the fireplace, with the lily of the Annunciation as a highlight, a pale question mark in the gloom, gave the room an oddly dramatic quality. Lisby had often thought—"It is like a room on the stage, in which the story of three sisters is about to unfold."

The passing reflections of Charlotte in red, Brenda in green made a faint shimmer on the walls as they drifted about, as if a herbaceous border were reflected momentarily in water.

"Charlotte dear, I've brought a friend. He was at Tobruk. Comes from South Africa, and doesn't know a soul over here," said Stephen Elyot. "He's just out of hospital."

"I am so glad!" said Charlotte glowingly, giving him both her hands. "You must come as often as you like."

His eyes dwelt on her dark, lovely face, and he said, "You don't know what it feels like to be in a drawing-room again."

"I can very well imagine. It must feel like the peace of God," said Brenda, in that soft, plangent voice of hers, which was so perfect an instrument for the inspired remarks that seemed to fall effortlessly from her lips.

She could say the most divinely right things without a throb of real sympathy, and would spend pounds on roses rather than write a letter of condolence. As for her 'cello playing, it was strange how deeply she could move one, while she herself remained quite aloof. It was because she knew what the music was meant to say and was thinking about the music all the time, and not of how she played or how she felt. It was a great charm in her.

Lisby said nothing. She had no poetic conception of herself to impose on the minds of others. However, she had her uses. She cut the sandwiches and made the coffee and threw herself into the breach when some unassuming guest seemed in danger of being neglected. And unassuming guests often were. Charlotte and Brenda had such brilliant friends—musicians and artists and writers. The truest thing about those girls was that they were charmers. Every other fact sank into insignificance beside that one supreme quality. Though each had her own strongly marked individuality, they had this in common: that by lamplight they acquired, in their trailing dresses, a timeless look, as if they might have stood for types of the seductive woman in any age. Not a modern girl; but the delicate creature who through the ages has been man's rose of beauty, or his cup of hemlock.

Always, destroying friendship, there was this allure—the glow, the fragrance, the what-you-will, which, sooner or later, ensnared every young man and made him the captive of one or the other of the two elder Misses Avery.

"Charlotte dear," said Stephen Elyot, wandering about the room with his coffee cup in his hand, "I wonder, with your exquisite taste, you let that picture hang there! It's all *wrong*, my dear, as I've told you before. A Watteau, now, or a Fragonard, for this eighteenth-century room. And yet your *décors* for the stage are so perfect! You are *quite* my favourite designer."

"Lisby would die if we banished the picture. It's been in the family for generations," said Charlotte.

"It has been loved by people who are dead, for its . . . holiness, not for aesthetic reasons; and that makes it spiritually precious," Simon Byrne said in a low voice to Lisby, by whom he chanced to be sitting.

She gave a little start. The thick white paint of the lily, and its golden tongue, had fascinated her as a child, making all lilies seem not quite earthly flowers. How did he know so quickly that the dark picture in the white room brought spiritual values into it, brought her mother saying, "Yes, darling; perhaps the angel has a queer face—perhaps he *is* a little bit like Miss Nettleton. How interesting that someone we know should have a face that an old master chose for the Angel Gabriel! I shall always think of Miss Nettleton as a very special kind of person."

"It almost seems as if he might be my kind of person," she thought. Perhaps one would have thought his face unremarkable if one had not caught that look on it. "He has known horror and violence, and is terribly vulnerable to beauty," she had said to herself, with one of her flashes of insight.

Brenda played that evening, and Simon Byrne never took his eyes off her. In her long green dress, with her gold hair like an inverted sheaf of corn, she held him spellbound. Or perhaps it was the music.

When she went to bed that night, Lisby caught herself hoping quite desperately that it was, after all, the music; and for such a foolish reason. Because as he was leaving he took her little willow tree in his long thin hands.

"So cool," he said, "and watery. Willows and water—I used to dream of them."

"In the desert?" she asked.

"When I was lost," he said, "and parched with thirst, and terribly frightened."

"It's the loveliest thing I have," she said.

It was made of jade and crystal and it stood on the lacquer cabinet in the hall. She had fallen in love with it in an antique shop and had expended on it, with wild extravagance, her first term's salary as a teacher. Charlotte and Brenda had thought her too utterly feckless—almost wicked. The sun by day and the moon by night made it throw a lovely shadow on the wall. She couldn't explain that what she loved was the *idea* of a willow that had been in the mind of the Chinese artist—the glitter and coolness and bewitchment. But he would know.

He came several times. "Naturally," thought Lisby, "one would like the house, wouldn't one? Its oldness and peace." And Charlotte arranged the flowers so beautifully and there were music and conversation: Brenda and her friends practising their quartets for concerts and Charlotte's friends talking of art. Anyone could come to the Court House as a place in which to forget the war. There was the strangeness of its being so near London and yet completely hidden in a wood, an oasis in the desert of ribbon development that had spread around it in the past few years. Many young men on leave found it a place of refuge.

He was a person one could talk to. The things that made Lisby laugh made him laugh too. Sometimes he would catch her eye and they would go off into a silent fit of laughter at some absurd thing that no one else had remarked. She knew, once or twice, the strange feeling of strings being plucked in her mind by a chance word or gesture of his, and he had a way of humming some tune that had been haunting her, even something she had not heard for a long time: a phrase from a symphony, perhaps, that had suddenly come back to her quite distinctly between sleeping and waking, as if a record had been put on in her mind.

And then, one day, Brenda, in her delicate way, appropriated his friendship. A person versed in Brenda-ish modes of behaviour could guess what she thought. When she said charming things a little frostily, as if offering an ice-chilled gardenia, when she smiled with dazzling sweetness one moment and raised her eyebrows rather coldly the next, one knew what was in her mind. She was dealing with a situation that required delicacy and tact. Love was sacred, even unwanted love. The little flame must not be allowed to go out. So one blew on it prettily one moment, and damped it down the next. For a conflagration meant the end of everything, it meant stamping on the heart in which it burned. And how, in wartime, could one bear to do that?

She said, "You know, Simon is rather an intriguing person. He can say rather divine things—when one is alone with him. Still waters, my dear, run deep."

Yes. He wouldn't wear his heart on his sleeve. But to be the person to whom he said "rather divine things" must be to feel oneself unimaginably exquisite.

There was that night they all went out into the garden when the all clear sounded. The scent of the tobacco plants was so sweet it was like a presence, like a naked nymph following one about, and the moon was so bright that the red roses kept their colour, and the white were luminous like the moths. Standing apart, Lisby was fascinated by his shadow lying clear-cut on the lawn. She stared at it, and then, looking up, saw it printed, gigantic, across the sky. It gave her a queer cold feeling, seeming to confirm an idea she had had of him lately: that everything he was concerned in here and now was the beginning of something that would go on happening outside this sphere. It would always be there, behind her eyelids.

After that, she couldn't go on trying to make up to him for the times that Brenda was too much occupied with someone else to bother about him. It would be a kind of mockery. The only thing was to keep out of his way.

But the last evening of his embarkation leave, when he came to say good-bye, it was she who had to see him to the front door. Brenda was fey that night, with a kind of febrile gaiety, because the favoured lover of the moment was home on forty-eight hours' leave, and she had no eyes for anyone but him; and Charlotte was deeply involved with Richard Harkness. When they said good-bye, they would doubtless be driven into each other's arms. One could see it in their eyes when they looked at each other.

Lisby's eyes fell on the little willow. She seized it and put it into his outstretched hand. "Please take it—for luck," she said.

"But you can't give this away, Miss Avery. It's—it's . . . much too lovely," he stammered.

"Please, please—it's more yours than mine."

"It's terribly kind of you. Your sisters—you've been so kind letting me come. I shall dream of this house."

"But you'll come again," said Lisby, speaking as lightly as she could.

"I'd try to . . . in the spirit, if not in the flesh," he said, with his crooked smile. Why must he say a thing so devastating?

"Look at Orion—like some secret heavenly diagram," said Lisby at the open door, because she had no word of comfort for him. (Oh, dear! He'll think I'm trying to be appealing, trying to be a poetical little puss, trying to get at him, she thought despairingly.) If only Brenda would come out for a moment and be very sweet in that way she had of being responsive to another's mood! She could have given him something to take away with him, some cryptic remark, that he could dwell upon and cherish, as if it were a tiny key she had put into his hand to unlock a door in the future. But she was caught away into a private heaven, and so he had to go without any hope.

He looked up at the heartbreaking glitter of Orion, so serene, so triumphant above the tortured world. "A lover might use it as a code," he said, almost under his breath. "Abelard signing his letters to Héloise."

He looked down at her, hesitating a moment, as if there were something he wanted to say. And then, with a sigh, he turned away. As he looked back at the gate to salute her, the little tree in his hand caught the starlight and shone with a faint blue fire.

He never wrote. Lisby, sorting out the post, sometimes looked wonderingly at a letter addressed to Brenda in a hand-writing she didn't know, but the name on the flap of the envelope was never his.

When the war was over at last, Richard Harkness, liberated from a prison camp in Germany, came back to claim Charlotte. Their wedding was fixed for the autumn.

"By the way, Brenda," Charlotte said casually one day, looking up from a letter she was writing, "I forgot to tell you. Richard says that Simon Byrne was a prisoner in the same Offlag. He died last year."

"Oh, poor darling!" said Brenda, in the sweet, hollow voice she used when the conventions demanded an assumption of sorrow. One's heart had been wrung so often that there had come a time when it recorded merely a mechanical spasm. She went on arranging the flowers with a set expression.

Lisby said nothing. She sat very still in the recesses of the armchair and clasped her knees to still their trembling. "So much death, one cannot bear it," she said at last, and got herself out of the room somehow. She always took things to heart—as if she suffered in her own body the agony of unknown millions.

"It's all very well for Lisby," said Brenda with a shrug. "But, after all, she hasn't had any *personal* loss in this war. Not like you and me. I mean, when someone's killed who's been in love with one, it makes it all so terribly poignant. I sometimes think I've felt so much, I can't feel any more. Those poor lambs!" She sighed and dipped her face into the roses, as if she would leave with them the expression of grief she could now decently abandon. It was almost as though she were leaving them on his grave to symbolise her thoughts of him, that would fade more quickly than they. "He was sweet, but rather dumb," she said.

"Did he ever——" asked Charlotte, looking over her tortoiseshell glasses.

"Not in so many words. You all took it for granted it was me. But perhaps, after all, *you* were the attraction, Charlotte." But the hint of doubt found no expression in the tones of her voice.

"Or Lisby. It really is rather awful the way we leave her out of account."

Charlotte sealed her letter and took off her glasses. She had a face like La Belle Ferronière, on which the glasses had the air of an amusing affectation. But Brenda had the flowerlike delicacy of a Piero della Francesca. Lisby had seen the resemblances and had made her sisters a present of them. But no one had noticed that she herself was like the watching girl who holds a basket on her head in the background of El Greco's *Christ in the Temple*.

"Of course," said Charlotte, affixing a stamp, "it wasn't I. That's a thing I never make a mistake about. A woman always knows."

"Well, I am not so cocksure about love as you seem to be. I mean, I'm inclined to say to myself, '*If* he does so and so, *if* he remembers what hat I wore the day before yesterday, *if* he bothers to look up the address I'm staying at in the telephone book, *then* I shall know for certain.' But I don't remember applying any such tests to Simon. Somehow we never got that far. Though I had my suspicions, of course."

Brenda carried the roses across the room and put them on the piano, in the midst of the numerous photographs, of young men in uniform. Surreptitiously she changed the place of one. He had been shot down over Hamburg, and his place was among the dead. Perhaps no one but herself, who was responsible for it, was aware of this arrangement of the photographs. She had a feeling about the matter of which she would not have spoken for the world. It did not exactly amount to a superstition. Perhaps it meant no more than did the meticulous dividing up of her books into their respective categories. It irritated her to find a novel thrust in between two volumes of poetry. Death, perhaps, was poetry, and life, prose. Or was it the other way round?

In the midst of preparations for the wedding, no one, it seemed, gave another thought to Simon Byrne.

"Lisby seems rather odd these days—sort of strung-up," said Charlotte one day. "Do you think, Brenda, that subconsciously she minds my getting married and your being engaged? I mean, it can't be much fun, poor child, seeing happiness through other people's eyes, as Shakespeare has already remarked." She snapped off a thread and took the pins out of a seam.

Brenda looked down with a preoccupied expression at the ring on her long pale hand, where it lay on a fold of crêpe de Chine she had been sewing. "How incredibly lucky we are that our two have come through alive!" she said. "Gerald doesn't know *how* lucky he is; because it *might* have been John. I don't know, but I *think* it might have been. I was devastated when he was killed. I dare say you are right about Lisby. But what can we do . . .?"

"That cyclamen colour you've chosen for the bridesmaids—of course, you'll look divine in it, but it's trying for Lisby. Heaven knows, she's sallow enough."

"But, my dear, what was I to do? We had the stuff and we've got no coupons. If only Gerald were back, we could have had a double wedding and both got out of Lisby's way. I feel we rather swamp her, you know—like two arc lamps putting out the moonlight. Now, isn't that a tribute to our Lis?"

Charlotte was married on a golden day. While they waited for her in the porch, Lisby thought that Brenda looked more like an Italian primitive than ever, pale and bright as an angel. (But we are all wrong for the blue horizon and the golden leaves—too shrill, too springlike, she thought.) Their reflections stained with pink the dew-drops in a spider's web slung between two tombstones.

A cab drove up to the lich gate, and Charlotte came down the path on the arm of an uncle, her dark eyes shining through her veil. She was so majestic, so withdrawn that they did not venture to speak to her, but spread out her train, whispering nervously together.

Richard Harkness stood at the altar steps. To Lisby he had rather a vulpine look. It argued a certain spirituality in Charlotte, not to be deceived by outward appearances, but to swoop unerringly on the qualities she wanted. But he hadn't been Simon's sort. He had never mentioned Simon's name in Lisby's presence. She was grateful to him for that, but she couldn't forgive him.

She stole a glance apprehensively at the best man. He had been in the camp too—a doctor, they said. He had a dark, ascetic face, sensitive and melancholy. One must keep out of his way.

The wedding reception was like any other: the strained hilarity, the desperate frivolity, lit with a perilous brightness as of unshed tears. Corks popped, the cake was cut, the toasts proposed. Charlotte came out of her trance, and Richard made a speech so charming that all her friends began to think they knew, after all, what she saw in him.

There was Brenda by the window, trying desperately to make conversation with Captain Oliver. When her voice was high and strained like that, one knew she was wilting, and there were those faint mauve shadows under her eyes. The man was difficult. He appeared to have no capacity for small talk.

"By the way, did you come across someone who was a friend of mine—Simon Byrne? He was in the tanks," she said.

Brenda . . . don't . . . Don't! Lisby cried out soundlessly, with a pain like cramp about her heart. His name seemed to sound through the room like a clash of cymbals. She felt that it must pierce every breastbone. It made a stranger of Brenda. It was incomprehensible that she could use it to make conversation, that to her it could be a name like any other.

Lisby saw the start that Captain Oliver gave. He turned quickly and looked at Brenda—a long, searching look.

"Yes, I knew Byrne," he said.

"He was such a dear. We liked him so much. Look, Charlotte has gone up to change. I must fly after her."

They were gone at last. Charlotte leaned out and waved. Someone threw a slipper after the taxicab.

In the throng at the gate, Lisby was aware of Captain Oliver edging his way toward her.

"Miss Avery," he said in her ear, "may I speak to you a moment alone?"

"In the morning room," said Lisby, very pale. For some unfathomable reason she picked up her bouquet from the hall table before preceding him into the little yellow room.

A picture glowing with evening appeared in the frame of the window. In the foreground, the black trunk of the mulberry tree, about which still dangled a few heart-shaped leaves of sour green, and to the right the long silver plumes of the pampas grass, had a strange significance, as if the words "black, gold, silver" were being reiterated in a poem. The blue October mist lay beyond, veiling the lawn, and a little sumac tree burned like a torch at the edge of the mist. A bird that had abandoned music for the winter made a grasshopper sound.

The pampas grass. Charlotte had tried to dig it up—a vulgar interloper, she had said. Lisby clung desperately to her thoughts. She did not want to hear what this man had to say. She sank down on the sofa and began mechanically to take her bouquet to pieces. The colour was drained out of her face, and she looked ghastly in the cyclamen shade that was so becoming to Brenda.

"So you knew Simon Byrne," said Captain Oliver, looking down at her. "I wonder . . . perhaps you could help me, Miss Avery? I was with him when he died."

"Have you, perhaps, a message . . . for my sister?" asked Lisby faintly, arranging little sprigs of heather on her knee.

"That's what I don't know," he said with a sigh. "There is something I'd like to tell someone—but not the wrong person. You see, Simon meant a great deal to me. Could you tell me, did she ever give him a little tree, a willow? I suppose it was one of those Chinese things."

"No," said Lisby, very low, "she never gave him anything."

"I am going to tell *you*," said Captain Oliver, as if making a sudden decision. "A secret would be safe with you, wouldn't it? He was badly hurt, you know. His wound never healed. He was terribly ill all the time; but the odd thing was that through it all, he was never less than himself. They couldn't do anything to Simon. They couldn't strip him of a single one of his qualities. It was as if he had some inward source of happiness, a core of peace in his heart. The camp was short of doctors and they were only too pleased to make use of me, so I was able to make things a little easier for him."

"I am glad," she said, bent over her flowers, "that he had you to look after him."

"The night before he died," went on Captain Oliver, in a low deliberate voice, "he dictated a letter to his mother in South Africa. He was a bit of a poet, you know. It was a very touching letter. I suppose she has it now, poor soul. I said, 'Is there no one else, Simon?' He shook his head. 'There was a girl' he said, 'but she never knew she was my girl,' I asked him to tell me about her, thinking it might comfort him. He said, 'She is a little, quiet creature—like mignonette—and her eyes go light and dark with her thoughts. I knew in my bones she was meant for me. Once, when the pain was very bad, I thought she came and kissed me. I felt her cheek against mine. It was soft and cool—like young buds, as I always imagined it would be. And the pain went away and I went to sleep. You know, Robert, she wouldn't mind my dreaming that. She has such exquisite compassion. When I said good-bye, she gave me the loveliest thing she had—a little willow tree. It was smashed to bits in my kit when the shell got us.' I thought to myself, 'Perhaps she did care, that girl.' He died toward morning, very peacefully, without speaking again."

Lisby sat very still. "So cold . . . so cold," she said, chafing her hands as if the hands of the dying lay between them.

"So *you* were his girl," said Robert Oliver.

"He was my dear, dear love," whispered Lisby. She bowed her head on her knees and wept soundlessly.

He thought, "It is sad for a girl when her first avowal of love has to be made to a third person." And, going softly to the door, he turned the key in the lock and let himself out by the window.

"Lisby cried her eyes out after you left," wrote Brenda to Charlotte. "But at night she looked so radiant, one might have thought it was *her* wedding day. There were dozens of letters for you by the evening post (I've sent them on) and some for me. I sorted them out, and said, as one usually does, 'None for you, I'm afraid, Lisby darling.' She looked at me so strangely, and said, 'I have had mine—one that was never written.' What could she have meant? I said, 'What on earth do you mean?' But I knew from the look on her face that it is one of those things she will never tell."

1 *AUGUST* 1917

HERBERT READ

During the First World War Herbert Read served as an infantry officer at the front in France. He wrote a sequence of letters to a young university friend, which he cast in the form of a diary; and this was first published in 1963. In a letter dated some weeks before the events described below, he wrote: "I've been chosen for a death or glory job soon to come off. I am very glad—glad in the first place because it gives me the first chance I've had of doing something—glad in the second place because it means that others recognize that I'm of the clan that don't care a damn for anything."

WELL, the "stunt" is over, so now I can tell you something about it. I, along with another officer, was detailed to get as many volunteers as we could from our company and, on a certain dark and dirty night, to raid the enemy's trenches, kill as many as possible and bring back at least one prisoner for identification purposes. Out of a possible 60 we got 47 volunteers . . . That was a jolly good start. We had about a fortnight to make our plans and rehearse. This we set about with enthusiasm—everybody was keen. Our plans were made with all the low villainous cunning we were capable of. When the battalion went into the front line we were left behind to train and take things easy. We two officers had to do a good amount of patrolling and observation. We had to discover the weak points in the enemy's wire, the best routes thither and as much of the enemy's habits as we could . . . This went on until the fateful night arrived. Picture us about midnight: our faces were blackened with burnt cork, everything that might rattle was taken off or tied up. We armed ourselves with daggers and bombs and various murderous devices to blow up the enemy's wire and dugouts—and, of course, our rifles or revolvers. The raid was to be a stealth raid and depended for its success on surprise effect. So out thro' our own wire we crept—our hearts thumping but our wills determined. We had 540 yards to traverse to the objective. The first half were simple enough. Then we began to crouch and then to crawl—about a yard a minute. Suddenly, about 150 yards from the German trenches, we saw and heard men approaching us. We were following one another in Indian file. They seemed scattered to the right and left as far as we could see. In a moment all our carefully prepared plans were thrown to the winds. New plans had to be made on the spur of the moment. Our position was tactically very weak. My fellow-officer began to crawl carefully back to reorganize the men into a defensive position, leaving me in front to deal with the situation if necessary. I could now see what was happening. The Huns were coming out to wire (had already started as a matter of fact) and were sending out a strong covering party to protect the wirers from surprise. This party halted and took up a line in shell-holes about twenty yards from us. Then some of them began to come forward to reconnoitre. We lay still, looking as much like clods of earth as we possibly could. Two Boche were getting very near me. I thought we had better surprise them before they saw us. So up I get and run to them pointing my revolver and shouting "Haende hoch." (hands up), followed by my trusty sergeant and others. Perhaps the Boche didn't understand my newly acquired German. At any rate they fired on me—and missed. I replied with my revolver and my sergeant with his gun. One was hit and shrieked out. Then I was on the other fellow who was now properly scared and fell flat in a shell-hole. "Je suis officier!" he cried in French. By this time there was a general fight going on, fire being opened on all sides. In a minute or two the guns were on and for five minutes it was inferno. The real object of the raid was achieved— a prisoner and a valuable one at that had been captured. So I began to make my way back with him whilst the other officer organized covering fire. In another five minutes we were back in our own trenches, and, all things considered, very glad to get there. Our casualties were only one missing and two slightly wounded. We must have inflicted twenty on the enemy, for, besides our rifle fire and bombs, we drove him back into a barrage put up by our trench mortars.

I took the prisoner along to Headquarters. He spoke a little French, so on the way we carried on a broken conversation. He told me his name, age, that he was married and where he came from. When we got to H.Q. there was an officer who spoke German and then the prisoner began to talk twenty to the dozen. We gave him a drink, cigarette, etc. He turned out to be an ex-schoolmaster of some sort and a very intelligent fellow. We got any amount of useful information from him. He was very interesting on things in general. Does not think we shall ever win this war, but neither will they. Says the new man, Michaelis, is a people's man and will gradually democratize the German government. But the Kaiser is still the people's hero and we must not expect the German nation to consent to his dethronement in the terms of peace. He says there is no chance of a revolution in Germany. Did not think much of the French, but was almost enthusiastic in his praise of the English. Said it was a mistaken idea to think the Germans hated the English. That was only an idea propagated by the German militarists and our own Press. We were of the same racial stock—should be allies—not enemies —etc., etc.

He himself won the Iron Cross at Verdun where he took 85 French prisoners.

We had to take him down to Brigade—an hour's walk. It was a beautiful early morning and everything was peaceful and the larks were singing. In our broken French we talked of music. He played both the violin and the piano and we found common enthusiasms in Beethoven and Chopin. He even admired Nietzsche and thenceforth we were sworn friends. He wrote his name and address in my pocket-book and I promised to visit him after the war if I ever came to Germany. By the time I handed him over to the authorities at the Brigade we were sorry to part with each other. And a few hours previously we had done our best to kill each other. *C'est la guerre*—and what a damnable irony of existence . . . at any rate a curious revelation of our common humanity.

I've got a beautiful automatic revolver as a souvenir.

In my next letter I'll answer the futile attack on *Art and Letters* in this week's *New Age*.

8 JUNE 1978

ALEXANDER SOLZHENITSYN

Mr Solzhenitsyn delivered this speech at the annual
commencement ceremony at Harvard University.

I am sincerely happy to be here with you on the occasion of the
327th commencement of this old and illustrious university. My
congratulations and best wishes to all of today's graduates.

Harvard's motto is "Veritas". Many of you have already found
out and others will find out in the course of their lives that truth
eludes us as soon as our concentration begins to flag, all the while
leaving the illusion that we are continuing to pursue it. This is
the source of much discord. Also, the truth seldom is sweet; it is
almost invariably bitter. A measure of bitter truth is included in
my speech today, but I offer it as a friend, not as an adversary.

Three years ago in the United States I said certain things that
were rejected and appeared unacceptable. Today, however, many
people agree with what I then said . . .

A World Split Apart

The split in today's world is perceptible even to a hasty glance.
Any of our contemporaries readily identifies two world powers,
each of them quite capable of utterly destroying the other.
However, the understanding of the split too often is limited to
this political conception: the illusion according to which danger
may be abolished through successful diplomatic negotiations or by
achieving a balance of armed forces. The truth is that the split is
both more profound and more alienating, that the rifts are more
numerous than one can see at first glance. These deep manifold
splits bear the danger of equally manifold disaster for all of us, in
accordance with the ancient truth that a kingdom—in this case,
our Earth—divided against itself cannot stand.

Contemporary Worlds

There is the concept of the Third World: thus, we already have
three worlds. Undoubtedly, however, the number is even greater;
we are just too far away to see. Every ancient and deeply rooted,
self-contained culture, especially if it is spread over a wide part
of the earth's surface, constitutes a self-contained world, full of
riddles and surprises to Western thinking. As a minimum, we

must include in this category China, India, the Muslim world and Africa, if indeed we accept the approximation of viewing the latter two as uniform. For one thousand years Russia belonged to such a category, although Western thinking systematically committed the mistake of denying its special character and therefore never understood it, just as today the West does not understand Russia in Communist captivity. And while it may be that in past years Japan has increasingly become, in effect, a Far West, drawing ever closer to Western ways (I am no judge here), Israel, I think, should not be reckoned as part of the West, if only because of the decisive circumstance that its state system is fundamentally linked to religion.

How short a time ago, relatively, the small world of modern Europe was easily seizing colonies all over the globe, not only without anticipating any real resistance, but usually with contempt for any possible values in the conquered peoples' approach to life. On the face of it, it was an overwhelming success, with no geographic limits. Western society expanded in a triumph of human independence and power. And all of a sudden the twentieth century brought the clear realisation of this society's fragility. We now see that the conquests proved to be shortlived and precarious, and this, in turn, points to defects in the Western view of the world which led to these conquests. Relations with the former colonial world now have switched to the opposite extreme and the Western world often exhibits an excess of obsequiousness, but it is difficult yet to estimate the size of the bill which former colonial countries will present to the West and it is difficult to predict whether the surrender not only of its last colonies, but of everything it owns will be sufficient for the West to clear this account.

Convergence

But the persisting blindness of superiority continues to hold the belief that all the vast regions of our planet should develop and mature to the level of contemporary Western systems, the best in theory and the most attractive in practice; that all those other worlds are but temporarily prevented by wicked leaders or by severe crises or by their own barbarity and incomprehension from pursuing Western pluralistic democracy and adopting the Western way of life. Countries are judged on the merits of their progress in that direction. But in fact such a conception is a fruit of Western incomprehension of the essence of other worlds, a result of mistakenly measuring them all with a Western yardstick. The real picture of our planet's development bears little resemblance to all this.

The anguish of a divided world gave birth to the theory of convergence between the leading Western countries and the Soviet Union. It is a soothing theory which overlooks the fact that these worlds are not at all evolving towards each other and that neither one can be transformed into the other without violence. Besides, convergence inevitably means acceptance of the other side's defects, and this can hardly suit anyone.

If I were today addressing an audience in my country, in my examination of the overall pattern of the world's rifts I would have concentrated on the calamities of the East. But since my forced exile in the West has now lasted four years and since my audience is a Western one, I think it may be of greater interest to concentrate on certain aspects of the contemporary West, such as I see them.

A Decline in Courage

A decline in courage may be the most striking feature which an outside observer notices in the West today. The Western world has lost its civic courage, both as a whole and separately, in each country, in each government, in each political party and, of course, in the United Nations. Such a decline in courage is particularly noticeable among the ruling and intellectual elites, causing an impression of a loss of courage by the entire society. There remain many courageous individuals, but they have no determining influence on public life. Political and intellectual functionaries exhibit this depression, passivity and perplexity in their actions and in their statements, and even more so in their self-serving rationales as to how realistic, reasonable and intellectually and even morally justified it is to base state policies on weakness and cowardice. And the decline in courage, at times attaining what could be termed a lack of manhood, is ironically emphasised by occasional outbursts of boldness and inflexibility on the part of those same functionaries when dealing with weak governments and with countries that lack support, or with doomed currents which clearly cannot offer any resistance. But they get tongue-tied and paralysed when they deal with powerful governments and threatening forces, with aggressors and inter- national terrorists.

Must one point out that from ancient times a decline in

courage has been considered the beginning of the end?

Well-being

When the modern Western states were being formed, it was proclaimed as a principle that governments are meant to serve man and that man lives in order to be free and pursue happiness. (See, for example, the American Declaration of Independence.) Now at last during past decades technical and social progress has permitted the realisation of such aspirations: the welfare state. Every citizen has been granted the desired freedom and material goods in such quantity and of such quality as to guarantee in theory the achievement of happiness, in the debased sense of the word which has come into being during those same decades. (In the process, however, one psychological detail has been overlooked: the constant desire to have still more things and a still better life, and the struggle to this end imprints many Western faces with worry and even depression, though it is customary to carefully conceal such feelings. This active and tense competition comes to dominate all human thought and does not in the least open a way to free spiritual development.) The individual's independence from many types of state pressure has been guaranteed; the majority of the people have been granted well-being to an extent their fathers and grandfathers could not even dream about; it has become possible to raise young people according to these ideals, preparing them for and summoning them towards physical bloom, happiness, possession of material goods, money and leisure, towards an almost unlimited freedom in the choice of pleasures. So who should now renounce all this, why and for the sake of what should one risk one's precious life in defence of the common good, and particularly in the nebulous case when the security of one's nation must be defended in an as yet distant land?

Even biology tells us that a high degree of habitual well-being is not advantageous to a living organism. Today, well-being in the life of Western society has begun to reveal its pernicious mask.

Legalistic Life

Western society has chosen for itself the organisation best suited to its purposes and one I might call legalistic. The limits of human rights and rightness are determined by a system of laws; such limits are very broad. People in the West have acquired considerable skill in using, interpreting and manipulating law (though laws tend to be too complicated for an average person to understand without the help of an expert). Every conflict is solved according to the letter of the law and this is considered to be the ultimate solution. If one is right from a legal point of view, nothing more is required, nobody may mention that one could still not be entirely right, and urge self-restraint or a renunciation of these rights, call for a sacrifice and selfless risk: this would simply sound absurd. Voluntary self-restraint is almost unheard of: everybody strives towards further expansion to the extreme limit of the legal frames. (An oil company is legally blameless when it buys up an invention of a new type of energy in order to prevent its use. A food product manufacturer is legally blameless when he poisons his product to make it last longer: after all, people are free not to purchase it.)

I have spent all my life under a Communist regime and I will tell you that a society without any objective legal scale is a terrible one indeed. But a society with no other scale but the legal one is also less than worthy of man. A society based on the letter of the law and never reaching any higher fails to take advantage of the full range of human possibilities. The letter of the law is too cold and formal to have a beneficial influence on society. Whenever the tissue of life is woven of legalistic relationships, this creates an atmosphere of spiritual mediocrity that paralyses man's noblest impulses.

And it will be simply impossible to bear up to the trials of this threatening century with nothing but the supports of a legalistic structure.

The Direction of Freedom

Today's Western society has revealed the inequality between the freedom for good deeds and the freedom for evil deeds. A statesman who wants to achieve something important and highly constructive for his country has to move cautiously and even timidly; thousands of hasty (and irresponsible) critics cling to him at all times; he is constantly rebuffed by parliament and the press. He has to prove that his every step is well-founded and absolutely flawless. Indeed, any outstanding, truly great person who has unusual and unexpected initiatives in mind does not get any chance to assert himself; dozens of traps will be set for him from the beginning. Thus mediocrity triumphs under the guise of democratic restraints.

It is feasible and easy everywhere to undermine administrative power and it has in fact been drastically weakened in all Western countries. The defence of individual rights has reached such extremes as to make society as a whole defenceless against certain individuals. It is time, in the West, to defend not so much human rights as human obligations.

On the other hand, destructive and irresponsible freedom has been granted boundless space. Society has turned out to have scarce defence against the abyss of human decadence, for example, against the misuse of liberty for moral violence against young people, such as motion pictures full of pornography, crime and horror. This is all considered to be part of freedom and to be counterbalanced, in theory, by the young people's right not to look and not to accept. Life organised legalistically has thus shown its inability to defend itself against the corrosion of Evil.

And what shall we say about the dark realms of overt criminality? Legal limits (especially in the United States) are broad enough to encourage not only individual freedom but also certain individual crimes. The culprit can go unpunished or obtain undeserved leniency—all with the support of thousands of defenders in the society. When a government earnestly undertakes to root out terrorism, public opinion immediately accuses it of violating the terrorists' civil rights. There is quite a number of such cases.

This tilt of freedom towards Evil has come about gradually, but it evidently stems from a humanistic and benevolent concept according to which man—the master of this world—does not bear any evil within himself, and all the defects of life are caused by misguided social systems which must therefore be corrected. Yet, strangely enough, though the best social conditions have been achieved in the West, there still remains a great deal of crime, there even is considerably more of it than in the destitute and lawless Soviet society. (There is a multitude of prisoners in our camps who are termed criminals, but most of them never committed any crime; they merely tried to defend themselves against a lawless state by resorting to means outside the legal framework.)

The Direction of the Press

The press, too, of course, enjoys the widest freedom. (I shall be using the word press to include all the media.) But what use does it make of it?

Here again, the overriding concern is not to infringe the letter of the law. There is no moral responsibility for distortion or disproportion. What sort of responsibility does a journalist or a newspaper have to the readership or to history? If they have misled public opinion by inaccurate information or wrong conclusions, even if they have contributed to mistakes on a state level, do we know of any case of open regret voiced by the same journalist or the same newspaper? No, this would damage sales. A nation may be the worse for such a mistake, but the journalist always gets away with it. It is most likely that he will start writing the exact opposite to his previous statements with renewed aplomb.

Because instant and credible information is required, it becomes necessary to resort to guesswork, rumours and suppositions to fill in the voids, and none of them will ever be refuted; they settle into the readers' memory. How many hasty, immature, superficial and misleading judgments are expressed every day, confusing readers, and are then left hanging? The press has the power to mould public opinion, and also to pervert it. Thus we may see terrorists treated as heroes, or secret matters pertaining to the nation's defence publicly revealed, or we may witness shameless intrusion into the privacy of well-known people according to the slogan that "Everyone is entitled to know everything". (But this is a false slogan of a false era: far greater in value is the forfeited right of people *not to know*, not to have their divine souls stuffed with gossip, nonsense, vain talk. A person who works and leads a meaningful life has no need for this excessive and burdening flow of information.)

Hastiness and superficiality—these are the psychic diseases of the twentieth century and more than anywhere else this is manifested in the press. In-depth analysis of a problem is anathema to the press, it is contrary to its nature. The press merely picks out sensational formulas.

Such as it is, however, the press has become the greatest power within the Western countries, exceeding that of the legislature, the executive and the judiciary. Yet one would like to ask: according to what law has it been elected and to whom is it responsible? In the Communist East, a journalist is frankly appointed as a state official. But who has voted Western journalists into their positions of power, for how long a time and with what prerogatives?

There is yet another surprise for someone coming from the totalitarian East with its rigorously unified press: one gradually discovers a common trend of preferences within the Western press as a whole (the spirit of the time), generally accepted patterns of judgment and maybe common corporate interests, the sum effect being not competition but unification. Unrestrained freedom exists for the press, but not for the readership because newspapers mostly transmit in a forceful and emphatic way those opinions which do not too openly contradict their own and that general trend.

A Fashion in Thinking

Without any censorship in the West, fashionable trends of thought and ideas are fastidiously separated from those which are not fashionable and the latter, without ever being forbidden, have little chance of finding their way into periodicals or books or being heard in colleges. Your scholars are free in the legal sense, but they are hemmed in by the idols of the prevailing fad. There is no open violence as in the East; however, a selection dictated by fashion and the need to accommodate mass standards frequently prevents the most independent-minded persons from contributing to public life and gives rise to dangerous herd instincts that block successful development. In America, I have received letters from highly intelligent persons, maybe a teacher in a far away small college, who could do much for the renewal and salvation of his country, but the country cannot hear him because the media will not provide him with a forum. This gives birth to strong mass prejudices, to a blindness which is perilous in our dynamic era. An example is the self-deluding interpretation of the state of affairs in the contemporary world that functions as a sort of a petrified armour around people's minds, to such a degree that human voices from seventeen countries of Eastern Europe and Eastern Asia cannot pierce it. It will be broken only by the inexorable crowbar of events.

I have mentioned a few traits of Western life which surprise and shock a new arrival to this world. The purpose and scope of this speech will not allow me to continue such a survey, in particular to look into the impact of these characteristics on important aspects of a nation's life such as elementary education, advanced education in the humanities and art.

Socialism

It is almost universally recognised that the West shows all the world the way to successful economic development, even though in past years it has been sharply offset by chaotic inflation.

However, many people living in the West are dissatisfied with their own society. They despise it or accuse it of no longer being up to the level of maturity attained by mankind. And this causes many to sway towards socialism, which is a false and dangerous current.

I hope that no one present will suspect me of expressing my personal criticism of the Western system in order to suggest socialism as an alternative. No, with the experience of a country where socialism has been realised, I shall certainly not speak for such an alternative. The mathematician Igor Shafarevich, a member of the Soviet Academy of Science, has written a brilliantly argued book entitled *Socialism*; this is a penetrating historical analysis demonstrating that socialism of any type and shade leads to a total destruction of the human spirit and to a levelling of mankind into death. Shafarevich's book was published in France almost two years ago and so far no one has been found to refute it. It will shortly be published in English in the US.

Not a Model

But should I be asked, instead, whether I would propose the West, such as it is today, as a model to my country, I would frankly have to answer negatively. No, I could not recommend your society as an ideal for the transformation of ours. Through deep suffering, people in our country have now achieved a spiritual development of such intensity that the Western system in its present state of spiritual exhaustion does not look attractive. Even those characteristics of your life which I have just enume-rated are extremely saddening.

A fact which cannot be disputed is the weakening of human personality in the West, while in the East it has become firmer and stronger. Six decades for our people and three decades for the people of Eastern Europe; during that time we have been through a spiritual training far in advance of Western experience. The complex and deadly crush of life has produced stronger, deeper and more interesting personalities than those generated by standardised Western well-being. Therefore, if our society were to be transformed into yours, it would mean an improvement in certain aspects, but also a change for the worse on some particularly significant points. Of course, a society cannot remain in an abyss of lawlessness as is the case in our country. But it is also demeaning for it to stay on such a soulless and smooth plane of legalism as is the case in yours. After the suffering of decades of violence and oppression, the human soul longs for things higher, warmer and purer than those offered by today's mass living habits, introduced as by a calling card by the revolting invasion of commercial advertising, by TV stupor and by intolerable music.

All this is visible to numerous observers from all the worlds of our planet. The Western way of life is less and less likely to become the leading model.

There are telltale symptoms by which history gives warning to a threatened or perishing society. Such are, for instance, a decline of the arts or a lack of great statesmen. Indeed, sometimes the warnings are quite explicit and concrete. The centre of your democracy and of your culture is left without electric power for a few hours only, and all of a sudden crowds of American citizens start looting and creating havoc. The smooth surface film must be very thin, then, the social system quite unstable and unhealthy.

But the fight for our planet, physical and spiritual, a fight of cosmic proportions, is not a vague matter of the future; it has already started. The forces of Evil have begun their decisive offensive; you can feel their pressure, yet your screens and publications are full of prescribed smiles and raised glasses. What is the joy about?

Shortsightedness

Very well-known representatives of your society, such as George Kennan, say: "We cannot apply moral criteria to politics." Thus we mix good and evil, right and wrong and make space for the absolute triumph of absolute Evil in the world. On the contrary, only moral criteria can help the West against Communism's well-planned world strategy. There are no other criteria. Practical or occasional considerations of any kind will inevitably be swept away by strategy. After a certain level of the problem has been reached, legalistic thinking induces paralysis; it prevents one from seeing the scale and the meaning of events.

In spite of the abundance of information, or maybe partly because of it, the West has great difficulty in finding its bearings amid contemporary events. There have been naïve predictions by some American experts who believed that Angola would become the Soviet Union's Vietnam or that the impudent Cuban expeditions in Africa would best be stopped by special US courtesy to Cuba. Kennan's advice to his own country—to begin unilateral disarmament—belongs to the same category. If you only knew how the youngest of the officials in Moscow's Old Square* roar with laughter at your political wizards! As to Fidel Castro, he openly scorns the United States, boldly sending his troops to distant adventures from his country right next to yours.

However, the most cruel mistake occurred with the failure to understand the Vietnam war. Some people sincerely wanted all wars to stop just as soon as possible; others believed that the way should be left open for national, or Communist, self-determination in Vietnam (or in Cambodia, as we see today with particular clarity). But in fact members of the US anti-war movement became accomplices in the betrayal of Far Eastern nations, in the genocide and the suffering today imposed on thirty million people there. Do these convinced pacifists now hear the moans coming from there? Do they understand their responsibility today? Or do they prefer not to hear? The American intelligentsia lost its nerve and as a consequence the danger has come much closer to the United States. But there is no awareness of this. Your shortsighted politician who signed the hasty Vietnam capitulation seemingly gave America a carefree breathing pause; however, a hundredfold Vietnam now looms over you. That small Vietnam had been a warning and an occasion to mobilise the nation's courage. But if the full might of America suffered a fully-fledged defeat at the hands of a small Communist half-country, how can the West hope to stand firm in the future?

I have said on another occasion that in the twentieth century Western democracy has not won any major war by itself; each time it shielded itself with an ally possessing a powerful land army, whose philosophy it did not question. In World War II against Hitler, instead of winning the conflict with its own forces, which would certainly have been sufficient, Western democracy raised up another enemy, one that would prove worse and more powerful, since Hitler had neither the resources nor the people, nor the ideas with broad appeal, nor such a large number of supporters in the West—a fifth column—as the Soviet Union possessed. Some Western voices already have spoken of the need of a protective screen against hostile forces in the next world conflict; in this case, the shield would be China. But I would not wish such an outcome to any country in the world. First of all it is again a doomed alliance with Evil; it would grant the United

---

* The Old Square in Moscow (Staraya Ploschad') is the place where the Headquarters of the Central Committee of the CPSU are located; it is the real name of what in the West is conventionally referred to as the Kremlin.

States a respite, but when at a later date China with its billion people would turn around armed with American weapons, America itself would fall victim to a Cambodia-style genocide.

Loss of Will

And yet—no weapons, no matter how powerful, can help the West until it overcomes its loss of willpower. In a state of psychological weakness, weapons even become a burden for the capitulating side. To defend oneself, one must also be ready to die; there is little such readiness in a society raised in the cult of material well-being. Nothing is left, in this case, but concessions, attempts to gain time and betrayal. Thus at the shameful Belgrade Conference free Western diplomats in their weakness surrendered the line of defence for which enslaved members of the Helsinki Watch Groups are sacrificing their lives.

Western thinking has become conservative: the world situation must stay as it is at any cost, there must be no changes. This debilitating dream of a *status quo* is the symptom of a society that has ceased to develop. But one must be blind in order not to see that the oceans no longer belong to the West, while the land under its domination keeps shrinking. The two so-called world wars (they were by far not on a world scale, not yet) constituted the internal self-destruction of the small progressive West, which has thus prepared its own end. The next war (which does not have to be an atomic one, I do not believe it will be) may well bury Western civilisation for ever.

In the face of such a danger, with such historical values in your past, with such a high level of attained freedom and, apparently, of devotion to it, how is it possible to lose to such an extent the will to defend oneself?

Humanism and its Consequences

How has this unfavourable relation of forces come about? How did the West decline from its triumphal march to its present debility? Have there been fatal turns and losses of direction in its development? It does not seem so. The West kept advancing steadily in accordance with its proclaimed social intentions, hand in hand with a dazzling progress in technology. And all of a sudden it found itself in its present state of weakness.

This means that the mistake must be at the root, at the very foundation of thought in modern times. I refer to the prevailing Western view of the world which was born in the Renaissance and has found political expression since the Age of Enlightenment. It became the basis for political and social doctrine and could be called rationalistic humanism or humanistic autonomy: the proclaimed and practised autonomy of man from any higher force above him. It could also be called anthropocentricity, with man seen as the centre of all.

The turn introduced by the Renaissance was probably inevitable historically: the Middle Ages had come to a natural end by exhaustion, having become an intolerable despotic repression of man's physical nature in favour of the spiritual one. But then, we recoiled from the Spirit and embraced all that is material, excessively and incommensurately. The humanistic way of thinking, which had proclaimed itself our guide, did not admit the existence of intrinsic evil in man nor did it see any task higher than the attainment of happiness on earth. It started modern Western civilisation on the dangerous trend of worshipping man and his material needs. Everything beyond physical well-being and the accumulation of material goods, all other human requirements and characteristics of a subtler and higher nature, were left outside the area of attention of state and social systems, as if human life did not have any higher meaning. Thus, gaps were left open for Evil and its draughts blow freely today. Mere freedom *per se* does not in the least solve all the problems of human life and even adds a number of new ones.

And yet, in early democracies, as in American democracy at the time of its birth, all individual human rights were granted on the ground that man is God's creature. That is, freedom was given to the individual conditionally, on the assumption of his constant religious responsibility. Such was the heritage of the preceding one thousand years. Two hundred or even fifty years ago, it would have seemed quite impossible, in America, that an individual be granted boundless freedom with no purpose, simply for the satisfaction of his whims. Subsequently, however, all such limitations were eroded everywhere in the West; a total emancipation occurred from the moral heritage of Christian centuries with their great reserves of mercy and sacrifice. State systems were becoming ever more materialistic. The West has finally achieved the rights of man, and even to excess, but man's sense of responsibility to God and society has grown dimmer and dimmer. In the past decades, the legalistic selfishness of the Western approach to the world has reached its peak and the world found itself in a harsh spiritual crisis and a political impasse.

All the celebrated technological achievements of Progress, including the conquest of outer space, do not redeem the twentieth century's moral poverty, which no one could have imagined even as late as the nineteenth century.

An Unexpected Kinship

As humanism in its development was becoming more and more materialistic, it also increasingly allowed its concepts to be used first by socialism and then by Communism. So that Karl Marx was able to say, in 1844, "Communism is naturalised humanism".

This statement has proved to be not entirely unreasonable. One does see the same stones in the foundations of an eroded humanism and of any type of socialism: boundless materialism; freedom from religion and religious responsibility (which under Communist regimes attain the stage of anti-religious dictatorship); concentration on social structures with an allegedly scientific approach. (This last is typical of both the Age of Enlightenment and of Marxism.) It is no accident that all of Communism's rhetorical vows revolve around Man (with a capital M) and his earthly happiness. At first glance it seems an ugly parallel: common traits in the thinking and way of life of today's West and today's East? But such is the logic of materialistic development.

The interrelationship is such, moreover, that the current of materialism which is farthest to the left, and is hence the most consistent, always proves to be stronger, more attractive and victorious. Humanism that has lost its Christian heritage cannot prevail in this competition. Thus, during the past centuries and especially in recent decades, as the process became more acute, the alignment of forces was as follows: liberalism was inevitably pushed aside by radicalism, radicalism had to surrender to socialism and socialism could not stand up to Communism. The Communist regime in the East could endure and grow due to the enthusiastic support from an enormous number of Western intellectuals who (feeling the kinship!) refused to see Communism's crimes, and when they no longer could refuse, they tried to justify these crimes. The problem persists: in our Eastern countries, Communism has suffered a complete ideological defeat, it is zero and less than zero. And yet Western intellectuals still look at it with considerable interest and empathy, and this is precisely what makes it so immensely difficult for the West to withstand the East.

Before the Turn

I am not examining the case of a disaster brought on by a world war and the changes which it would produce in society. But as long as we wake up every morning under a peaceful sun, we must lead an everyday life. Yet there is a disaster which is already very much with us. I am referring to the calamity of an autonomous, irreligious humanistic consciousness.

It has made man the measure of all things on earth—imperfect man who is never free of pride, self-interest, envy, vanity and dozens of other defects. We are now paying for the mistakes which had not been properly appraised at the beginning of the journey. On the way from the Renaissance to our days we have enriched our experience but we have lost the concept of a Supreme Complete Entity which used to restrain our passions and our irresponsibility. We have placed too much hope in political and social reforms, only to find out that we were being deprived of our most precious possession: our spiritual life. It is trampled by the Party mob in the East, by the commercial one in the West. This is the essence of the crisis: the split in the world is less terrifying than the similarity of the disease afflicting its main sections.

If, as claimed by humanism, man were born only to be happy, he would not be born to die. Since his body is doomed to death, his task on earth evidently must be more spiritual: not a total engrossment in everyday life, not the search for the best ways to obtain material goods and then their carefree consumption. It has to be the fulfilment of a permanent, earnest duty so that one's life journey may become above all an experience of moral growth: to leave life a better human being than one started it. It is imperative to reappraise the scale of the usual human values; its present incorrectness is astounding. It is not possible that assessment of the President's performance should be reduced to the question of how much money one makes or to the availability of gasoline. Only by the voluntary nurturing in ourselves of freely chosen and serene self-restraint can mankind rise above the world stream of materialism.

Even if we are spared destruction by war, life will have to change in order not to perish on its own. We cannot avoid reassessing the fundamental definitions of human life and human society. Is it true that man is above everything? Is there no Superior Spirit above him? Is it right that man's life and society's activities should be ruled by material expansion above all? Is it permissible to promote such expansion to the detriment of our integral spiritual life?

If the world has not approached its end, it has reached a major watershed in history, equal in importance to the turn from the Middle Ages to the Renaissance. It will demand from us a spiritual blaze, we shall have to rise to a new height of vision, to a new level of life where our physical nature will not be cursed as in the Middle Ages, but, even more importantly, our spiritual being will not be trampled upon as in the modern era.

This ascension will be similar to climbing on to the next anthropologic stage. No one on earth has any other way left but— upward.

From
Alexander Solzhenitsyn Speaks to the West

BOUNCERS

DICKIE BIRD

THE mistake I made was to hit Frank Tyson's first three deliveries for four. I might have known the next ball in that match at Scarborough would be a bouncer. As he bowled it, Frank said, "Hit that bastard for four."

I was half on the front foot, looking to drive again, when the ball smashed into the side of my jaw and knocked me to the ground. There was blood all over my face and inside my mouth. I was dazed but not completely out. Faintly, I could hear the "ting, ting, ting" of the ambulance. People seemed to be laughing. I was carried off the field and lifted into the ambulance. At the hospital, the X-ray showed that my jaw wasn't broken but the wound needed a stitch or two. I was patched up and went back to resume my innings.

At the time Tyson was probably the fastest bowler in England. Not long before, he'd earned the nickname "Typhoon" in Australia as he demolished the Australian batsmen in the 1954-5 series. He was very fast, but not as fast as Holding or Thomson.

I had encountered bouncers before but that was the first one that had really maimed me. Tyson never apologized. Norman

Yardley, the former Yorkshire captain and a member of the committee, said it was my own fault, I should have expected a bouncer. I should have been on the back foot. We were tough in those Yorkshire days.

The other time I was hit on the head was against Hampshire at Ilkley. Butch White bowled a reasonable bouncer in his day and this particular one struck me a glancing blow on the head and went on to bounce off the top of the sightscreen. The umpire signalled four leg byes. I sank to my knees, more in shock than pain and Willie Watson, who was batting with me at the time, said sternly, "Get up and get on with it. You're all right."

I might have lost some teeth on another occasion when Lancashire's Colin Hilton bounced one at me in a county match which saw Leicester bowled out for 38 on a dicey wicket. I played it down in front of my face off the knuckle part of the glove, fracturing one of the small bones in my hand.

Perhaps the most serious case of a bouncer injuring a batsman was the Charlie Griffith v. Nari Contractor incident in Barbados when Contractor, the Indian opening batsman, was on the danger list for a week after ducking into a Griffith bouncer.

Contractor had a steel plate put in his head and I've been told is still troubled by it today.

Some people are very unlucky. Tom Pugh, once the Gloucester captain, ducked into a bouncer which never got up and was given out lbw. He would have retired hurt anyway because the blow fractured his jawbone. The worst incident I ever saw was in a match at Paignton, when Jeff Tolchard, now with Leicester, was hit in the face by a local bowler. His glasses were smashed and bits of glass went into his eye. He was lucky not to suffer more permanent damage.

The bouncer is a dangerous ball but it is part of the game and I would never agree with those who say it should be outlawed. It is a legitimate part of the fast bowler's armoury. Without it, the game would be much less exciting. Some of the most dramatic moments in Test cricket come when a bowler drops it short and the batsman hooks it spectacularly for four. West Indians and Australians, brought up on hard, fast wickets, usually rise to the challenge. To stop bowlers bowling bouncers to someone like Clive Lloyd would rob the game of one of its finest sights.

The trouble comes when bowlers start peppering the batsmen with bouncers and the bouncer becomes an intimidating weapon. This happened, apparently, on the final session's play in the England v. West Indies Test at Old Trafford in 1976 when Mike Holding, Andy Roberts, and Wayne Daniel overdid it against Brian Close and John Edrich. Edrich felt so upset about it that he said later he felt like coming off the field. "Surely cricket hasn't come to this," he said.

Many deliveries flew over their heads and only 21 runs were scored in eighty minutes. Several times Close was hit about the body and arms as he stood there, often not trying to avoid the ball. Eventually, Bill Alley had a word with the West Indians and later Lloyd admitted his bowlers had bowled badly and had got carried away. There was to be no repetition.

The matter is adequately covered in the laws. The relevant section says, "The persistent bowling of fast short-pitched balls is unfair if, in the opinion of the umpire at the bowler's end, it constitutes a systematic attempt at intimidation. In such event, he must adopt the following procedure:

(a) When he decides that such bowling is becoming persistent he forthwith cautions the bowler.

(b) If this caution is ineffective, he informs the captain of the fielding side and the other umpire what has occurred.

(c) Should the above prove ineffective, the umpire at the bowler's end must:

(i) At the first repetition call "Dead ball" when the over is regarded as completed.

(ii) Direct the captain of the fielding side to take the bowler off forthwith. The captain shall take the bowler off as directed.

(iii) Report the occurrence to the captain of the batting side as soon as the interval of play takes place. A bowler who has been taken off as above may not bowl again during the same innings.

From
Not Out

11 *JANUARY 1664*

SAMUEL PEPYS

WAKED this morning by 4 a-clock by my wife, to call the maids to their wash. And what through my sleeping so long last night and vexation for the lazy sluts lying so long against their great wash, neither my wife nor I could sleep one winke after that time till day; and then I rose and by coach (taking Captain Grove with me and three bottles of Tent, which I sent to Mrs. Lane by my promise on Saturday night last) to White-hall and there with the rest of our company to the Duke and did our business; and thence I to the Tennis Court till noon and there saw several great matches played; and so by invitation to St. James's, where at Mr. Coventry's chamber I dined with my Lord Barkely, Sir G. Carteret, Sir Edwd. Turner, Sir Ellis Layton, and one Mr. Seymour, a fine gentleman; where admirable good discourse of all sorts, pleasant and serious.

Thence after dinner to White-hall; where the Duke being busy at the Guinny business—the Duke of Albemarle, Sir W. Rider, Povy, Sir J. Lawson and I to the Duke of Albemarle's lodgings and there did some business; and so to the Court again and I to the Duke of Yorkes lodgings, where the Guinny Company are choosing their Assistants for the next year by balletting. Thence by coach with Sir J. Robinson, Lieutenant of the Tower; he set me down at Cornhill; but Lord, the simple discourse that all the way we had, he magnifying his great undertakings and cares that have been upon him for these last two years, and how he commanded the city to the content of all parties, when the loggerhead knows nothing almost that is sense.

Thence to the Coffee-house, whither comes Sir W. Petty and Captain Grant, and we fell in talk (besides a young gentleman I suppose a merchant, his name Mr. Hill, that hath travelled and I perceive is a master in most sorts of Musique and other things) of Musique, the Universall Character—art of Memory—Granger's counterfeiting of hands—and other most excellent discourses, to my great content, having not been in so good company a great while. And had I time I should covett the acquaintance of that Mr. Hill.

This morning I stood by the King, arguing with a pretty Quaker woman that delivered to him a desire of hers in writing. The King showed her Sir J. Minnes, as a man the fittest for her quaker religion, saying that his beard was the stiffest thing about him. And again merrily said, looking upon the length of her paper, that if all she desired was of that length, she might lose her desires. She modestly saying nothing till he begun seriously to discourse with her, arguing the truth of his spirit against hers. She replying still with these words, "O King!" and thou'd him all along.

The general talk of the towne still is of Collonell Turner, about the robbery; who it is thought will be hanged.

I heard the Duke of Yorke tell tonight how letters are come that fifteen are condemned for the last plot by the judges at Yorke; and among others, Captain Otes, against whom it was proved that he drow his sword at his going out; and flinging away the Scabbard, said that he would either return victor or be hanged.

So home, where I find the house full of the washing and my wife mighty angry about Will's being here today talking with her maids, which she overheard, idling of their time, and he telling what a good maid my old Jane was and that she would never have her like again—at which I was angry; and after directing her to beat at least the little girl—I went to the office and there reproved Will, who told me that he went thither by my wife's order, she having commanded him to come thither on Monday morning. Now God forgive me how apt I am to be jealous of her as to this fellow, and that she must need take this time, when she knows I must be gone out to the Duke; though methinks, had she that mind, she would never think it discretion to tell me this story of him, to let me know that he was there; much less to make me offended with him, to forbid him coming again. But this cursed humour I cannot kill in myself by all the reason I have; which God forgive me for and convince me of the folly of it—and the disquiet it brings me.

So home—where, God be thanked, when I came to speak to my wife my trouble of mind soon vanished, and to bed. The house foul with the washing and quite out of order against tomorrow's dinner.

26 *MAY* *1703*

JOHN EVELYN

THIS day died Mr Sam: Pepys, a very worthy, industrious and curious person, none in England exceeding him in the knowledge of the Navy, in which he had passed through all the most considerable offices, Clerk of the Acts, and Secretary to the Admiralty, all of which he performed with great integrity. When King James II went out of England he laid down his office, and would serve no more: but withdrawing himself from all public affairs, lived at Clapham with his partner (formerly his Clerk) Mr. Hewer, in a very noble house and sweet place, where he

enjoyed the fruit of his labours in great prosperity, was universally beloved, hospitable, generous, learned in many things,
skilled in music, a very great cherisher of learned men, of whom
he had the conversation. His library and other collections of
curiosities was one of the most considerable, the models of ships
especially. Beside what he boldly published of an account of the
Navy, as he found and left it, he had for divers years under his
hand the History of the Navy, or *Navalia* as he called it; but
how far advanced and what will follow of this is left, I suppose,
to his sister's son Mr. Jackson, a young gentleman whom his
uncle had educated in all sorts of useful learning, travel abroad,
returning with extraordinary accomplishments, and worth to be
his heir. Mr. Pepys had been for near 40 years so my particular
friend, that he now sent me Complete Mourning, desiring me to
be one to hold up the pall at his magnificent obsequies; but my
present indisposition hindered me from doing him this last office.

The King of Portugal has at last entered into the Confederacy
against France, offensive and defensive. The weather was so very
wet, as threatened great loss to farmers.

FORGET WHAT DID

PHILIP LARKIN

Stopping the diary
Was a stun to memory,
Was a blank starting,

One no longer cicatrized
By such words, such actions
As bleakened waking.

I wanted them over,
Hurried to burial
And looked back on

Like the wars and winters
Missing behind the windows
Of an opaque childhood.

And the empty pages?
Should they ever by filled
Let it be with observed

Celestial recurrences,
The day the flowers come,
And when the birds go.

A STORY OF DON JUAN

V. S. PRITCHETT

IT is said that on one night of his life Don Juan slept alone, though I think the point has been disputed. Returning to Seville in the spring he was held up, some hours' ride from the city, by the floods of the Quadalquiver, a river as dirty as an old lion after the rains, and was obliged to stay at the finca of the Quintero family. The doorway, the walls, the windows of the house were hung with the black and violet draperies of mourning when he arrived there. God rest her soul (the peasants said), the lady of the house was dead. She had been dead a year. The young Quintero was a widower. Nevertheless Quintero took him in and even smiled to see a gallant spattered and drooping in the rain like a sodden cockerel. There was malice in that smile, for Quintero was mad with loneliness and grief; the man who had possessed and discarded all women, was received by a man demented because he had lost only one.

"My house is yours," said Quintero, speaking the formula. There was bewilderment in his eyes; those who grieve do not find the world and its people either real or believable. Irony inflects the voices of mourners, and there was malice, too, in Quintero's further greetings; for grief appears to put one at an advantage, the advantage (in Quintero's case) being the macabre one that he could receive Juan now without that fear, that terror which Juan brought to the husbands of Seville. It was perfect, Quintero thought, that for once in his life Juan should have arrived at an empty house.

There was not even (as Juan quickly ascertained) a maid, for Quintero was served only by a manservant, being unable any longer to bear the sight of women. This servant dried Don Juan's clothes and in an hour or two brought in a bad dinner, food which stamped up and down in the stomach like people waiting for a coach in the cold. Quintero was torturing his body as well as his mind, and as the familiar pains arrived they agonized him and set him off about his wife. Grief had also made Quintero an actor. His eyes had that hollow, taper-haunted dusk of the theatre as he spoke of the beautiful girl. He dwelled upon their courtship, on details of her beauty and temperament, and how he had rushed her from the church to the marriage bed like a man racing a tray of diamonds through the streets into the safety of a bank vault. The presence of Don Juan turned every man into an artist when he was telling his own love story—one had to tantalize and surpass the great seducer—and Quintero, rolling it all off in the grand manner, could not resist telling that his bride had died on her marriage night.

"Man!" cried Don Juan. He started straight off on stories of his own. But Quintero hardly listened; he had returned to the state of exhaustion and emptiness which is natural to grief. As Juan talked the madman followed his own thoughts like an actor preparing and mumbling the next entrance; and the thought he had had when Juan had first appeared at his door returned to him: that Juan must be a monster to make a man feel triumphant that his own wife was dead. Half-listening, and indigestion aiding, Quintero felt within himself the total hatred of all the husbands of Seville for this diabolical man. And as Quintero brooded upon this it occurred to him that it was probably not a chance that he had it in his power to effect the most curious revenge on behalf of the husbands of Seville.

The decision was made. The wine being finished Quintero called for his manservant and gave orders to change Don Juan's room.

"For," said Quintero drily, "his Excellency's visit is an honour and I cannot allow one who has slept in the most delicately scented rooms in Spain to pass the night in a chamber which stinks to heaven of goat."

"The closed room?" said the manservant, astonished that the room which still held the great dynastic marriage bed and which had not been used more than half-a-dozen times by his master since the lady's death—and then only at the full moon when his frenzy was worst—was to be given to a stranger.

Yet to this room Quintero led his guest and there parted from him with eyes so sparkling with ill-intention that Juan, who was sensitive to this kind of point, understood perfectly that the cat was being let into the cage only because the bird had long ago flown out. The humiliation was unpleasant. Juan saw the night stretching before him like a desert.

What a bed to lie in: so wide, so unutterably vacant, so malignantly inopportune! Juan took off his clothes, snuffed the lamp wick. He lay down conscious that on either side of him lay wastes of sheet, draughty and uninhabited except by the nomadic bug. A desert. To move an arm one inch to the side, to push out a leg, however cautiously, was to enter desolation. For miles and miles the foot might probe, the fingers or the knee explore a friendless Antarctica. Yet to lie rigid and still was to have a foretaste of the grave. And here, too, he was frustrated; for though the wine kept him yawning, that awful food romped in his stomach, jolting him back from the edge of sleep the moment he got there.

There is an art in sleeping alone in a double bed but, naturally, this art was unknown to Juan; he had to learn it. The difficulty is easily solved. If you cannot sleep on one side of the bed, you move over and try the other. Two hours or more must have passed before this occurred to Juan. Sullen-headed he advanced into the desert and the night air lying chill between the sheets flapped, and made him shiver. He stretched out his arm and crawled towards the opposite pillow. Mother of God, the coldness, the more than virgin frigidity of linen! Juan put down his head and, drawing up his knees, he shivered. Soon, he supposed, he would be warm again, but in the meantime, ice could not have been colder. It was unbelievable.

Ice was the word for that pillow and those sheets. Ice. Was he ill? Had the rain chilled him that his teeth must chatter like this and his legs tremble? Far from getting warmer he found the cold growing. Now it was on his forehead and his cheeks, like arms of ice on his body, like legs of ice upon his legs. Suddenly in superstition he got up on his hands and stared down at the pillow in the darkness, threw back the bed-clothes and looked down upon the sheet his breath was hot, yet blowing against his cheeks was a breath colder than the grave, his shoulders and body were hot, yet limbs of snow were drawing him down; and just as he would have shouted his appalled suspicion, lips like wet ice unfolded upon his own and he sank down to a kiss, unmistakably a kiss, which froze him like a winter.

In his own room Quintero lay listening. His mad eyes were exalted and his ears were waiting. He was waiting for the scream of horror. He knew the apparition. There would be a scream, a tumble, hands fighting for the light, fists knocking at the door. And Quintero had locked the door. But when no scream came, Quintero lay talking to himself, remembering the night the apparition had first come to him and had made him speechless and left him choked and stiff. It would be even better if there were no scream! Quintero lay awake through the night building castle after castle of triumphant revenge and receiving, as he did so, the ovations of the husbands of Seville. "The stallion is gelded!" At an early hour Quintero unlocked the door and waited downstairs impatiently. He was a wreck after a night like that.

Juan came down at last. He was (Quintero observed) pale. Or was he pale?

"Did you sleep well?" Quintero asked furtively.

"Very well," Juan replied.

"I do not sleep well in strange beds myself," Quintero insinuated. Juan smiled and replied that he was more used to strange beds than his own. Quintero scowled.

"I reproach myself: the bed was large," he said. But the large, Juan said, were necessarily as familiar to him as the strange. Quintero bit his nails. Some noise had been heard in the night—something like a scream, a disturbance. The manservant had noticed it also. Juan answered him that disturbances in the night had indeed bothered him at the beginning of his career, but now he took them in his stride. Quintero dug his nails into the palms of his hands. He brought out the trump.

"I am afraid," Quintero said, "it was a cold bed. You must have *frozen.*"

"I am never cold for long." Juan said, and, unconsciously anticipating the manner of a poem that was to be written in his memory two centuries later, declaimed: "The blood of Don Juan is hot, for the sun is the blood of Don Juan".

Quintero watched. His eyes jumped like flies to every movement of his guest. He watched him drink his coffee. He watched him tighten the stirrups of his horse. He watched Juan vault into the saddle. Don Juan was humming and when he went off was singing, was singing in that intolerable tenor of his which was like a cock crow in the olive groves.

Quintero went into the house and rubbed his unshaven chin. Then he went out again to the road where the figure of Don Juan was now only a small smoke of dust between the eucalyptus trees. Quintero went up to the room where Juan had slept and stared at it with accusations and suspicions. He called the manservant.

"I shall sleep here to-night," Quintero said.

The manservant answered carefully. Quintero was mad again and the moon was still only in its first quarter. The man watched his master during the day looking towards Seville. It was too warm after the rains, the country steamed like a laundry.

And then, when the night came, Quintero laughed at his doubts. He went up to the room and as he undressed he thought of the assurance of those ice-cold lips, those icicle fingers and those icy arms. She had not come last night; oh what fidelity! To think, he would say in his remorse to the ghost, that malice had so disordered him that he had been base and credulous enough to use the dead for a trick.

Tears were in his eyes as he lay down and for some time he dared not turn on his side and stretch out his hand to touch what, in his disorder, he had been willing to betray. He loathed his heart. He craved—yet how could he hope for it now?—the miracle of recognition and forgiveness. It was this craving which moved him at last. His hands went out. And they were met.

The hands, the arms, the lips moved out of their invisibility and soundlessness towards him. They touched him, they clasped him, they drew him down, but—what was this? He gave a shout, he fought to get away, kicked out and swore; and so the manservant found him wrestling with the sheets, striking out with fists and knees, roaring that he was in hell. Those hands, those lips, those limbs, he screamed, were *burning* him. They were of ice no more. They were of fire.

SOURCES AND ACKNOWLEDGEMENTS

"Paradise" by Laurie Lee: from *I Can't Stay Long* (André Deutsch, 1975)
"The Mysteries of the Kingdom" by E. R. Norman: from the last of six Reith
Lectures broadcast by the B.B.C. in 1978, reprinted by permission of the author
"Islanders" by John Fowles: from *Islands* (Jonathan Cape, 1978)
"George Moore" by Tom Stoppard: reprinted by permission of Faber & Faber Ltd
from *Jumpers* (1972)
"Philosophy" by Isaiah Berlin and Brian Magee: reprinted by permission of the
authors from *Men of Ideas* (B.B.C. publications, 1978)
"Ying Chü" by Gerald Brenan: from *Thoughts in a Dry Season* (Cambridge
University Press, 1978)
"In the Hours of Darkness" by Edna O'Brien: from *Mrs Reinhardt and Other Stories*
(Weidenfeld & Nicolson, 1978)
"Three Brothers" by Joyce Grenfell: from *Stately as a Galleon* (Macmillan London
Ltd, 1978) reprinted by permission of Richard Scott Simon Ltd
"Woman" by James Thurber: from "The Ladies of Orlon" in *Alarms and Diversions*
(Harper and Row, 1957), copyright © 1957 James Thurber, originally printed in *The
New Yorker*
"Data" by Philip Howard: from *Weasel Words* (Hamish Hamilton, 1978)
"Below Stairs" by Mark Girouard: from *Life in the English Country House* (Yale
University Press, 1978)
"The Landlady" by Roald Dahl: from *Kiss Kiss* (Michael Joseph, 1962, and Penguin
Books; republished under the title *Tales of the Unexpected*, 1979)
"A Stay in Cologne" by Patrick Leigh Fermor: from *A Time of Gifts* (John Murray, 1977)
"Walking Bare" by Ted Hughes: reprinted by permission of Faber & Faber Ltd from
Cave Birds (1978)
"Storm Force" by Clare Francis: from *Come Wind or Weather* (Pelham Books, 1978)
"Alone on a Wide Sea" by Naomi James: from *At One with the Sea* (Hutchinson/
Stanley Paul, 1979)
"The Highest Point in the World" by Peter Habeler: from *Everest, Impossible Victory*
(Arlington Books, 1979)
"Crete" by Lawrence Durrell: reprinted by permission of Faber & Faber Ltd from
The Greek Islands (1978)
"The Gentleman Abroad" by Douglas Sutherland: from *The English Gentleman*
(Debrett's Peerage, 1978)
"9 May 1956" by Harold Nicolson: from *The Diaries and Letters* of Harold Nicolson,
edited by Nigel Nicolson (Collins, 1968)
"June 1967" and "September 1970" by Cecil Beaton: from *The Parting Years*
(Weidenfeld & Nicolson, 1978)
"Oysters in Green Waistcoats" by Michel Guérard: reprinted by permission of
Macmillan, London and Basingstoke, from *Cuisine Gourmande* (1978)
"Food is a Profound Subject" by Iris Murdoch: from *The Sea, The Sea* (Chatto &
Windus, 1978)
"The Restaurant" by Noel Blakiston: from *The Collected Stories of Noel Blakiston*
(Constable Publishers, 1977)
"The Beginning" by Lord Rothschild: from *Meditations of a Broomstick* (Collins, 1977)
"The King's Departure" by Frances Donaldson: from *Edward VIII: The Road to
Abdication* (Weidenfeld & Nicolson, 1978)
"11 December 1936" by Sir Henry Channon: from *Chips: The Diaries of Sir Henry
Channon*, edited by Robert Rhodes James (Weidenfeld & Nicolson, 1967)
"28 January 1937" by Marie Belloc Lowndes: from *The Diaries and Letters of Marie
Belloc Lowndes*, edited by Susan Lowndes (Chatto & Windus, 1971)
"Dreaming" by J. Z. Young: reprinted by permission of the Oxford University Press
from *Programs of the Brain*, © J. Z. Young 1978
"Psychobabble" by R. D. Rosen: from *Psychobabble* (Wildwood House, 1978)
"16 January 1923" by Virginia Woolf: reprinted by permission of the Author's
Literary Estate and the Hogarth Press from *The Diary of Virginia Woolf*, Vol. II,
edited by Anne Olivier Bell
"Diary of a Somebody" by Christopher Matthew: from *The Diary of a Somebody*
(Hutchinson, 1978)
"Thoughts on 'The Diary of a Nobody'" by John Betjeman: from *Collected Poems*
(John Murray, 1958)

"The Door in the Wall" by H. G. Wells: reprinted by permission of the Estate of the Late H. G. Wells

"True Strange Story" by J. B. Priestley: from *Outcries and Asides* (Heinemann, 1974)

"To a Poet a Thousand Years Hence" by John Heath-Stubbs: from *The Watchman's Flute* (Carcanet, 1978)

"Inventing the Future" by Lyall Watson: reprinted by permission of Hodder & Stoughton Ltd from *Lifetide* (1979)

"Cosmic Evolution" by Arthur Koestler: from *Janus: A Summing Up* (Hutchinson, 1978)

"The Compulsive Communicators" by David Attenborough: from *Life on Earth* (Collins/B.B.C., 1979)

"Bad Backs" by Brian Inglis: from *The Book of the Back* (Ebury Press, 1978)

"Self-Help" by Jonathan Miller: from *The Body in Question* (Jonathan Cape, 1978)

"Seaside Sensation" by D. J. Enright: from *Paradise Illustrated* (Chatto & Windus, 1978)

"Jane Austen's Secret" by David Cecil: from *A Portrait of Jane Austen* (Constable Publishers, 1978)

"Rudyard Kipling" by Lord Birkenhead: from *Rudyard Kipling* (Weidenfeld & Nicolson, 1978)

"A Picture of Faulkner" by Paul Theroux: from *Picture Palace*, © 1978 Paul Theroux (Hamish Hamilton)

"The Filming of 'Death in Venice'" by Dirk Bogarde: from *Snakes and Ladders* (Chatto & Windus, 1978)

"Modern Music" by Hugo Cole: from *The Changing Face of Music* (Gollancz, 1978)

"Mannerisms to Impress" by Michael Schäffer: reprinted by permission of Kaye & Ward Ltd from *The Language of the Horse* (1954). © 1974 Nymphenburger Verlagshandlung GmbH. English translation © Kaye & Ward Ltd 1975

"Vet in a Spin" by James Herriot: reprinted by permission of David Higham Associates Ltd from *Vet in a Spin* (Michael Joseph, 1978)

"The Black Cat's Conversation" by Elizabeth Jennings: reprinted by permission of David Higham Associates Ltd from *After the Ark* (Oxford University Press, 1978)

"Ace High" by Peter Fleming: reprinted by permission of the Author's Literary Estate from *A Story to Tell and Other Tales* (Jonathan Cape, 1942)

"The Little Willow" by Frances Towers: reprinted by permission of the Author's Literary Estate from *Tea with Mr Rochester and Other Stories* (Michael Joseph, 1948)

"1 August 1917" by Herbert Read: from *The Contrary Experience* (Secker & Warburg, reissued 1973)

"8 June 1978" by Alexander Solzhenitsyn: reprinted by permission of The Bodley Head from *Alexander Solzhenitsyn Speaks to the West* (1978)

"Bouncers" by Dickie Bird: from *Not Out* (Arthur Batker, 1978)

"11 January 1664" by Samuel Pepys: reprinted by permission of A. D. Peters & Co Ltd from *The Diary of Samuel Pepys*, Vol. V, edited by R. Latham and W. Matthews (Bell & Hyman, 1971)

"Forget What Did" by Philip Larkin: reprinted by permission of Faber & Faber Ltd from *High Windows* (1974)

"A Story of Don Juan" by V. S. Pritchett: reprinted by permission of A. D. Peters & Co Ltd

Illustrations by

Rene Eyre pp. 11, 16, 18, 22, 38, 73, 93, 109, 114, 134, 139, 146, 153, 155, 157, 162, 165, 175, 197, 200, 220, 238, 244, 256, 268, 269, 275, 281.

Lucina Della Rocca Hay pp. 98, 108.

Kathryn Hunt pp. 40, 49, 51, 89, 265.

Carole Johnson pp. 4, 27, 30, 43, 44, 52, 54, 61, 65, 79, 83, 130, 224, 225, 234, 254.

Sheilagh Noble pp. 76, 85, 136, 211, 229, 232, 249, 306, 313, 315.

Sarah Pring p. 144.

Roger Pring pp. 178, 192, 223.

The illustration on p. 206 is reproduced by permission of Cadbury Schweppes Ltd, London, and that on p. 218 by permission of De Luca Editore, Rome.